A Romani Women's Anthology

Published in Canada by
Inanna Publications and Education Inc.
210 Founders College, York University
4700 Keele Street, Toronto, Ontario M3J 1P3
Telephone: (416) 736-5356 Fax (416) 736-5765
Email: inanna.publications@inanna.ca Website: www.inanna.ca

The publisher gratefully acknowledges the support of the Canada Council for the Arts and the Ontario Arts Council for its publishing program. We also acknowlege the financial assistance of the Government of Canada through the Canada Book Fund.

Note from the publisher: Care has been taken to trace the ownership of copyright material used in this book. The author and the publisher welcome any information enabling them to rectify any references or credits in subsequent editions.

Cover artwork: Monica Bodirsky, "14th Street," 2015, watercolour, ink, photograph, map, postcard, 9 x 11 inches. www.monicabodirsky.com.

Cover design: Val Fullard

Library and Archives Canada Cataloguing in Publication

A Romani women's anthology : spectrum of the blue water / edited by Hedina Tahirović-Sijerčić and Cynthia Levine-Rasky.

Issued in print and electronic formats.
ISBN 978-1-77133-401-3 (softcover). — ISBN 978-1-77133-401-3 (softcover). —
ISBN 978-1-77133-402-0 (epub). — ISBN 978-1-77133-403-7 (Kindle). —
ISBN 978-1-77133-404-4 (pdf)

1. Women, Romani—Canada—Biography. 2. Women, Romani—Canada—Social conditions—21st century. 3. Canada—Biography.
I. Tahirović-Sijerčić, Hedina, 1960–, editor II. Levine-Rasky, Cynthia, 1958–, editor

DX125.S64 2017   305.891'497   C2017-900326-7
                                              C2017-900327-5

Printed and Bound in Canada.

MIX
Paper from
responsible sources
FSC® C004071

Spectrum of the Blue Water

edited by
Hedina Tahirović-Sijerčić and Cynthia Levine-Rasky

INANNA Publications and Education Inc.
Toronto, Canada

TABLE OF CONTENTS

v

To all Romani women who, despite living in dozens of countries around the world, speaking many languages, and following many spiritual traditions, share dreams of community. We hope that in expressing personal stories, their voices will contribute to the decolonization of knowledge about the Roma peoples.

ACKNOWLEDGEMENTS

We wish to thank all of the contributors who together created this unique and important volume attesting to the power and creativity of Canadian Romani women. Included in our circle of gratitude are the women whose images appear in Chad Evans Wyatt's contribution to the book, *RomaRisingCA*. Our respect for each other—in our plurality—is enduring.

At Inanna Publications, editor-in-chief Luciana Ricciutelli believed in the book from the start, advocated for it, and made it a reality. We acknowledge her invaluable support and assistance.

We express our gratitude to Ronald Lee for his consultation on Romani issues. We thank translators Suzan Searle and Peter Hajnal for their work on Sarah Barbieux's and Tímea Ágnes Daróczi's chapters, respectively, and Mike Thoms for his transcription services. Monica Bodirsky is the visual artist who created the startlingly beautiful cover art for which we are much indebted.

We recognize the quality of our co-editorial partnership that is so robust that it makes our considerable physical distance irrelevant.

Finally, we thank our families and friends, especially our children—Edis and Zerin Sijerčić, and Adam and Elia Rasky—

without whom nothing is possible and with whom everything is made meaningful.

INTRODUCTION

A Spectrum of Voices

CYNTHIA LEVINE-RASKY AND HEDINA TAHIROVIĆ-SIJERČIĆ

THE POEM "CV 6," by co-editor Hedina Tahirović-Sijerčić, and from which the title of this book comes, tells of the life, the death, and the afterlife of Mehmed, a Romani man. Denied dignity after death, Mehmed's soul seeks and finds peace in a vision of the sky replete with clouds, rain, and lightning. Journeying to India on a "golden path," his soul dismounts from its horse and descends to the Ganges. While his horse returns to the "spectrum of the blue sky," Mehmed's soul returns to the "spectrum of the blue water." The title is a perfect reflection of Romani women in Canada. It is simple in naming a singular category—blue water—a ubiquitous, beautiful, and necessary thing. But it is also complex, summoning a multiplicity—a spectrum—a thing that exists in tension with what on its watery surface appears to be a singularity. One need only look more closely at the blue water's surface to realize its depths. Mehmed's soul returns to its origins, a location identified by a legendary river that evokes a double meaning.

This book is a literary meeting place to which twenty authors do not return, but arrive for the first time. They do so both as a single category—women—and as a multiplicity. An assemblage of elements without becoming a totality (Roffe), multiplicity preserves subjectively meaningful components of belonging to a group, but rejects an assumption of sameness in their quality.

There are many claims we can make about this book: it is the first of its kind in North America and maybe anywhere, in

1

English; it embodies the multiplicity of Romani women with dynamic implications for the Roma peoples; it makes axiomatic the epistemic privilege of Romani women in which their critical insights are recognized as authoritative on the basis of their authentic and personal knowledge; it embraces the collaborative spirit of a group of friends and colleagues in a shared project of creativity; it collects an array of writing styles reflecting the panoply of women's voices made poignant for never having been heard together. The contributors who are not Roma count themselves as staunch allies in the struggle for Romani rights having enacted their commitment on the street, in their professional labour, and in cultural venues. In support of the directive that informs community empowerment, *Khanchi pa amende bi-amengo* (nothing about us without us), allies are aware of the ethics that flow from this orientation affecting our positionality, our identities, and the intersecting circuits of power and privilege in which we all move. We respect what Romani feminists Jelena Jovanović, Angéla Kóczé, and Lidia Balogh acknowledge as the mutual exchange of knowledge and experiences that can occur between Romani and non-Romani women (11).

The book is a consummate collection of the work of twenty individuals—Melaena Allen-Trottier, Sarah Barbieux, Julianna Beaudoin, Monica Bodirsky, Elizabeth Lisa Ann Csanyi, Gina Csanyi-Robah, Jennifer Danch, Tímea Ágnes Daróczi, Arielle Dylan, Chad Evans Wyatt, Ildi Gulyas, Gyongyi Hamori, Lynn Hutchinson Lee, Delilah Lee, Cynthia Levine-Rasky, Julia Lovell, Viktoria Mohacsi, Hedina Tahirović-Sijerčić, Bluma Teram, and Saskia Tomkins. Most of the contributors have worked together in various ways, with some collaborations beginning years ago. Many of us continue to work together and commune together. We are twenty individuals, a multiplicity of friends. The authors are Romani women, women of mixed Romani heritage, and non-Romani allies. The book consists of a dynamic blend of life writing, creative work, research essays about identity, childhood, immigration, work, art, memory, love, spirituality, activism, advocacy, leadership, and other themes affecting the lives of Canadian Romani women. The sole male contributor, Chad Evans Wyatt contributes a selection from his international photography exhibit, *RomaRising*. Comprised of black and white portraits of Canadian Romani women taken in 2013 and 2014, Wyatt's work puts faces to contributors' words, conveying the multi-dimensionality of his subjects. Reflecting the diversity of women's voices, the chapters link everyday experience to a social critique of the factors that enable and constrain women's lives. It consolidates distinct expressions of agency and collectivity.

In her chapter, Tahirović-Sijerčić observes that, "Romani literature by Roma and in the voice of Roma remains invisible." This is especially the case for women. Romani American writer Qristina Zavačková-Cummings expresses her dismay at the general inattention to Romani literature:

> When I look at all the wonderful work that Romani writers, artists, musicians, and others have done it breaks my heart to realize that much of it is already fading away. Who outside of Romani culture has heard of Ceija Stojka, Dušan Marinkovic, or Helena Červeňáková-Laliková? What's worse is that many Romani haven't heard of them either.

This regrettable fact needs to be challenged. *A Romani Women's Anthology: Spectrum of the Blue Water* occupies a space, however small, in a growing stock of literary artifacts created by Roma around the world. Contributors are as plural as their subject matter. North American Romani women are impressively diverse in their identities and their attachments. The chapters in this book—stories, essays, poems, art—communicate this multiplicity. Contributors are activists, artists, academics, community leaders, educators, professionals, and cultural and community workers. They are dedicated to human rights and to the arts, to community development and education, and to the dignity of Romani lives in Canada and Europe.

ROMANI WOMEN AND INTERSECTIONALITY

The theory of intersectionality proposes that racism, sexism, and class exploitation (to take three salient categories) interconnect and operate simultaneously resulting in both oppression and privilege. The effects are not additive; one cannot deduce "double" and "triple" oppression from the number of categories one occupies. Instead, intersectionality is "multiply, simultaneously, and interactively determined by various significant axes of social organization" (Stasiulus 347). Reflecting the complexity of exclusion that stems from multiple sources, intersectionality affirms more than a mere combination of factors. Multiple intersections of race, class, gender, infers that ethnicity, ability, religiosity, culture, nationality, and transnationality are decidedly untidy, non-uniform, and in continuous dialogue with power. Avtar Brah and Ann Phoenix offer a particularly valuable definition:

> We regard the concept of "intersectionality" as signifying the complex, irreducible, varied, and variable effects, which ensue when multiple axis [sic] of differentiation—economic, political, cultural, psychic, subjective, and experiential—intersect in historically specific contexts. (76)

For Brah and Phoenix, no one kind of difference is given privileged status. This avoids the risk of "adding up" factors of marginalization by eschewing identity categories like gender or ethnicity. The categories themselves are not assumed to contain meaning; indeed, the authors do not use the language of social difference at all. Instead, they look at the *effects* of differentiation, not at the categories produced by differentiation. They abandon the convention of asserting *what* difference is significant by signaling *how* intersectionality is an effect of differentiation. This is more meaningful than determining who is affected by acts of differentiation. "Axes of differentiation" goes well beyond the usual categories of race, gender, and class, to highlight broader forces: the economic, political, cultural, and so on. Race is understood, therefore, in its economic, cultural, and political context, not just as an outcome of membership in a racialized group. This is important because categories of difference—gender, ethnicity, class—tend to supersede questions about how such categories came to have the meanings and the relative value they have, and why and how they become the focal point of resistance or oppression. Rather than giving difference a central role, the theory of intersectionality taims at an analysis of structural arrangements in which difference has come to matter. This means that it is not just "being" Roma that matters, or even a Romani woman, or a Canadian Romani woman. Privilege and oppression do not directly follow from one's social location. What matters is how these categories were produced through "economic, political, cultural, psychic, subjective, experiential" and historical processes of differentiation. It is the effects of that differentiation for social actors in relation to each other that need to be examined.

Romani women's lives should be understood from the perspective of intersectionality. Angéla Kóczé affirms that "Romani women experience multiple and intersecting inequalities" (14) and specifically, that "the categories of race/ethnicity, gender, and class are ubiquitous and thus constantly overlapping in the lives of Romani women" (23). In its call for strategies for gender equality in Europe, the European Agency for Fundamental Rights recognizes "the multiple and intersectional forms of discrimination that certain groups of women face," and the necessity of "developing specific actions to strengthen the rights of these different groups of women, among them Roma women." For the Roma, life in Europe is characterized by flagrant and public anti-Roma racism in Europe (see Fekete; Council of Europe 2012; European Roma and Travellers Forum), often against Romani women (Oprea; Council of Europe 2013; Szalai and Zentai). In Bulgaria, the Czech Republic, France, Greece, Italy, Hungary, Poland, Portugal, Romania, Slovakia and Spain, the average situation of Roma women in core areas of social life such as education, employment and health, is worse than that of Roma men (European Union Agency for Fundamental Rights 45). In its influential report, the Council of Europe (2010) reports that:

> Romani women in Europe face multiple [forms of] discrimination, based on their ethnicity and their gender.

This negatively impacts all areas of their daily life, including housing, healthcare, employment, education, political or civic participation and family relationships. Furthermore, they have often been victims of atrocious human rights violations: trafficking, racially-motivated violence, hate crimes and coercive sterilization.

In 2006, the European Parliament passed a resolution on the situation of Romani women in the European Union. Its wording reveals the depth of the problem: "Romani women [are] among the most threatened groups and individuals in the member States and accession and candidate countries" (Council of Europe nd: 3-4).

Research such as this shows the forms of oppression that affect Romani women specifically. It registers not the "fact" of difference, but the economic and political contexts in which Romani women are differentiated and treated inequitably. Romani women's ethnicity and gender interest, not at the expense of their class and nationality, but simultaneously. And not all contexts for Romani women's inequalities are situated in dominant society. They may also found in Romani communities, embedded in traditional social organization. In her chapter, Tahirović-Sijerčić explains that Romani women's voices "are mostly ignored by the community which is still influenced by power of the men.... Because of their ideals, their education, and their knowledge, these women are discriminated against not just by non-Romani people, but also by their own people, both men and women, making the situation more difficult."

These formidable challenges notwithstanding, Romani women are organizing themselves at international conferences, in publishing, and in activism. One example is the Council of Europe's International Conference of Roma Women first held in Sweden in 2007, with the fifth and most recent held in Skopje, Macedonia, in October of 2015. The delegates, over 100 political figures, government representatives, and experts in Romani women's rights from twenty countries, built on the Strategy for the Advancement of Romani Women and Girls developed at the Fourth International Conference held in Helsinki, Finland, in 2013 (Council of Europe 2015). One priority was the mainstreaming of gender in national Roma integration strategies and local action plans. Other priorities were empowerment and political participation, and violence against Roma women, especially trafficking and child marriage.

Debra Schultz counts no fewer than 135 Romani women's organizations in Central and Eastern Europe. Their proliferation does not imply unified politics, of course. The International Romani Women's Network and the Joint Roma Women's Initiative, for example, represent conservative and radical traditions respectively (Jovanović, Kóczé, and Balogh). Jelena Jovanović, Angéla Kóczé, and Lidia Balogh advise that the Romani women's movement "is a complex term that implies multiple forms of Romani women's struggles at the political level and a diversity of contexts, and does not imply singularity or exclusively joint steps that they have been taking" (3). But even in cases where Romani women's organizations do not support feminism, their programs reflect the intersectionality of gender, race, and class (Stancu 58).

Another example of the rise of Romani feminism is the website romawoman.org, "I'm a European Roma Woman," hosted by Romedia Foundation and funded by the Decade of Roma Inclusion, Open Society Foundations, and other organizations. The site posts dozens of videos of European Romani women speaking about their personal experiences and their political engagement. The intersectionality of gender, ethnicity, and class is a theme running through the narratives. Organizations dedicated to the improved status of Romani women do not assume that these achievements are sufficient. The Council of Europe notes that despite gains made, "Romani women and girls at national and local level have received very limited attention, while the pool of Romani women's NGOs and women's activists at national levels is largely under-represented and under-equipped" (nd: 6). Serena D'Agostino provides more evidence for concern: despite European Parliamentary (EP) resolutions in 2006 and 2013 on the situation of Romani women and their empowerment, gender policy development at the EP level "seems to have come to a standstill" (14).

THE VALUE OF METAPHOR

The Roma are a non-territorial nation whose common language is in the process of becoming standardized, and for whom extant traditional practices and self-identifications are as diffuse as their dynamic expressions in relation to dominant cultures. While systemic racism divides a people, the Roma embrace pluralistic subjectivities that are active in public life and reactive to dominant culture but in idiosyncratic ways affected by migration, by inter-generational change, by mass culture, and public policy. As Tahirović-Sijerčić indicates in her chapter, "any reference that speaks about the Roma as a homogenous group is an ideological and political construct. The Romani community is a non-homogeneous social and cultural ethnic group structured with hierarchy" (21). For diasporic groups in particular, differences in migration history and citizenship status in their host country are significant. This has special relevance for Canadian Roma for whom, as Annabel Tremlett claims about European Roma, intra-group diversity is just as critical as inter-group diversity. Like other communities in Canada, the Roma are impressively diverse in their country of origin, language, religion, immigration status, and transnational practices, intersecting dimensions that segment their communities (832). In their multiplicity—a group without the assumption of homogeneous terms of belonging— Roma women are a spectrum for what Nicoleta Bițu calls "a feminism of multiethnicity" (17).

A Romani Women's Anthology: Spectrum of the Blue Water blends a diversity of voices into a stimulating hybrid of a project. In this, it is a montage. Borrowed from film studies, the montage is a kind of film in which many pictures or designs are juxtaposed or superimposed. In cultural studies, montage is a way of presenting disparate elements, written, image-based, or other forms of text, that reflect a range of voices, perspectives, and angles. Literary, poetic, journalistic, fictional, cinematic, documentary, factual, and ethnographic writing and representation cohabit. Experimentation with narrative involves story, poetry, dialogue, first-person accounts, autobiography, and image that are integrated into a single text expanding possibilities for understanding the complexity of social life. Not a methodological novelty free of ethics, the montage is intimately attached to principles of social justice. It is a form of "new writing, [that] asks only that we conduct our ground-level criticism aimed at the repressive structures in our everyday lives" (Denzin 142). The montage is an appropriate creative response to the challenge in representing the assemblage of research, accounts, voices, and images on a topic as wide as the Canadian Romani women. As an approach to presenting disparate perspectives, it is one inspiration for this unique book.

WORKS CITED

Bițu, Nicoleta. *Romani Women and Feminism.* PhD Dissertation: Thesis summary. University of Bucharest, Romania, 2014. Print.

Brah, Avtar, and Ann Phoenix. "Ain't I a Woman? Revisiting Intersectionality." *Journal of International Women's Studies* 5.3 (2004): 75-86. Print.

Council of Europe. "International Review Conference of Romani Women: Advancing Despite Everything." Skopje, 6-7 October 2015. Web.

Council of Europe. "Final Report of the Fourth International Romani Women's Conference." 17-18 September 2013, Helsinki. Strasbourg, FR. Web. Accessed 11 June 2016.

Council of Europe. 2012. "Human rights of Roma and Travellers in Europe." Commissioner of Human Rights. Strasbourg: Council of Europe Publishing, 2012. Web. Accessed 28 November 2014.

Council of Europe. 2010. "Declaration Of Romani Women Networks 2010, 'I Am A European Roma Woman' Conference." Athens, January 11-12, 2010. Web. Accessed 11 June 2016.

Council of Europe. nd. "Strategy on the Advancement of Romani Women and Girls, 2014-2020." Web. Accessed 11 June 2016.

Crowley, Niall, Angela Genova, and Silvia Sansonetti. "Empowerment Of Roma Women Within The European Framework Of National Roma Inclusion Strategies." European

Parliament Directorate General For Internal Policies, Policy Department C: Citizens' Rights And Constitutional Affairs— Gender Equality. 2013. Web. Accessed 16 June 2016.

D'Agostino, Serena. "Five Years of EU Roma Integration Policies: Vanishing Gender Awareness." Institute for European Studies, Brussels. 2016. Web. Accessed 16 June 2016.

Denzin, Norman K. 2003. *Performance Ethnography: Critical Pedagogy And The Politics Of Culture.* Thousand Oaks, CA: Sage Publications, 2003. Print.

European Union Agency for Fundamental Rights. "Roma Survey–Data in Focus. Education: The Situation of Roma in 11 EU Member States." Vienna, 2014. Web. Accessed 24 November 2014.

Fekete, Liz. "Europe against the Roma." *Race and Class* 55.3 (2014): 60–70. Print.

Jovanović, Jelena, Angéla Kóczé, and Lidia Balogh. "Intersections of Gender, Ethnicity, and Class: History and Future of the Romani Women's Movement." Centre for Policy Studies. Budapest: CEU Press, 2015. Print.

Kóczé, Angéla. 2009. "Missing Intersectionality: Race/Ethnicity, Gender, and Class in Current Research and Policies on Romani Women in Europe." Central European University Center for Policy Studies. Budapest: CEUPress, 2009. Web. Accessed 8 June 2016.

Oprea, Alexandra. "Romani Feminism in Reactionary Times." *Signs* 38.1 (2012): 11-21. Print.

Roffe, Jonathan. 2010. "Multiplicity." *The Deleuze Dictionary,* revised edition. Ed. A. Parr. Edinburgh: Edinburgh University Press, 2010. 181. Print.

Romedia Foundation. "I'm a European Roma Woman." 2011. Web. Accessed 5 October 2012.

Schultz, Debra L. 2012. "Translating Intersectionality Theory into Practice: A Tale of Romani-Gadže Feminist Alliance." *Signs* 38.1 (2012): 37-43. Print.

Stancu, Monica. *Discovering Roma Women's Voices: Roma Women's Activist Movement in Post-Communist Romania.* PhD Dissertation. Sarah Lawrence College, 2011. Print.

Stasiulus, Daiva K. "Feminist Intersectional Theorizing." *Race and Ethnic Relations in Canada,* 2nd ed. Ed. Peter S. Li. Toronto: Oxford University Press, 1999. 347-398. Print.

Szalai, Júlia and Violetta Zentai, eds. *Face and Causes of Roma Marginalization in Local Contexts.* Hungary: Centre for Policy Studies, Central European University, 2014. Print.

Tremlett, Annabel. "Making a Difference Without Creating a Difference: Super-diversity as a New Direction for Research on Roma Minorities." *Ethnicities* 14.6 (2014): 830-848. Print.

Zavačková-Cummings, Qristina. "Instituting History." August 6, 2015. Web. Accessed 6 August 2015.

ROMANI IDENTITY

HEDINA TAHIROVIĆ-SIJERČIĆ

Roma: a European nation with Indian roots. The Indian origin and affiliation of the Roma is most obvious linguistically, by the language still spoken by many members of this heterogeneous ethnicity. The Roma consist of various groups, which are labelled with different ethnonymes—self-designations as well as external designations: Arlije, Calé, Gurbet, Kaale, Kalderaš, Lovara, Manuš, Sepečides, Sinti, Ursari, etc.; many groups also use the self-designation Roma. Usually all these groups are summarized—sometimes even together with population groups of non-Indian origin—by the pejorative denomination "Gypsies." (Halwachs)

FOR CENTURIES, the culture and traditions of the Roma have been abundantly generalized by majority societies. This tendency contributes to the preservation of old stereotypes and the construction of new stereotypes about the Roma. These stereotypes eventually transform into acts of discrimination and racism against Roma simply because they are "different," and ultimately create a wall of "otherness" between majority and minority peoples and other ethnic groups. A barrier in communication is created because "otherness" is manifest not only in appearance, but also in cultural and linguistic terms. The history of the powerful and dominant has created images of the

13

Roma that, as they are transmitted and updated, play a large role in the creation of Romani identity and in the racism that is projected towards them.

Dominant ideology and culture erroneously understand Romani as an oral language and not as written, and Romani literature as a folk literature with no focus on contemporary creation. However, international Romani authors do, in fact, write in Romani and publish in its different dialects, and the written language is used in Romani networks, email, and chatrooms. Linguist Yaron Matras states that,

> No unification effort will succeed in bringing dozens or even hundreds of authors and thousands of other users of written Romani under the control of one, single authority. And, conversely, no language policy that ignores or tries to bypass these pioneers of written Romani will have a chance to succeed. (2005: 11)

This problem is produced not only by dominant ideology and politics, but also by Romani language and culture activists. Traditionally, there is no dominant class within Romani society, and there will be no dominant speech that can be accepted by all until Romani activists assert consensus about leadership. Dominant ideology co-opts elements of Romani culture, language, and history, and controls both education about Romani and instruction in the language. Because of internal struggles for prestige, and because of the lack of information and representation, many educated Roma are not accepted by their own people, their identity often shifting to that of the dominant culture. In such a situation, it is no wonder that the term, "Gypsy scholar" is met with an audible sneer. It is a racism that neither recognizes the written word of Romani authors nor the literary creativity of Roma. Ultimately it implies a kind of abnormality subsumed under the category of Other.

When we say the Other, we usually refer to groups and individuals who are in marginalized positions in society and who are exposed to various forms of stereotyping, stigmatization, and discrimination. In this sense, we recognize the Other most often as those who are poor; women; disabled; have different religious, cultural, and political views; or those who have a different skin colour or different sexual orientation; and so on. Otherness as stated by Jelisaveta Blagojević,

> cannot be a specific characteristic of an individual / individuals or social groups, but rather represents a way for every single human being to be in relation to the dominant discourse in relation to culture. Understood in this way, it means that the subject is never the same and identical with itself because it is always already produced in relationships with others, with multitudinous others, understood as another culture, another language, another person, another sex, etc. Culture and others, otherness of culture or cultures of others are political themes because culture always implies the relationship between nature and culture, humanity and non-humanity, the relationship between the "I" or "we" and somebody "other" and as such raises questions of power, domination, hierarchy, manipulation, and stigmatization.[1] (32)

The otherness of Romani culture is also a political theme that raises questions of power, domination, hierarchy, and manipulation. The relationship between humanity and non-humanity is a complex issue inclusive of the relationship between "we" and "other." Research on stereotypes about the Roma in Bosnia and Herzegovina suggest that stereotypes reflect an ambivalent attitude of the majority society (Bošnjaks, Serbs, and Croats) towards the Roma community (Puhalo 2009), and a tendency to generalize about the Roma in absolute terms. Their characteristics are considered fixed and are unjustifiably transposed and attributed to all members of the global Roma community.

A Pew Center study in 2009 found that 84% of Czechs expressed a dislike of Roma, as did 78% of Slovaks, 69% of Hungarians, and 84% of Italians. Across Europe, studies have found Roma are seen less favourably than

Black, African, Muslim, Jewish, or gay people. *Wired Magazine* noted in 2016 that the top two hate speech terms used in tweets from the UK are anti-Gypsy slang words. Anti-Gypsy bias is Europe's and Britain's most socially acceptable bigotry. (Nirenberg)

This treatment of the Roma has created a classic kind of racism, the traces of which can be found even in academic research papers. As A. Donovan McFarlane suggests, stereotypes, positive as well as negative, are based on insufficient knowledge of another culture:

[S]tereotyping and stereotypes serve more than an identity preservation or reactionary purpose—they serve to cover our inability and limitations when it comes to our understanding of others, and consequently, performs a progressive function by arming us with presumptions upon which we can strive to ascertain truth or factual knowledge of the others (other people and cultures) to eliminate these stereotypes or at least reduce them until self-knowledge becomes more possible or is accomplished. (142-43)

Following McFarlane, I seek possible ways to reduce stereotypes about Roma. One may be found in the contents of this book, where Romani women find space for their voices and produce self-knowledge accompanied by non-Romani women's knowledge. In this way, Romani and other cultures work together to eliminate stereotypes.

One form of stereotype arises through the perception of the Roma as nomadic people; this creates both positive and negative stereotypes about them. According to Marija Dalbelo,

[T]he "gypsy" stereotype in art and literature is designed in accordance with the romantic temperament, like the one that tends to melancholy and restlessness, and which epitomizes the ideal of freedom that takes place outside of all social institutions. In literature, the positive stereotype of Gypsies has crystallized, and, without exaggeration, it can be said that Roma in the Western European cultural context have achieved the status of the most universal and predominant stereotypes, so that they have become a literary metaphor for themselves. (436-7)

The pattern of prejudice and stereotypes in writing by non-Roma about Romani communities and the Romani language[2] reflects a belief in an extant imaginary community where Roma speak many different dialects often incomprehensible to each other, and have different religions, customs, and traditions imposed by the majority community (Šakaja and Užarević 2014: 37). This diversity confirms many Romani sayings: "Hundreds of Romani settlements, hundreds of Romani speeches" (Vukanović 1983: 339); "How many Gypsies—so many customs..." (339). In their diffusion and variety, Roma communities are unable to function as one.

Fiction—the literary art that has created positive stereotypes about Roma—generalizes everything that is "Gypsy" in accordance with romantic images: "gypsy music," "gypsy fashion," "gypsy love," "gypsy fire," "fiery gypsy men," "fiery gypsy women," the people who are black, tall, handsome, and beautiful, good singers, musicians, dancers, and symbols of love. The abundant use of these stereotypes in literary and artistic representation illustrates that the definition of Romani identity rests in many hands, but not in those of the Roma.

> For a very long time, Gypsy identity has been in the hands of the non-Gypsy specialist, especially politicians and academics, whose ideas about who and what we are have given sustenance to the Gypsy Image. (Hancock 2007b: 6)

At the same time, however, it is not rare to find Romani men and women authors, such as in case of Amela Avdić's song, "Warm is the Gypsy Soul," who also make use of stereotypes. In so doing, the positive stereotypes observed in literature survive, perpetuated not only by the dominant but also by the oppressed. Consider the following example:

Život i pjesma, vatre su vječne
U nama sreća i radost tinja
Sretni smo u čergi punom dušom
Pored vatre dok kiša tiho rominja.

Life and song, eternal fire are
Happiness and joy smoldering in us
We are happy in the tent and our soul is fullfilled
By the fire while the rain is still drizzling[3]

Even if the stereotype transmitted might be considered positive, continued use of the word "gypsy" written in small letters connotes negativity. A generalizing term, it indicates ignorance and/or repudiation of *Romanipe(n)* as well as those who create and make up *Romanipe(n)*: Romani women and Romani men. Its usage can be intentional as much as unintentional. *Rromanipe(n)* */Romanipe(n)* is the common denominator of all that is considered or believed to make up the essential characteristics of all Romani people around the world. The term is derived from the name of Roma/Rroma.[4] It refers to the feeling of belonging to the same people, to the same history, culture, and habits despite the differences that are specific to sub-groups.

Non-Roma researchers and other authors have contributed to the preservation of stereotypes about the Roma as a marginalized and misunderstood people, a subaltern group. Rajko Djurić notes that "astonishing and humiliating is the fact that, in literary lexicons and in literary histories of European countries and peoples, there is no mention of any Romani writer" (2010: 150). Ian Hancock describes his related experience:

I spent a couple of hours in a local bookshop going through several works with such titles as *An Encyclopedia of Western Culture, A History of Europe, A Compendium of European History, A History of the Western World*, etc., but no Romanies graced their pages. For whoever wrote them, we were not considered to be part of European history or culture. (Hancock 2007-2008)

National or ethnic stereotypes in general constitute the most common form of stereotyping and are a basic element of expressing nationalistic views. They are transmitted to the press and mass media, to publishing houses and through published media including textbooks.[5] In the case of the Roma, stereotyping is closely linked to issues of representation. When faced with the stereotyping that occurs in national canons and in mass media, Romani scholars and researchers have not been able to speak for themselves, nor have they been able to effectively represent themselves and their people.[6] The socio-political status of countries where the Roma live creates and determines their status. In this sense, Gayatri Spivak raises a relevant question: "With what voice-consciousness can the subaltern speak?" (27). After centuries-long persecution of the Roma, it is not surprising to find that in literary encyclopedias and in the literary history of Europe, there is no mention of a single Romani writer or author. This is the case even today; Romani literature by Roma and in the voice of Romani authors remains invisible.

IDENTIFICATION BEFORE IDENTITY IS PREFERABLE

Because of the history of discrimination, racism, and persecution, the majority of Romani men and women do not identify themselves by their ethnicity. Because of the continual expulsions they undergo, Roma are ambivalent in terms of their very self-identification. In this way, they directly and consciously determine their own destiny. From the very start, not identifying their *Romanipe(n)* implies that they lose their Romani identity. Those who decide to non-identify mainly live outside of Romani settlements; they are generally racialized as white, do not speak the Romani language, and are educated. In accepting non-Romani identification they accept the non-Romani identity of those who are dominant and powerful in the majority society. In so doing, they assimilate. Their children of course do the same, and the tradition of non-identification continues from one generation to the next. In this way, their identification with the most powerful people in their society—their heritage, accomplishments, and symbols—all provide them with a sense of belonging to a larger, more highly valued group of people. In this way, Roma who associate themselves with the more powerful members of society provide another image of themselves; they align themselves with another identity. This "newly" adopted identity, they reason, is more valuable than their original Romani one. They assume it brings them more respect and more prosperity for themselves and their children. In this sense, they presume to escape the stereotypical characteristics of their Romani identity. Yet their new identity consists of a mixture of both. T. Minh-ha Trinh illustrates this point: "The moment the insider steps out from the inside, she is no longer a mere insider (and vice versa). She necessarily looks in from the outside while also looking out from the inside" (198). However, there will always be something missing, something that brings him or her into a position of not belonging fully to either identity: "She knows she is different while at the same time being Him. Not quite the Same, not quite the Other..." (Trinth 198).

Roma who make professional presentations about the Roma generally speak either about the group they have grown up with themselves or about a group designated to be of great interest to non-Roma who know nothing about Roma except through stereotypes. As a result, wrong or poorly researched information about Romani people is circulated. Ethnocentrism and the assessment of Romani values by non-Roma have led to harsh treatment whereby the Roma are denoted as a unique ethnic group. Researchers generally show features that are based on Romani sub-groups that are recognizable to society— the poorest and least educated—consolidating the stereotypes already in place about the Roma population at large. Under such circumstances, the Roma who belong to groups that are of little interest to researchers—the domestic, settled, and native-born, and those who are employed, educated, and otherwise assimilated into dominant society—accept their own identity with some reservations. They denounce their Romani identity because they do not see, feel, or know its value when it is reduced to a stereotype.

When identity no longer has any value for its members, and when their own image in relation to the Other is negative, the group begins to disintegrate, change, or may be "lost" in terms of an individual's identification (Kyuchukov and Hancock 21). This is the process of assimilation.

> Two or more groups may unite to form a new group, larger and different from any component parts. This is referred to as *amalgamation.* Alternatively, one group may lose its identity by merging into another group, which retains its identity. This is called *incorporation.* On the other hand, there is a possibility of proliferation: a new group comes into existence without its parent group (or groups) losing its (or their) identity. (Horowitz qtd in Kyuchukov and Hancock 21)

Roma/Romani identities are very complex and can be interpreted differently not just by non-Roma but also by Roma themselves. Identities associated with Romani men and women differ from one group to another and very often from family to family. In the context of presenting Romani identity, any reference that speaks about the Roma as a homogeneous group is an ideological and political construct. The Romani community is a non-homogeneous social and cultural ethnic group with a hierarchical structure. Different sub-groups each have their own ethno-social and ethno-cultural characteristics, differences that affect the creation of their multidimensional identity (Marushiakova and Popov 56-58).

SELF-EVALUATING ONE'S IDENTITY:
A CASE OF INTERPRETATION

It is important to create a set of criteria that is relevant for internal relationships within Romani society and for external relationships with others. As Ian Hancock, an American linguist and an expert in Romani Studies, notes that: "one simple political distinction functions as the most accurate definition of the perceived status of the Roma in society: they are Roma, and all the others are not" (qtd. in Mirga and Mruz 171). Nicolae Gheorghe, a Romanian academic who, like Hancock, is of Romani origin, speaks about Roma or Gypsy identity not as a naturally given fact, but as a role that shapes and reflects personality. In turn, this produces criteria for establishing relationships. Subjective feelings about beliefs, customs, and religions intertwine with educational level and familiarity with language(s). Objective feelings develop in relation to the content of subjective feelings about our ethnic identity. The process is necessary for our social existence.

A naturally given fact is that birth is fundamental for a blood bond (Gheorghe). In *Roma Differences and Intolerance,* Andžej Mirga, a Polish academic of Romani origin, elaborates on identity, describing several characteristic values of Romani identity among which gender and cultural dichotomy stand out: any persons who by nature belong to the group by birth, through their parents, are classified as Roma (Mirga and Mruz 169-176). The authors base their analysis on the formation of male identity; gender difference is seen through a patriarchal framework and tradition is understood from a male perspective. For my purposes, I will highlight six basic types of identity criteria most commonly used by Roma when referring to their Romani identity. Also indicated is a critique of their value as I experience it with respect to Roma in the Balkans.

The first criterion concerns native Rom or Rom born to two Romani parents. This criterion also concerns marriage partners. Mixed marriages are not infrequent. In this case, the status of a non-Romani partner, despite the fact that he/she fully participates in the life of the group, is marked as *Gadjo-Rom* or *Gadjo-Romni*. Roma recognize others when and how they prefer to do so. In the case of a mixed marriage, there is a heavy burden placed on the non-Romani spouse. It involves a duality and politics of identity that Roma use automatically with reference to themselves and to others. Children from mixed marriages acquire the full status of Roma if they meet all the criteria, provided that they remain in the group. This criterion conflicts with the Universal Declaration of Human Rights (UDHR) that states the right of individuals to declare his or her own identity regardless of their parentage or circumstances of birth (Article 15, clauses 1 and 2).[7]

The second identity criterion is associated with social behaviour and it is regulated by rules of ritual purity, respect or appreciation, and age. Purity laws, or "mahrime/marime" in Romani, are still respected by most Roma. These affect many aspects of life, and they are applied to people, actions, and things. For example, parts of the human body are considered impure (fingernails, toenails, the genital organs), and this standard affects washing rituals for clothes, the body, dishes, and children. Childbirth, death, menstruating women, and some animals are also regarded as impure. This criterion is relevant to the current living conditions of many Romani groups but should not be generalized. Many Roma groups and subgroups live surrounded by contaminated materials, and without water and sewage systems. In those living conditions, they are not able to meet the criteria of "mahrime/ marime."

Respect and appreciation are gained through the life course. For example, age implies having authority or being the elder of a family or leader of a group in accordance with the function being carried out. The structure in the traditional Romani family vests power in the oldest man or grandfather. In general, men have more power and command more respect than women. Young women start to gain some authority when they give birth and have children. Appreciation of older women increases as they age.

The issue of power brings with it the issue of exploitation of the powerless (i.e., women and children), which invites criticism of this criterion. This issue is of great importance, especially for certain groups of Roma such as the nomad Gurbeti group, Kalderaš, and Arli. In such groups, male and female children are workers who bring goods and money into the family and as such gain respect as adults. Most of them behave like adults. Once female children achieve adulthood, they are no longer respected and are often exposed to all forms of violence. Older women and men are not protected or respected, and due to alcoholism, drug addiction, and gambling, they are often abused and exploited by younger family members. For this reason, we cannot make general claims about respect toward all Romani elders since many, if not most, live without adequate care and in very bad conditions.

The third identity criterion is related to the Romani language, i.e., any Romani dialect in its relationship with any non-Romani language. The language performs the role of symbolic separation from the non-Romani world. Use of the Romani language determines an ethnic boundary and performs basic communication functions within the group. There are groups of indigenous (locally-born) Roma who speak the language(s) of the countries they live in as their first language. Their use of the Romani language has only a secondary value; the assurance of the secrecy needed in relation to non-Roma who do not understand that language takes precedence. In this case, the use of the Romani language is not a sign of Romani identity. This context implies a loss of the original/old identity, leading to a loss of the native language as a core identity value and the creation of a "new" identity among Roma.

The fourth criterion is related to the acceptance of exclusions that arise from the social organization of the group. These relationships are related to age, sex, kinship, and legal and religious traditions. These prohibitions are determined by the power accorded to men within the mindset of the Romani group. The position of girls and young women is thus represented by traditional and historical subjugation, and their bodies are a source of exploitation for men in every way. This affects the education of girls in particular (Tahirović-Sijerčić 2012: 79). Moreover, as stated by Mirga and Gheorge,

> traditional families and groups are convinced that education would result in the disappearance of Roma identity. Therefore they oppose the education of their children. Thus the crux of the matter is: how to win equality and stay different. (39-40)

The dominance of men in the Romani community manifests itself through established cultural and traditional laws in addition to the informal institutions that are organized to resolve disputes within the Roma community, i.e. the so-called

Romani *kris* (Heinschick and Teichmann 2). The Romani *kris* is a traditional court that applies Romani laws to resolve conflicts inside and outside the Romani community. Laws are bound to ritual taboos. Those related to Romani women are designed to regulate customs of early arranged marriage, adultery, and sexual behaviour, but they also convey sanctions against theft and fraud inside and outside of the Romani community. In general, their aim is dominance over women and girls who fall victim to their oppression and subjugation.

The laws created by the "respectable" members of the group, the men, are accepted and governed by the Romani *kris*. The degree of power accorded to the men determines the level of integration of the group, and its hierarchy among, and solidarity with, other Roma and non-Roma. The institution of the *kris* enhances men's status and provides opportunities for jobs and other activities within Romani and non-Romani society. The role of younger women in these groups is to fulfill husbands' and children's needs. They do not have the right to accept or reject laws, and are forbidden to attend Romani *kris* sessions. Using cultural traditions or even inventing new traditions often justifies the control and oppression of women. This is intensified in situations in which individual men, or the whole community, feel threatened.

Romani *kris*, just like *Romanipe*, is undergoing reconstruction and change. Although their voices are mostly ignored by the community, Romani women are approaching Romani men and reminding them of the traditional meaning of the Romani *kris*. In their fight for Romani women's rights, they are very often misunderstood. Because of their ideals and their knowledge, Romani women are discriminated against not just by non-Romani people, but also by their own people, both men and women. Because of that, they are often alienated; their "otherness of other" can result in deep disappointment, sickness, and death. The Polish Romani poet Bronislawa Wajs Papusza is a famous case in point.

The fifth identity criterion involves a certain model of the Roma's economic dependence on the exploitation of the *Gadjo* world.[8] Even though the Romani *kris* supports and advocates for economic dependence on non-Roma, this criterion seems to be the most conspicuous in public discourse. This is evidenced by the exploitation of Romani children both in early marriages arranged for profit motives, and in work such as begging, washing cars, cleaning shoes, as well as by the reliance on Romani women who are involved in begging, prostitution, theft, and other illegitimate activities (Tahirović-Sijerčić 2012: 80). There is a false belief that Roma do not subject their own members to acts of exploitation. But these practices also exploit non-Roma because in cases such as begging and stealing, the *Gadje* are the exclusive target.

The last and sixth identity criterion involves all of the visual signs and traits by which the Roma identify themselves as Roma. These may be akin to anthropological characteristics, for example having a style of movement that is distinctive, or wearing particular decorations, costumes and the like. Obviously, these can vary depending on the group and time, but members of a given group can easily distinguish the characteristics they use for self-definition. Visual signs are not "read" exclusively by Roma to increase their own visibility and to promote their identity among each other. They are also used by non-Roma who follow so-called Gypsy fashion, Gypsy music trends, and so on. These six criteria for the interpretation of Romani identity and identity politics develop within Romani society with specific modalities of power. Whoever has power is able to exercise exclusion. As Stuart Hall emphasizes, identities are products that mark differences and exclusions (1996: 219). They are constructed through differences rather than outside of them.

ROMA AS A TRANSNATIONAL PEOPLE THROUGHOUT HISTORY

It is impossible to talk about Romani identity—its change and its deconstruction, its creation and loss of identities—without talking about Romani suffering. The Romani trail of suffering started a long time ago in India, between the fifth and seventh centuries of the European Middle Ages (Djurić 1987: 40). When the Roma settled in Europe in search of better living conditions and prosperity, they were not accepted by the local populations. The Roma have been persecuted for centuries across Europe,[9] tortured and burned as witches and supporters of the devil, hanged, and even held in bondage. In the modern era, when Nazi racial reasoning served as a justification for the genocidal destruction of the Roma people—as the Other and among the Other—the Roma arrived in Bergen-Belsen, Sachenhausen, Dachau, Auschwitz-Birkenau, and dozens of other concentration camps. At Auschwitz-Birkenau, Romani children were a favourite subject of research for Joseph Mengele. Almost no child survived his "experiments." According to Nazi philosophy, human life could survive only through preserving the strongest of the "race." The Holocaust, or *Porrajmos*, as Roma refer to it, means "devouring." "Devoured" were more than 500,000 Roma, which at that time comprised between one-third and two-thirds of the European Roma population. For Roma, the Holocaust was not only a specific case of genocide, but also a continuation of the suffering that has extended through hundreds of years of slavery, persecution, and exile.

Discrimination, intolerance, mass extermination, killings, and persecution of the Roma continue to put them on the margins of society. As a result, they are considered unacceptable, unequal, and less worthy as a people, wherever they live. The Roma have been targeted and killed by skinheads and neo-Nazis, and daily assaults, beatings, and other forms of violence are prevalent.[10] Now, at the beginning of the twenty-first century, the Roma still live below the minimum standard in the social, economic, and educational development enjoyed by other human beings. Moreover, the Roma have come to believe that they cannot obtain any form of protection from law-enforcement agencies in the countries where they live. They believe that the state cannot or will not protect them from violence. They are forced, therefore, to displace themselves by moving long distances with their families. In this situation, there is no opportunity to be concerned with education, the key to prosperity and survival for any ethnic group. In their fight against poverty and to achieve the bare necessities of life, education has become the lowest-priority problem for the Roma. The cycle of movement and migration continues.

The majority of the Roma from the ex-Yugoslav region, the Balkans, and Eastern European countries have been forced to move to Western Europe (Germany, France, Belgium, Austria, the Netherlands, Italy), and to the U.S. and Canada. There are Romani migrants living in diaspora all over the world. According to NGO Romani activists, there are about fifteen million Roma living in Europe, and about eighteen million in the world. They are a global population, both inside and outside of the Balkans, from Europe and the Americas to Australia. To find a job, to access education, and to be accepted in their new countries of residence, "they are forced to change their identity, either to displace internally, or to move on to other countries" (Tahirović-Sijerčić 2012: 74). The migration and displacement of Roma depends on the laws of the countries to which they migrate.

> According to UNHCR, today about 300,000 people that were relocated due to the Balkan conflicts of the 1990s are still away from home. The internally displaced persons (IDPs) in the [Balkan] region number 218,500 and include 80,000 members of the Roma, Ashkali, and Egyptian (RAE) groups. (Cherkezova and Tomova 22)

National and international migration statistics are cited in general terms; there is no research about Romani populations specifically and the problems that cause their migration. Until recently, there have been no statistics on Romani migration or Romani migrant quotas. However, Cherkezova and Tomova provide comparative research on the migration of Roma and non-Roma along with statistics on its possible motives, which include the need for better living conditions and access to employment:

> The ranking of motives for a possible migration is identical for all countries. The majority of respondents, who intend to relocate abroad, indicate "better chances of finding employment" as the main reason for migration (64% among Roma and 56% among non-Roma). Next are the

"better pay / better working conditions"—16% among Roma and 20% among non-Roma. Thirdly, motives are related to "better living conditions / social and health care system / political situation"—15% for Roma and 16% for non-Roma. The differences are significant in terms of the weight of each reason, given by the proportion of respondents by country and ethnicity. (Cherkezova and Tomova 35)

Migration is a phenomenon that affects the formation of "new" identity/identities, and this in turn is dependent on identity politics in the country where the Roma live and from which they migrate. It is important to note that the movement of majority populations is classified as migration, but Romani movement is traditionally, and continues to be, identified by the majority of people as "nomadism." This is the case even though the "term nomad is not suitable because there is just a small number of Roma, Sinti, Gitana, and Travellers who are truly nomads, [and] it can also mark other travelling groups or communities" (Djokić 2011). Non-Roma never ask whether Romani migrations occur by force of circumstance.

In the case of the Roma, nomadism is not merely a state of mind and cannot be separated from exile. While seeking protection, Roma are constantly moving, but still living a traditional life (Djurić 1987: 181). Nomadism, in the eyes of the non-Roma, is a cultural tradition that has shaped and defined their perceptions of Roma identity. In reality, the necessity of movement has been caused by economic, social, and political hardship; persecution; discrimination; attacks; and wars in countries where the Roma have lived. Scholars and experts have not spoken about Romani migration in terms of an internally forced displacement or about how these forces have resulted in a lack of education. This "nomadism by force of law" has led to problems in identifying the national characteristics and dominant cultural heritage of the Roma, and in distinguishing their nationalities, customs, and languages. The globalization of Romani identity, of their cultural and traditional values, and of the Romani lifestyle, has led to a loss of Romani national consciousness. This situation has incurred the loss of educated Roma whose numbers are already small. These individuals often change their identity and attempt to identify with the dominant, powerful nations (Tahirović-Sijerčić 2012). As Stuart Hall explains, cultural identity

> is "a matter of "becoming" as well as "being". It belongs to the future as much as to the past. It is not something which already exists, transcending place, time, history, and culture. Cultural identities come from somewhere, have histories. But, like everything which is historical, they undergo constant transformation. (1990: 225)

The problem of Romani identity is underexplored. Academic debate exists and is diverse, but it is one in which Roma do not participate; the few experts who could do so are usually unwelcome. This situation further reinforces the prejudices that continue to fuel misconceptions about the Roma population, exacerbating the problems of racism that exist in all areas of their lives. Hancock is instructive on this point, and on the contradictions it raises:

> There are three approaches to formalizing a consensus on Romani identity: treating us either as Europeans, or else as Asians, or as both. Each is attended by arguments, for and against. The case for being considered European, for some at least, rests upon the fact that over the centuries our genetic makeup has acquired a generous infusion of European "blood," for some Romani populations clearly far outweighing the original gene pool. Secondly, we might be considered European because of our widespread geographical dispersion as a truly transnational people. But as Mirga and Gheorghe have pointed out, we are a global, not just a European, population. Are the Romanies in Peru also "true Europeans?" One's identity has to be evaluated in terms not only of what one perceives oneself to be, but also by whether members of the population that one sees oneself as identifying with also share that perception. And it depends, furthermore, upon the

attitudes of the out-group, which is the third dimension; in other words, one might be attempting to become part of a population which has no intention of letting one in. (Hancock 2007b:16)

When thinking about identity politics and the dominance of the powerful category of "white," it is useful to look at the writings of bell hooks, who recognizes multiple African-American identities and "multiple blackness." What exactly does "multiplicity" mean for Roma identity? Could hooks' framing of identity as "multiple blackness" be applicable to Roma? Are the two ethnicities comparable? Not only in the former Yugoslavia, Balkans, Eastern Europe, and Europe but throughout the world, the Roma are treated as "Black" regardless of the fact that the majority of them are "White." According to bell hooks, there are social class differences among African-Americans that affect the question of skin colour. Poverty creates divisions of social class for Roma as well—those who are "White" but poor. We can recognize the differences that constitute the Roma even as they create distinctions among themselves. Skin colour creates differences within one's own community and between other Romani groups. Those who have a lighter skin are more dominant. These individuals tend to be chosen as community mediators and representatives of the community, creating a hierarchy within local Roma communities.

There are entities in the Americas who translate the language of African Americans into the language of Whites so that it can be understood. Hatred, discrimination, and racism by the dominant and powerful prevent understanding of a common language when it is spoken by the powerless. This situation may be comparable to the situation of the Roma. The intermediaries—bilingual or multilingual Roma who are elected by the dominant to present community needs—serve the dominant culture as a kind of proof to show that they have succeeded. Their social elevation allows them to believe that they rank higher as a class. Their social status increases and they become socially mobile. In the creation of all these classes, the woman is associated with the lower class. She is the "Other," "different," and even "different from different."

In reading the works of African-American women, I recognize in them the voice of Romani women:

> [The] everyday life experience of being a black woman in this culture was to be aware of the social realities of the diversity of the white men, white women, even black men, but I did not know how to explain this difference (hooks 150).

IDENTITY THROUGH THE PRISM OF LITERARY EXPRESSION

Dominant culture and ethnonationalism can strongly marginalize the literature of those who are "different" and reinforce stereotypes. According to their language, the language of the Other, Romani writers are identified by their own communities and by others as "different." At the same time, Romani writers are proposing new ideas through writing and education. The perception of difference and "diversity" begins from birth, and becomes a burden for those who are subordinate. They carry this feeling with them through their lifetime. Audre Lorde in her biomythography, *Zami: A New Spelling Of My Name*, talks about "diversity" in these words:

> As a child, I always knew my mother was different from the other women I knew. (15)

> Pain was always right around the corner. Difference had taught me that, out of the mouth of my mother. And knowing that, I fancied myself on guard, safe. I still had to learn that knowing was not enough. (205)

> I remember how being young and Black and gay and lonely felt. (176)

> The question of acceptance had a different weight for me. In a paradoxical sense, once I accepted my position as different from the larger society as well as from any single sub-society—Black or gay—I felt I didn't have to try so

hard. To be accepted. To look femme. To be straight. To look straight. To be proper. To look "nice." To be liked. To be loved. To be approved. What I didn't realize was how much harder I had to try merely to stay alive, or rather, to stay human. How much stronger a person I became in that trying. (181)

"Difference" increases or becomes more visible in situations where individual men or entire communities feel threatened by Others. Such was the case of the Polish Romani poet Bronislawa Wajs Papusza, who belonged to a group of nomadic Roma. Her officially registered, yet contested, date of birth is 30 May 1910 in Lubin; she died on 8 February 1987 in Wrocław. She did not attend school; a Jewish woman taught her to read and write. Because of her literacy, the Roma community became suspicious of her. Her work became known through the Polish writer Jerzy Ficowski and the Polish lyricist Julian Tuwim. Papusza wrote of her own "difference of difference" within the Romani community and of her literacy as its cause:

When I was thirteen,
I was lean and agile as
a squirrel on a tree,
I've only been black.
I have read and Roma
Ridiculed me because of it and spit on me.[11]

She was aware of how her dark skin set her apart from the non-Roma community:

But who knows, maybe a new skin grows on me,
perhaps a more beautiful one [12]

"Otherness" created by people other than those to whom you belong is intolerable, but the "Otherness" created by one's own people is more than that. This "Otherness," where the Other are one's own people, creates an improper/inappropriate Otherness whose consequences are alienation, loneliness, and disappearance. The problem of "Otherness" for Romani women, or even more precisely, for educated Romani women writers, resides in their "thirdness" within their own community. Recognition of selves that entails a connection to the Other's mind while accepting one's own separateness sustains a subjectivity that is destroyed, negated, and modified by the Other. Such a selfhood seeks to find "the freedom from any intent to control or coerce" (Benjamin 1-2).

The issues of identity and subordination in this context have yet to be fully explored and remain a fertile area for further research. Through bilingualism/multilingualism and self-translation, Romani writers who write in *Romani čhib* [Romani language] find ways to preserve and keep the vitality of the language and its dialects. Through their literary expression, they are on their path to decolonizing the mind; representing their own work honestly, without stereotypes; and honouring their own knowledge, culture, religion, and customst[13] (Denzin, Lincoln, and Smith 2), to changing a centuries-long silence into a voice that tells the truth about our people, their position, and their situation around the world.

Romani: XXX

Ako tumen den vorba gova si džuvdipe
Me dživiv.
Ako tumen den vorba gova si baxt
Me sem baxtali.
Ako tumen den vorba gova si šukaripe (miro)
Me sem šukarimaha.

Von uštaven (čalaven prnenca thaj phiraven prdal pe)
amaro barikanipe.
Cikniven amari čhib,
Traden amaro narodo.

Ako tumen den vorba gova si e Devlestar dino,
O Devel na dija amen khanči.

—Hedina Tahirović-Sijerčić

34

English: XXX

If you call it life
Then, I live.
If you call it luck
Then, I'm lucky.
If you call it peace
Then, I'm tranquil.

You trample on our dignity.
You underrate our language,
You torment our people.
If you say they were given to us by God,
God gave us nothing.

—Hedina Tahirović-Sijerčić

[1]The English translation is mine.

[2]"Romani, the common language of the Roma, the Sinti, the Kale, and other European population groups summarized by the pejorative denomination "gypsies," belongs to the Indo-Aryan branch of the Indo-European language family and is the only new Indo-Aryan language spoken exclusively outside of the Indian subcontinent" (Zatreanu and Halwachs 3).

[3]From Amela Avdić's unpublished manuscript, "Topla je duša ciganska. / Warm is the *gypsy* soul."

[4]Alternative spellings and pronunciations reflect dialectical and regional differences.

[5]Another stereotype that persists among Roma people is the distrust of learning from books.

[6]Until the twentieth century, the Romani language was a spoken language only (Djurić 2010: 6). "Romani … is the only Indo-Aryan language spoken exclusively in Europe, as well as by emigrant population in the Americas and Australia" (Matras 2006: 1).

[7]Article 15. (1) "Everyone has the right to claim a nationality. (2) No one shall be arbitrarily deprived of his nationality nor denied the right to change his nationality." The Universal Declaration

of Human Rights (UDHR) is a milestone document in the history of human rights. Drafted by representatives with different legal and cultural backgrounds from all regions of the world, the Declaration was proclaimed by the United Nations General Assembly in Paris on 10 December 1948. General Assembly Resolution 217A declares a common standard of achievement for all peoples and all nations. It sets out, for the first time, fundamental human rights to be universally protected.

[8]*Gadjo* is the name used by Roma to refer to non-Romani people.

[9]See Hancock, "The Roots of Antigypsyism: To Holocaust and After." "Romanies were first documented in German-speaking Europe in 1407; the first anti-Gypsy law was issued in 1416, the beginning of centuries of legal discrimination. Bischoff wrote that "in Germany, the greatest number of decrees of banishment were published against them ... this unhappy people was persecuted, strung up without exception as thieves and robbers when caught and, guilty or innocent, destroyed by the thousands" (1827: 3). By 1417, commentaries on their frightening physical appearance were beginning to be recorded; Hermann Cornerus wrote of the Romaines' "very ugly" and "black" faces, and likened them to the Tatars (in Eccard, 1723), while in 1435 the Roman Catholic monk Rufus of Lübeck wrote disparagingly of their dark skin and black hair (Grautoff, 1872). The first accusations of the Roma as spies, carriers of the plague and traitors to Christendom were made in 1496 and again in 1497, and yet again in 1498. In 1500, all Roma were banished from Germany on pain of death by Maximilian I, while German citizens were told that killing Romanies was not a punishable offense. In 1543, in a diatribe directed at both Jews and Romanies, Martin Luther recommended that Jews be rounded up and put into stables "like Gypsies," in order to be reminded of their lowly status in German society (Gilbert 1985: 19), and in a sermon he gave in 1543, he said Romanies charged high prices, gave away information and were traitors, that they poisoned the wells, started fires, kidnapped children and cheated the public in all sorts of ways intended to cause harm (Luther 1883: 19-24). While the Lutheran Church has officially apologized to the Jewish people for Luther's anti-

Semitic remarks, they have yet publicly to acknowledge his racism directed at Romanies" (Hancock 2012: 26).

[10]For more on this issue, see: ERRC; RVN; and Lee (1998): "The number of assaults against Roma is not admitted to by the Czech, Hungarian, or Romanian governments. However, the American researcher Paul Polansky, in his book, *Dvakrat Tim Samym [Living Through It Twice]*, published in 1997, reports that over 2,000 cases were recorded at that time" (Tahirović-Sijerčić 2012: 74).

[11]Cited in Hübschmannová.

[12]"Cigani I Njihov Put (1): Iz Papuszinih usta [Gypsies and their Journey (1): From Papusza's mouth]." Zurnal. Centar za razvoj medija i analize. July 14, 2009. Adapted from Fonseca.

[13]"The work must represent Indigenous persons honestly, without distortion or stereotype, and the research should honour indigenous knowledge, customs, and rituals. [R]esearchers should be accountable to indigenous persons. They, not Western scholars, should have first access to research findings and control over the distribution of knowledge" (Denzin and Lincoln 2008: 2).

WORKS CITED

Avdić, Amela. "Topla je duša ciganska [Warm is the Gypsy Soul]." Unpublished manuscript.

Benjamin, Jessica. "Intersubjectivity, Thirdness, and Mutual Recognition." Presentation to the Institute for Contemporary Psychoanalysis, Los Angeles, 2007. Web. Accessed 4.06.2016.

Blagojević, Jelisaveta. "Kulture Koje Dolaze: Drugi i Kultura (Incoming Cultures: Others and Cultures)." *Kultura, Drugi, Žene [Culture, The Other, Women]*. Eds. J. Kodrnja, S. Savić, S. i Slapšak. Zagreb: Plejada, 2010, 25-37. Print.

Cherkezova, Stoyanka and Ilona Tomova, eds. *An Option of Last Resort? Migration of Roma and Non-Roma from CEE Countries*. Roma Inclusion Working Papers. UNDP Europe and CIS, Bratislava Regional Centre, 2013. Print.

Dalbelo, Marija. "Prilog bibliografiji o Romima (Ciganima) u SFRJ's posebnim obzirom na etnološku i folklorističku građu u periodici [Bibliography of the Roma in Yugoslavia with

Special Reference to the Ethnological and Folkloristic Material in Periodicals.]." *Jezik i kultura Roma* [*The Language and Culture of Roma*]. Ed. M. Šipka. Sarajevo: Institute for the Study of National Relations, 1989. 421-441. Print.

Denzin, K. Norman, Yvonna S. Lincoln and Linda Tuhiwai Smith, eds. *Critical-Indigenous Methodologies*. Los Angeles: Sage, 2008. Print.

Djokić, Ana. *Jean-Pierre Liegeois: Romi preispituju Europu, njene sastavnice* (Vijesti: 30.05.2011). Interview from French, 2011. Translated by Ema Pongrašić. Web. Accessed 11.08.2013.

Djurić, Rajko. *Istorija Romske Književnosti/History of the Roma Literature*. Vršac: Biblioteka Vetrokaz, 2010. Print.

Djurić, Rajko. *Seobe Roma – Krugovipaklai Venacsreće*. Beograd: Beogradski izdavačko-grafički zavod, 1987.

European Roma Rights Center (ERRC). Web.

Fonseca, Isabel. *Sahranite me uspravno: Cigani i njihov put* [*Bury Me Standing: The Gypsies and Their Journey*]. New York: Vintage Books, 1995. Print.

Gheorghe, Nicolae. "The Romani identity between victimization and emancipation: Nicolae Gheorghe in Dialogue with Iulius Rostaşi." *Rom Sau Ţigan. Dilemele Unui Etnonim În Spaţiul Românesc* [*Roma or Gypsy: The Dilemmas of an Ethnonym in the Romanian Society*]. Eds. I. Horvath and L. Nastasă. Romanian Institute for Research on National Minorities and Soros Foundation Romania, 2012. Trans. I. M. Nistor. Web. Accessed 04.06. 2016.

Hall, Stuart. "Introduction: Who Needs Identity?" *Questions of Cultural Identity*. Eds. S. Hall and Paul du Guy. London: Sage, 1996. 1-17. Print.

Hall, Stuart. "Cultural Identity and Diaspora." *Identity: Community, Culture, Difference*. Ed. Jonathan Rutherford. London: Lawrence and Wishart, 1990. Web. Accessed 15.06.2016.

Halwachs W. Dieter. "[Romani] Project 2012." Universität Graz/ Dieter W. Halwachs, 2012. Web. Accessed 25.11.2015.

Hancock, Ian. "On Romani Origins and Identity." 2007-2008. Web. Accessed 10.01. 2014.

Hancock, Ian. "On Romani Origins and Identity: Questions for

Discussion." *Gypsies and the Problem of Identity: Contextual, Constructed and Contested.* Eds. A. Marsh and E. Strand. Istanbul: Swedish Research Institute, 2006. Print.

Hancock, Ian. "Our Need for Internal Diplomatic Skills." *Roma Diplomacy.* Eds. V. Nicolae and Hanna Slavik. Brussels: European Roma Information Office, 2007a. Print.

Hancock, Ian. *Porrajmos: A Selection of Essays on the Romani Genocide.* Buda, 2012. Print.

Hancock, Ian. "The Struggle for the Control of Identity." *Road Memories: Aspects of Migrant History.* Ed. Michael Hayes. Newcastle, UK: Cambridge Scholars Publishing, 2007b. Print.

Heinschick, F. Moses and Michael Teichmann. "Kris." Graz: Rombaze, 2008. Web. Accessed 20.11.1914.

hooks, bell. *Feminist Theory, Talking Back: Thinking Feminist, Thinking Black.* Cambridge, MA: South and Press, 1989. Print.

Hübschmannová, Milena. "Papusza (Bronislawa Wajs)." ROMBASE, 2003. Web. Accessed 18.09.2012.

Kyuchukov, Hristo and Ian Hancock. *Roma Identity.* Prague: NGO Slovo 21, 2010. Print.

Lee, Ronald. *Why Roma Are Coming to Canada.* Toronto, 1998. Updated by Paul St. Clair, March, 2007. Web. Accessed 24.07. 2012.

Lorde, Audre. *Zami: A New Spelling of My Name.* Berkeley, CA: The Crossing Press, 1983. Print.

Marushiakova, Elena and Vesselin Popov. *Gypsies (Roma) in Bulgaria.* Frankfurt am Main: Peter Lang, 1997. Print.

Matras, Yaron. "The Status of Romani in Europe." Report submitted to the Council of Europe's Language Policy Division. Strasbourg: Council of Europe, 2005. Print.

Matras, Yaron. "Romani." *Encyclopedia of Languages and Linguistics.* 2nd edition. Ed. Keith Brown. Oxford: Elsevier, 2006. Web. Accessed 02.03.2017.

McFarlane, A. Donovan. "A Positive Theory of Stereotyping and Stereotypes: Is Stereotyping Useful?" *Journal of Studies in Social Sciences* 8.1 (2014): 140-163. Web. Accessed 15.05.2016.

Mirga, Andžej and Nicolae Gheorge. "Romski Narod U Istorijskom Kontekstu [The Roma in Historical Perspective]." *Romološke Studije/Romology Studies* Series I, Vol. I, August-

December, 1997. Print.

Mirga, Andžej and Leh Mruz, eds. *Roma/Differences and Intolerance*. Beograd: AKAPIT, 1997. Print.

Nirenberg, Jud. "They are Europe's Largest Minority, and Also Its Most Despised." *HNN History News Network*. May 15, 2016. Web. Accessed 17.05.2016.

Puhalo, Srđan. *Etničkadistancai (Auto) Stereotipigrađana-bosneihercegovine / Ethnic Distance And (Self) Stereotypes Of Citizens of Bosnia and Herzegovina*. Sarajevo: Freidrich Ebert Stiftung BiH, 2009. Print.

Roma Virtual Network (RVN). Web.

Spivak, C. Gayatri. *"Can the Subaltern Speak?" Marxism and the Interpretation of Culture*. Eds C. Nelson and L. Grossberg. London: Macmillan, 1988. Web. Accessed 16.05.2016.

Šakaja, Laura and Josip Užarević. "Tko mnogo luta, mnogo zna: O civilizacijskome nomadizmu Roma." *Nomadizam*. Zbornik znanstvenih radova u spomen na profesora Aleksandra Flakera. Ed. Jasmina Vojvodić. Zagreb: DISPUT, 2014. Print.

Tahirović-Sijerčić, Hedina. "Migration and its Implications for the Educational System: The Case of the Roma in Bosnia, Germany and Canada." *Formal and Informal Education for Roma, Different Models and Experience*. Eds. R. Bešter, V. Klopčić and M. Medvešek. Ljubljana: Institut for Ethnic Studies, 2012. 72-83. Print.

Tahirović-Sijerčić, Hedina. *"XXX." Like Water/Sar o paj*. Chandigarh, India: Kafla Inter-Continental, 2009. 21-22. Print.

Tahirović-Sijerčić, Hedina, ed. *Like Water/Sar o paj*. Chandigarh, India: Kafla Inter-Continental, 2009. Print.

Trinh, T. Minh-ha. *When the Moon Waxes Red: Representation, Gender and Cultural Politics*. New York and London: Routledge, 1991. Print.

Universal Declaration of Human Rights (UDHR). 1948. Web. Accessed 04.06.2016.

Zatreanu, Mihaela and W. Dieter Halwachs. "Romani in Europe." Ministry of Education and Research – Bucharest Romania/Department of Linguistics at the University of Graz / Austria, 2003. Web.Accessed 01.2014.

LIFE STORIES IN POETRY

HEDINA TAHIROVIĆ-SIJERČIĆ

CURRICULA VITAE of Romani people do not often meet the requirements prescribed by people in power. My poems are CVs for life. While not requirements for jobs, they are intended as requirements for a better life. After six CVs and the poem "The Earth," I call Romani woman to our tradition and culture, to our knowledge and experience, and to protect life and humanity on the earth.

CV 1

Me bijandilem ande Rusija.
Me đelem ande škola ande Poljska.
Me ćerdem bući sar sikadi ande Romania.
Me đelem rromehte ande Serbija.
Me ćerdem bući ande Bosna.

Angluno čhavo bijandem ande Kroacija.
Dujto čhavo ande Francuska, trinto ande Španija,
štarto ande Germanija,
Thaj pandžto ande Belgija.

Me boldinajdem ande Serbija.
Me bijandem šovto čhavo ande Serbija.
Musaj te našavav ande Italija,

thaj kote bijandem mrno eftato čhavo.
Me bijandem kote dujorre čhavore jekhethane.

Seha-man bari tragedija: Mo čhavo mula thaj von phende sar
vov tasavda
ande pajeste. Von trade amen, von phabarde amen, thaj von
mangen amare
najendar vurma. Thaj e čhavorendar.
Me sem daravni. Von ćerde gova jekhvaratar ando nakhlo
vakto. Daravni sem.

Me peklem našipe ande Holandija.
Me bijandem dešto čhavo.
Me bijandem dešojekhtato čhavo ande Švedska.
Me sem saranda berš phuri.
Me vaćarav Rromani (mrni dejaki čhib), Ruski, Slovački,
Rumunski, Srpski, Bosnaki, Hrvatski, Talijanski, Francuski,
Španski, Germanski, Holandski thaj cira Engleski.

Mrni familija mangel thaj trubuj šajipe pala lačhi edukacija.
Amen phenas pe hamisardine Evropske čhiba. Odolese, amen
das vorba pe Evropski čhib.
Mo ćher si jekh "Cikni Evropa."
Phurilem.

Ako si mrno ćher "Cikni Evropa " athoska si Evropa "Bari
Evropa."
Angluno uladipe maškare amende: Cikni Evropa si bilivarni
                                 Bari Evropa si livarni.
Dujto uladipe maškare amende: Cikni Evropa naj-la love pala
džuvdipe, numaj von san jekhethane.
Bari Evropa hi-la but love pala džuvdipe numaj...
Trito uladipe...

Phendem kaj phurilem. Me paruvdem mrni vorba. E vorbasa
musaj te džav ando mrno trajo.

Astardem šovto čhavoresko čhavo.

Ćerdem jekh turvinjipe e " Ciknese Evropese" te džas ande Kanada.
Kote si šajipe pala amen pala škola thaj šaj te sikavas Engleski
čhib, savore, phure tu.
Me dijem alav e čhavorende pala avindipe.

Ačhen Devleha!

CV 1

I was born in Russia.
I went to school in Poland.
I worked as an apprentice in Romania.
I married in Serbia.

I got a job in Bosnia.

I had my first child in Croatia.

I had my second child in France, the third in Spain,
the fourth in Germany,
The fifth in Belgium.

I returned to Serbia.
I had my sixth child in Serbia.
I had to escape to Italy, after the birth of my seventh child.
I had twins.

I endured the biggest tragedy: my child was found dead and
they said he drowned in
the sea. They drove me away, burned my roof,
and they wanted to take my
fingerprints. And those of my children too.
I am scared. They did it once like that before, with the
fingerprints, not so long ago. I am scared.

I escaped to Holland.
I had my tenth child.
I had the eleventh child in Sweden.

I am forty.
I speak Romani (my mother tongue), Russian, Slovakian,
Romanian, Serbian, Bosnian,
      Croatian, Italian, French, Spanish, German, Dutch,
and a little bit of English.

What my family needs is literacy, and a fair chance to have a
good education.
We speak mixed European languages. We speak European.
My house is "Europe-in-miniature."
I am getting old.

If my house is "Europe-in-miniature" then Europe is
"Europe-in-large."
The first difference between us: Europe-in-miniature is illiterate
                         Europe-in-large is literate.
The second difference between us: Europe-in-miniature has no
money to exist but she keeps a communal spirit.
Europe-in-large has more than enough money to exist but....
The third difference....

I told you I am getting old. I switched themes. I should follow
my CV.

I had my sixth grandchild.
I proposed to "Europe-in-miniature" that we move to Canada.
I found out there we could go to school and study English,
regardless of how old we were.
I promised my children and grandchildren a future.

Stay with God!

CV 2

Bijandilem ande Germanija.
Dživinas ande Holandija.
Našas ande Belgija.

Ansurisardem.
Ćerdem bući: ćidem phuro sastruno pe dromende.
Bijanda mo angluno čhavo.
Me ćidem phuro sastruno.
Bijanda mo dujto čhavo.
Durder ćidem phuro sastruno pe dromende.
Bijanda mo trinto čhavo.
Rodem ažutipe. Na dije mandje.
Naj man papira (lila)!

Thaj durder ćidem phuro sastruno pe dromende, so aver te ćerav.
Von akušle mrni "Rromani dej" thaj čungarde pe mrne mujeste.
Me akušlem len.
Von phande man ande phandipeste.
A naj-man papira (lila)?!

Mi Rromni ćerdarisarda: djeli kataro udar džiko
aver udar thaj mangla.
Bijanda mo štarto čhavo.
Mrni Rromni durder mangla kataro udar džiko aver udar.
Von akušle laki "Rromani dej" thaj čungarde
pe lako mujeste.
Voj mangla te nakhel.
Von phande las ande phandipeste.
A naj-la papira (lila)?!

Rodem bući: na dije mandje khanči.
Naj-man papira (lila)!

Naj-man čhavore bizo papiri.
Naj-man bući bizo papiri.
Naj-man mahno bizo papiri.

Mora te džav durder.

Kaj?
Naj-amen papiri!
Kaj bizo papiri!

CV 2

I was born in Germany.
We use to live in Holland.
We escaped to Belgium.

I married.

I got a job: I gathered old scraps on the streets.
I had my first child.
I gathered old scraps.
I had my second child.
I still gathered old scraps.
I had my third child.
They forbade me to gather scraps.

I asked for help. They didn't help me.
I didn't have identity papers.
I still gathered old scraps on the streets.
What else could I do?
They swore at my "gipsy mother" and they spat at my honour.
I tried to protect myself.
They imprisoned me.
But I have no identity papers?!

My wife started to work: she begged at the doors.
I had my fourth child.
She still begged at the doors.
They swore at her "gipsy mother" and they spat at her honour.
She tried to escape.
They imprisoned her.
But she has no identity papers?!

I asked for a job: they wouldn't give me work.
I have no papers!

I have no children without identity papers.
I have no job without papers.

I have no bread without papers.
I have to go far away.

But where?
We have no identity papers.
Where to go without papers?

CV 3

Bijandilem ande Rumunija.
Ande Rumunija astardem te džav ande škola.
Amen djelam ande Engleska.
Djelem ande skola ande Engleska.
Amen djelam ande Belgija.
Gatisardem škola ande Belgija.
Ćerdem bući kote.

Mo dad mardilo man.
Mi dej mardili man.

Von dije man e rromese. Opro mrni vodji.
Sar von mangle. Pala love.

Vov bićinda ćilime pe bićindate.
Me kamnisajlem.
Vov astarda te marel man.
Bijandem angluno ćhavo.
Vov mardilo man durder.
Oprosarda man te džav te ćerav.
Bijandem dujto ćhavo.
Vov mardilo man durder.
Astarda te pijel thaj te kuravel.
Na djelo te bićinel ćilime pe bićindate.
Seha-leh dujti rromni thaj ćhavo.
Anda len ando ćher, amendje.

Rodem ažutipe e dadestar thaj e dejatar.

Na dije man.
Rodem ažutipe e amalendar.
Na dije man.
Rodem ažutipe e gadjendar.
Na dije man.

Astardem te mangav e čhavorenca pe dromende thaj pe ćherende.
Ladž sasa mande. Musaj te magav.
Mangljem e čhavorenca. Sasto djive.
Rodem ažutipe.
Khonik na ažutina man.
Gadje phende "Rromani bući, von gova si rromano siklipe."
Rroma phende "Gadija musaj te avel, gova si amaro siklipe."

Mangljem durder.
Vov trada man thaj mardilo man pe dromeste. Lelo mrne love.
Vov pija thaj dželo e averenca džuvljenca.
Cira si leske duj ande ćhereste.

Phirdem e čhavorenca pe dromende thaj mangljem.
Čhavoren rovde. Me rovdem.
Kataro drom džiko aver dromeste, kataro ćher džiko aver ćhereste, kataro hudumić džiko aver hudumićeste.
Pala cira mahno. Pala cira miro (lačhipe).

Phuro gadžo dikhla man e hudumićestar. Ande jakha.
Sasa mange ladžavno pala mrno džuvdipe thaj problemurja.
Phuro gadzo dikhla man. Ande jakha.
Sasa mange ladžavno pala gova so aver manuša ćerde man.
Ladž lija mrni vorba.
Phuro gadžo haćarda man.

Našlem e čhavorenca ande Engleska.
Ćerdem bući ande fabrikate.
Čhavore džele ande čhavoreski edukacijski bošćin.
Khonik na marel man.
Sikljovav ande škola uzo bući. Sociologia.

Ažutinav e džuvljendje, a majbut amarendje.
Džanav sar si gova, dživisardem gova džuvdipe.

Khonik na marel man.
Me Dživiv.

CV 3

I was born in Romania.
In Romania I started to go to school.
We moved to England.
I went to school in England.
Then we moved to Belgium.
I finished school in Belgium.
I got a job.

My father beat me.
My mother beat me.

They married me off. Against my will.
As they liked. For money.

He sold carpets on the markets.
Then I got pregnant.
He started to beat me.
I had my first child.
He still beat me.
He kept me from doing my job, and I lost my job.
I had my second child.
He still beat me.
He started to drink and go with other women.
He didn't sell carpets on the markets anymore.
He had another woman and child.
He brought them into our house, to us.

I asked for help from my father and mother.
They didn't help me.
I asked for help from my friends.

They didn't help me.
I asked for help from social services.
They didn't help me.

I started to beg with my children, around streets and houses.
I was embarrassed. But I had no choice.
I begged with my children. Whole days (from morning until
night).
I asked for help.
Nobody helped me.
Gadze said "Gipsy things, this is their custom."
Our people said "It must be like that, this is our custom."

I begged again.
He followed me and beat me on the streets. He took the money
I'd begged for.
He drank and went with other women.
It was not enough that there were two of us in the house.

I walked with my children around the streets, and I begged.
The children cried. I cried too.
From street to street, from house to house, from doorstep to
doorstep.
For a bit of bread. For a bit of peace.

An old gadzo man looked compassionately at me from his
doorstep. Into my eyes.
I was embarrassed about my own life and problems.
An old gadzo man looked compassionately at me from his
doorstep. Into my eyes.
I was embarrassed about what the other man was doing to me.
Embarrassment had silenced my voice.
The old gadzo man understood me.

I ran away (escaped) with my children to England.
I got a job in a factory.
My children went to kindergarten.
No one beats me.

I study (along with my job). Sociology.
I help women, and especially my Roma women.
I know how it is, I have lived that life.

No one beats me.
I live.

CV 4

Me sem dešošovbrđengi rakli.
Džav ande škola.
Mo dad thaj mi dej logode man.
Von dije vorba pala man.
Von lije love pala bijav.

Gova si amari tradicija: von phende man.
Mora te tradav la.
Mora te astarav la.

Gova si amaro siklipe/adet: ćiravde man.

Muklem škola.

Trubuj te džav rromehte.
Sigo.
Pala duj-trin đivengo.

Mora te avav džuvli.
Mora te avav dej.

Gova si mo džuvdipe: našti te našav.

CV 4

I am a sixteen-year-old girl.
I go to school.
My parents engaged me.

They promised me to them.
And they took the money for a celebration.

This is our tradition, they told me.
I have to follow it.
I have to accept it.

This is our way, they persuade me.

I left school.
Soon I'll be married.
Very soon.
In just a few days.

I have to be a woman.
I have to be a mother.

This is my life: I can't escape it.

CV 5

Mo anav si Karolina.
Bišothajefta sem.
Bešav ande Češka.
Kate bijandilem.
Na djelem ande škola.
Von den amendje o than numaj ande škola pala dile.
Sikljovdem korkori te djinavav thaj romasarav.
Prandosardem.
Ande mande si trin saste thaj normalne čhaven.
Majbaro trubuj te džal ande škola.
Pala les numaj o than ande škola pala dile.
E mrne čhavorende na trubuj gova "šansa".
Von na den amendje te ćeren bući.
Naj ma bući pala Rromen.
Von mudarden amen.
Ćeren bombe ande šiše.

Ašundem krlo: "Phabar, mudar Cigane!"
Čhude bomba ando mrno ćher.
Phabarde thaj mudarde mrno majterno ćhavo.
Dukhal ma te phurdav. Dukhal ma te phenav.
Ranisajven amen.
Phabarde amaro ćher.
Naj-amen o ćher.
Khonik na paćavel amen.
Phenen, "rromani baći" von phabardisarde korkore peske.
Xoxaven.
Musaj te našav e duj ćhavorenca thaj e Rromensa.
Angla deso von mudaren amen.
Amare phenen: Ande Kanada na mudaren Rromen.
Musaj te našaven.
Amen roden o džuvdipe.

CV 5

My name is Karolina.
I am twenty seven.
I live in Czech Republic.
I was born here.
I didn't go to school.
They have accepted us just in classes for mentally retarded
children.
I learned by myself to read and write.
I married.
I gave birth to three healthy and normal children.
The oldest one should go to school.
They accepted him just in the class for mentally retarded
children.
Neither my children don't need this "chance."
They don't give us to work.
There is no work for Roma.
They kill us here.
They make bombs in bottles.
I heard the voice: "Burn them, kill *Cigane/Gypsies*!"
They threw one of these at my house.

They burned and killed my youngest one.
It hurts me to breathe. It hurts me to talk.
They wounded us all.
They burned our house.
We are without a home.
Nobody believes us.
They say, *"Ciganski/Gypsy businesses,"* they burned themselves.
They lie.
I must flee with two children and a husband to Canada.
Before they kill us all.
Our people say: In Canada they do not kill Roma.
We must flee.
We seek life.

CV 6

Mo anav sasa Mehmed. Bijandilem thaj dživisardem
ande Bosna. Ćerdem xarkumaće šeja, kazane thaj kotlove.
Phurisardem. Seha man pinda thaj pandž brš.

Mulisardem.

Amare mangle te praxosaren man, von na dije. Nane o than
pe lengi limori. Ande lengi kali phuv. Mrno trupo astarda
te rispisarel. Athoska 15 djive von dije mandje kotor kale
phuvjako. Dure e cahretar. Pe thaneste kaj khonik našti te rodel
man. Pe thaneste kaj knonik našti te dikhel man.

Mrno trupo raspisarda thaj pharuvda ande kali phuv.

Akana akharav Odji. Ujrav pe plavo delesko duripeste.

Rodav miro.

Iklav po nuvera. Paruvav nuvera sar ćhindile grasta. Bršind
thovel mo muj. Bahval vaćarel mansa. Devlehći jag del mandje
zuralipe. Ujrav pe plavo delesko duripeste. Paruvav nuvera sar

ćhindile grasta. Kham ćerel mandje sumnakuno drom koring
Indija. Talo nuvera mothovel pes Indija.

Izdrav. Huljardem ande Gangeski xar. Grast boldisarada e
plave delese.
Me boldisardem e plave pajese.

CV 6

My name was Mehmed. I was born and I lived in Bosnia.
I tapped cauldrons and copperboilers. I was getting old.
I was fifty-five years old.
I died.

They tried to bury me, but it wasn't allowed. There was no
place in their cemetery. In their black earth. My body began
to crumble. After fifteen days they allowed me a piece of black
earth. For hygienic reasons. Far away from the tent.
In a place where no one will find me. At the place where
no one will visit me.

My body was scattered and merged with the earth.

Now, my name is Soul. I fly on the range of the blue shades of
sky.

I seek peace.

I ride on the clouds. I exchange the clouds as I would tired
horses. Rain washes my face. Wind talks to me. Lightning
charges me with power. I fly on the range of the blue shades
of sky. I exchange the clouds as tired horses. The sun builds for
me a golden path to India. Below the clouds is the silhouette
of India.

I'm shivering. I dismounted in the valley of the Ganges.
The horse returned to the spectrum of the blue sky. I returned
to the spectrum of the blue water.

Phuv

Rromnije!
Pala mule thaj džuvinde,
Pala e Rroma,
Del armaja e phuvjaće,
Te našjares šimijake
Te našjares dušmaja.

Rromnije!
Pala mule thaj džuvinde,
Pala e Rroma,
Thuv telešoreha e phuv
Thaj del armaja kale sudbinaće
Te xoxajves bilaće
Te xoxajves kali jrat.

Rromnije!
Pala mule thaj džuvinde,
Pala e Rroma,
Del e phuvjaće ćoxanipe thaj del ćo mrtik pala o kamipe
Nek e jag na thuvljardel
Nek o dumutnipe na buhljarel.

Del o ćohanipe, Rromnije, del ćo mrtik pal las
Voj si ćiri, mrni thaj Devleski dej
PHUV.

The Earth

Romnije!
Because of all the dead and all the living,

Because of the Roma
Put a curse on the Earth
To destroy the rats
To destroy the enemy.

Romnije!
Because of all the dead and all the living,
Because of the Roma
Turn the Earth upside down
And predict black destiny
To distract the devil
To distract the black night.

Romnije!
Because of all the dead and all the living,
Because of the Roma
Cast magic upon the Earth and predict love.
Predict a fire without smoke
Predict damnation with the end.

Cast a magic spell, Romnije, save her!
She is yours, she is mine, Mother of God
THE EARTH.

Romnije!—Roma woman!
To distract the devil—evil forces.

SPEAKING OF SUBJECTIVITIES

CYNTHIA LEVINE-RASKY

THE DOCUMENTATION of women's lived experience has occupied the centre of feminist research since the inception of the second wave of the women's movement. Gender as the centre of inquiry, women as subjects in their own right rather than as objects for men, affirmation of the private, the relational, and the intimate, and the everyday experiences of women are the guiding principles of feminist research. The scope of feminist research expanded dramatically when racialized feminists led a vigorous challenge against a movement they correctly criticized as representing only white, middle-class women (Oleson). Goals shifted from a liberal feminist vision of women's equality to a more incisive, intersectional vision of women's equity concerned with the effects of discrimination not only on the basis of gender, but also class, ethnicity, race, ability, age, religion, sexuality, and other "axes of differentiation" (Brah and Phoenix 76). Intersectional theorizing goes beyond a proliferation of categories, however, to the way they reticulate with each other in particular ways for particular women. Adrien Wing asserts that the experience of Black women, to take an instructive example, "must be seen as a multiplicative, multilayered, indivisible whole…. This experience is characterized not only by oppression, discrimination and spirit murder, but by strength and love and transcendence as well" (200). Exclusion affects individuals and groups marked by multiple categories of difference whose meanings are subject to change in response to social forces (Crenshaw). These forces, together with historical and political processes, construct difference and the power relations that produce terms of exclusion and inclusion. Colonialism, capitalist expansion, global trade, migration, security regimes, and nationalism are among the contexts in which oppression and privilege arise.

How do these general contexts affect the particular? For European Romani women, gender, ethnicity, and class intersect (Jovanović, Kóczé, and Balogh) to produce oppression in the form of coercive sterilization, poor labour market participation, children's exclusion from mainstream schooling, poor health outcomes, and sexual violence (Council of Europe 2015; Kóczé). In Canada, Romani women are free of many of the egregious injustices observed in Europe. But complex intersections of gender, ethnicity, class, immigration status, religion, and country of origin, in addition to other categories of identity, can be observed in various policies. These include those circumscribing education (Brown), multiculturalism (Hatfield), settlement (Fiorito 2013), policing (Connor), international relations (Patterson), and in institutions such as schools (Fiorito 2012a), media (Catalano), justice (Green), health care (Fiorito 2012b), religion (Marmur), and the arts (Ciampini). In the particularly intense discussion of Romani refugee claimants, the Roma have been constructed both positively (Ayed; Brosnahan; Murphy) and negatively (Boesveld; Cohn; Keung). Such debates have bearing upon the identities of those who are its subjects.

The women whose words I present in these pages were interviewed as part of a critical ethnographic research project at the Toronto Roma Community Centre (RCC). Working as an active volunteer at the Centre since 2011, I recorded interviews with forty-six individuals of different ages, countries of origin, immigrant statuses, and Romani sub-groups, many of whom either played active roles at RCC, or were users of its services. Of this group, twenty were women. I asked questions about Romani identities, migration (if applicable), quality of life in Toronto, cultural practices and adaptations, public perceptions of the Roma, and community building. For this chapter, I isolated excerpts on a range of themes and avoided imposing an order upon them. Neither a "vertical slice" of key themes nor a "horizontal slice" of individual profiles, what I present are some portions of stories conveying depth and significance. I make no grandiose claims to have captured a representative sample or even a meaningful segment of the tens of thousands of Romani women who live in Toronto. I chose these six excerpts on the basis of their substantive content, their infusion with personal meaning that I expect has resonance for many others, and their reticulation with social relationships situated well beyond the personal.

In addition to their content and implications, the significance of these passages also lies in the way the six speakers cogently communicate a key assertion about the Roma. I conceive of the Roma in the city not as a singular community but as a multiplicity of communities. Borrowing from French social theorist Gilles Deleuze, the term "multiplicity" is an assemblage of elements without totality and without integration as a whole (Roffe 181). A multiplicity preserves collectively practiced and subjectively meaningful components of belonging to a group, but it rejects an assumption of sameness in their quality. This position is antagonistic to that of some intellectuals and European state actors who either deny the Roma as a people or recognize them only as political entities (see Matras 2011). It also conflicts with the perspective of many members of the general public, who see in the Roma only a racialized and inferior category of persons. The idea of multiplicity assumes a critical place in my growing understanding of the group whose social and cultural differences are too deep to allow their reduction to a monolithic category. The Roma might even demonstrate what Steven Vertovec calls a "super-diversity," which moves well beyond ethnicity to include country of origin, legal status, socio-economic status, religion, education, migration, access to jobs, residential patterns, technology, transnational practices, enjoyment or restriction of rights, responses by local authorities and residents, local context, and other components of modern life. With no congruence across the groups that comprise the local Roma community, we may instead explore the complexity of Romani subjectivities in the multiple cultures in which they, like everyone else, participate.

Found in Romani narratives are tensions between myth and practice, politics and subjectivity—endogenous and exogenous factors that slip and slide with the conditions in which these social actors finds themselves. Romani identities reflect on myth even as they resist their injuries, they practice *Romanipe* in degrees from orthodoxy to none at all, they identify with the Roma rights movement to lesser and greater extents. Some preserve a sense of the past and others do not. Some prefer to call themselves "Gypsy" and others prefer "Roma." Some respect traditional occupations and others do not. Some seek to align themselves with each other while others prefer the support of non-Roma. Some seek to further their education while others eschew such opportunities. Some regard social mobility highly while others are suspicious of it. Some proclaim their ethnicity publicly, while others prefer invisibility. Some know about past efforts to mobilize and others are unconcerned. Some want to fight against unjust Gypsy myths while others' priorities lie elsewhere. Some have developed a critical consciousness about the social inequalities for Roma, and others do not reflect on the impact of politics and ideology on their exclusion. Some feel a connection to world Roma, but not all do.

I am not a Romani woman. Elsewhere, I reflect on the ethical questions that arise from my researcher role (see Levine-Rasky 2015, 2016). Most crucial of these are related to representation and authority. In publications, my written word represents "them," a diverse group of men and women who have consented to my work with earnest and generous trust—and with whom I stand as an ally. But I am also an outsider. Deploying the power of representing their lives, I become a conduit for information about them, as I explain the Roma to readers. Since general information about the Roma is scant and often erroneous, I find myself in the role of authority, mediating the communicative space between the public and the Roma. The risk is that my perspective may be regarded as more authoritative than that of the community members themselves, whom few people take the initiative to consult. The act of representing a group implies that participants cannot speak for themselves; they are an undifferentiated mass. This is ethically problematic in its exclusion of the very people upon whom a researcher is dependent. Moreover, a researcher's claim to authority produces unequal benefits. Professional benefits are conferred upon a researcher who takes credit for producing an academically sound text. Participants' social conditions are written about, but they are unchanged as a result of the research (Cameron and Gibson).

There is no easy reconciliation of these problems. On the one hand, community-based researchers are never free from the elite positions we occupy, regardless of how well we collaborate with our participants. As advocates for the community-based approach advise, we "need to be vigilant about our own power, and never unquestioningly assume benevolence" (Pain, Kindon, and Kesby 15). On the other hand, by disconnecting my labour at the Centre from my researcher role, I facilitated programming, hiring, and public education about the Roma. I assisted families with their refugee claims and other needs. And, as the grant-writer, I found important sources of revenue for the organization. As I write elsewhere, working with the Roma in an accountable way cannot always be separated from work done for them or about them (see Levine-Rasky 2015). On the question of research ethics, Uma Narayan encourages "methodological humility": a tentativeness in making claims and an expectation of making errors (37). This principle informs my actions. Moreover, I recognize that my research derives from "something like love, or a passion" rather than from something like sympathy or compassion (Bergo 154).

SUBJECTIVITIES AS METHOD

Narrating the subjective and lived experience of women is a valid methodological approach in the qualitative research tradition, especially that informed by critical and feminist perspectives. Subjectivities must be understood on their own terms, not as a repositories for social markers like gender or ascribed statuses like ethnicity. How may this be done? In order to understand a community in depth, it is necessary to conduct an "analysis of the predominantly oral culture of the groups themselves" (Csepeli and Simon 135). But that is insufficient. Subjectivities cannot be expected to reflect the totality of a culture, and it is unreasonable to load a small group of interview participants with this conceptual weight. Instead, researchers seek to conjoin what Rogers Brubaker et al. call the "big structures" of social analysis—ideology, politics, institutions, history—to everyday experience conveyed ethnographically. Brubaker and colleagues emphasize that ethnicity and nationhood are expressed "in everyday encounters, practical categories, commonsense knowledge, cultural idioms ... social networks, and institutional forms," but that the same can be said of any "axis of differentiation" such as gender or social class (6-7).

Romani subjectivities are both individualistic and collective. Like members of other ethnic groups, they involve a complex mix of unique factors in selfhood and group membership. The meaning of a Romani identity is produced both by a unique social agent—the I—and attachments to things larger than the I—the We. These elements stand in tension with each other. They are made and unmade, formed and reformed through interactions with other selves, and in increasingly wide zones of sociability that fan out from the self. Society surrounds us as an outer zone, permeated with the effects of history, ideology, economic realities, and the inevitability of cultural change. Selfhood, therefore, is not atomistic; it does not stand in a social vacuum. Indeed, it is meaningful only insofar as it stands in relation to other selves and to social conditions.

Shaped by power relations, socially nuanced subjectivity is contingent upon the prevailing culture, the interpretive community, and particular relations of power (Rattansi 2007). Systemic discrimination against the Roma bears upon Romani subjectivities (Brooks; Sachdev). Such discrimination occurs in Canada (Catalano; Do; Elliott), but in Europe, it is characterized by flagrant and public anti-Roma racism (Fekete; Council of Europe 2012; European Roma and Travellers Forum), often against Romani women (Oprea; Council of Europe 2013; Szalai and Zentai). In Bulgaria, the Czech Republic, France, Greece, Italy, Hungary, Poland, Portugal, Romania, Slovakia, and Spain, the average situation of Romani women in core areas of social life—such as education, employment, and health—is worse than that of Roma men (European Union Agency for

Fundamental Rights 45). In their comprehensive survey of European Roma, the United Nations Development Program found that only 15 percent of Romani women are employed compared to 38 percent of Romani men. On average, Romani women earn only 45 percent that of Romani men, and only 54 percent of earnings received by non-Romani women in equal jobs. Sixty-six percent of Romani women have no income whatsoever (UNDP 2015).

Romani women are constructed in the public imaginary as being of a certain "kind," irrespective of the particularities of their experience. Sources are historical. So common was the image of the exotic Gypsy woman—for example, Esmeralda in Victor Hugo's 1831 novel *Hunchback of Notre Dame* and Carmen in George Bizet's 1875 opera—that her body became an acceptable symbol for taboo female eroticism (Bogdal). Meanings are also contemporary. Siren, mystic, beggar, thief, philistine, anachronistic, are popular images of Romani women that are offered up to a public eager for sensationalized TV (Matras 2015). Misrepresentations of "Gypsy" traditions intersect with social class and gender in the reality TV show 'My Big Fat Gypsy Wedding,' which was broadcast initially in 2011 and has since inspired spin-offs and a mini-series (Tremlett). Angéla Kóczé and Julija Sardelic explain the psychical dimensions of the "Gypsy" woman in relation to the exalted status of the White woman:

> The cultural canon about Romani woman is constructed as a counterpart to the 'benevolent white woman' who demonstrates filial piety, chastity, innocence, obedience and approval of the white patriarchy. Romani women represent moral freedom, evilness, transgressions, arrogance and treacherous behaviour. This perceived behaviour lends legitimacy to efforts now and in the past to demonize and marginalize them as dangerous women who threaten the patriarchal infrastructure across Europe.

Not wishing to imply that Romani women are without agency, the authors emphasize their everyday acts of resistance:

> Romani women in their everyday lives have to be heroes:
> they are smart, and reflexive because they are constantly
> contesting the power structures of patriarchal society by
> irony and by putting up a mirror to reflect those structures
> back with the image of their very existence.

While anti-Roma racism may be a near-universal experience, evoking its vastness leaves little room for the unique ways in which individuals know it, resist it, or work with it. For most non-Roma, there is little knowledge about this differentiation of experience and often less interest in exploring it. Negative generalizations about a people soothe the need to assert one's own positive belongingness. The brand of generalization known as racism usually escapes identification as such, often substituted by more neutral aspersions directed to "culture" (Rattansi 2007: 95). One consequence of anti-Roma racism is the will to deny the nuances of individual experience within the pluralistic category known as Romani woman (and Roma generally).

There exists some discussion of Romani women's subjectivities in the scholarly literature. A collection of essays on this topic appears as a special 2012 issue of the scholarly feminist journal, *Signs*. In her semi-auto-ethnography, Petra Gelbart writes of how the possibility of a feminist Romani woman challenges established gender roles, but not in a way that can be mapped directly onto a feminist prototype. Romani women's subjectivities can exceed the conventions of feminist methodology. Romani women's power, and their interpretations of their power—whether in relation to domestic work or to income-earning—demonstrate how "Romani gender dynamics intersect with and parallel larger structures, including the gender roles and inequalities of the broader societies in which they are embedded, while also taking some of their own quite plural trajectories" (Gelbart 27). Carol Silverman makes a similar point. Despite having to endure control over their sexualities, young Macedonian Romani women in New York craft new identities through their education and non-traditional employment (33-34).

In two Romani communities in Northern Hungary, Judit Durst finds a heterogeneity among the women that is manifest in their reproductive behaviour and family structures. The two groups diverge from both the majority society and from each other. One group of women seeks to distinguish themselves from other Roma by improving their social status through marriage, adopting Hungarian names, leaving town, obtaining an education, and by having relatively few children. The second group, while also identifying as *Romungro*, has more children, lower incomes, and, while they aspire to mobility, they have not achieved it. The author concludes, too hastily in my view, that "it is not worth talking about 'Roma culture'" since no homogeneity of practice exists (Durst 28).

Some accounts of Romani women's lives emphasize the individual. Paloma Gay y Blasco tells the life story of Agata González, a Gitano woman in Spain who diverged from life as a conventional wife and mother to build a new life with another man. She found her old life unimaginable after a change of consciousness through her active involvement with a parents' association. Departing permanently and dramatically from traditional Gitano life, Agata challenges strict norms of propriety and morality, despite its profound emotional cost to her and to her children. In her ethnography of two Romani women in the Czech Republic, Natasha Beranek provides another example of radical subjectivity. Despite their differences in age, socioeconomic status, and educational attainment, Alžběta and Zdeňka struggle against the "entrapment" of their ethnicity through their familial relationships and their relationships with men. As Romani women in the post-communist world, their subjectivities—while making space for some freedoms—are still affected by the myth of essentialized Romani immorality.

Like the Toronto-based Romani women I interviewed, those in Hungary, Spain, and the Czech Republic communicate the particularities of their social and personal lives. Their knowledge of themselves is grounded on sometimes-painful interactions with members of their own communities. They are both object and subject of social policy affecting immigration, welfare, education, national security, multiculturalism, and minority rights, the "big structures" to which their narratives are conjoined. In the interview excerpts below, we hear subjectivities impelled by memory, family, marriage, inter-generational change, employment, policing, racism, and diaspora. Pam attempts to unearth the vestiges of a Romani life that was deliberately suppressed even as they make vague but regular appearances in her home. Eugenia struggles with the shame of a low social status for Roma that clashes with her relationships to non-Roma. Eszter describes the consequences of marginalization as a Romani woman, wife, and refugee. Gail reflects on family members' disavowal of their Romani identity as she laments her isolation from community. Marta seeks a safe passage for herself between the shoals of tradition and the new landscape of contemporary life in Toronto. Rose's journey lights upon elements of her Romani identity whose name, once found, is uttered at the risk of rejection. Each woman speaks as an individual, but not irreducibly so. In their words lie the sensibility of memory and community, and all that lies beyond. The tension we hear conveys a dynamic interaction between the subjectivities and the questions to which they are responding.

ROMANI WOMEN SPEAK

The women whom I interviewed spoke to me about the meaning of being Romani, of childhood and youth, change and stasis, belonging and the impossibility of belonging, difference and its ironies, integration and its costs. They spoke of factors that separate the Roma from each other and those that unify the Roma as a community. They are candid about their opinions about the potential for Roma to express themselves as a collectivity, about the impact of the past, and about options in the future. My preference is to let the women speak for themselves, even though a text absolutely unmediated by an author's decisions is impossible. All names are pseudonyms, and I provide minimal information about individuals to protect their privacy. The only changes made were minor grammatical corrections where these errors may have affected comprehension. Ellipses piece together the most relevant elements from long excerpts. After each excerpt, I offer some analysis about its implications, but mainly I preserve the stories as they were delivered, at some length.

They do not affirm a particular experience or perspective. Indeed, it is not their convergence but their divergence that is pivotal. These interlocutors evince the multiplicity of Romani women—a collectivity without necessary affinity.

Who are my twenty adult female interview participants? Aged between 21 and 67, they are refugee claimants, Geneva Convention refugees, Permanent Residents, naturalized citizens, and Canadian-born. Occupation, religion, and Romani sub-group are also diverse. Artists, retail clerks, a cleaner, homemakers, and teachers, they are Catholics, Evangelicals, and other Christians, Muslim, atheists or non-religious, or they follow other spiritual traditions. To my knowledge, all are heterosexual. At the time of the interview, twelve were married, in common-law relationships, or otherwise attached. Six were divorced, and of the two women who were unattached, neither had immediate plans for marriage. While most partners were Romani, there were three non-Romani partners.

All individuals form subjectivities that actively draw from Romani histories and knowledge of systemic exclusion. Their subjectivities reveal "a multiplicity of subject positions" inhabiting communities as diverse "as the social relations in which we participate," themes developed further in the next section (Mouffe 37, 44).

> *I think my father did what maybe some immigrants do. He decided he was going to be a Canadian and was going to ... erase the past. And because he had such a difficult relationship with his family, everything, I think he probably decided everything would go, which is a pretty huge and.... I would say [pause], a very rare thing for a [sub-group withheld] to do, because for [sub-group], family is the centre of everything. Your identity is the centre of everything, and you know there were only a few little leftovers that entered into my life as a child from his—mokkadi ... and just modesty and personal hygiene ... that was what I grew up with.... These codes were not imparted to me as something that belonged to [sub-group], this was just what came to*

me from my father ... you know he was so desperate to [pause], to distance himself, to not identify as [sub-group] in Canada. He [pause], he would not ascribe an ethnic origin to these practices.... They were, I guess they were things I clung to from him because I didn't really have much else to cling to. (Pam)

Pam's reflections are delivered with some apprehension as she ponders the basis of her father's life decision to extinguish his Romani ethnic identity in his adult years in Canada. Pam refers to a few extant practices, *mokkadi* among them, a term for the purity code also known as *marime*. These practices were not passed on to her under the Romani rubric of Roma or her father's sub-group, but individualistically; she understood them as something her father happened to believe in. Pam animates them to some degree in her private life, but laments her general disconnectedness from her father's memories. She compensates for this loss in her activism for Roma rights and as a self-identified Romani woman who was intensely involved in the local community.

The [sub-group withheld] Roma are known to get by by whatever means necessary ... because that's all they know within their own social class when they grew up...there is [so] much else available there for what you could do, so why choose the informal economy than if you could have a normal.... It's not about making a lot of money. It's about not wanting to integrate into society because of the fear of losing yourself ... losing your Roma identity and becoming part of the Gadje and then you're done! This is the whole mind-frame and the whole outlook ... the biggest fear is that oh my God, you don't want to become part of the Gadje. What is so wrong with the Gadje? [laughing] This is my opinion. You're living in a country. Doesn't matter where.... I believe in integration. You have to integrate. If you don't integrate, then you find other ways. Then when you find other ways, then the whole stereotype comes into existence. (Eugenia)

While dedicated to Romani causes, Eugenia is very largely a product of the integration that she values so highly. Perhaps due to her North American education, she not only criticizes some groups of Roma for their lack of integration, she also holds them responsible for the consequences of what appears to her as their choice. Work in the informal economy reinforces a stereotype, Eugenia believes, and affects all Roma. For Eugenia, this choice is unfortunate because Canada offers open opportunities to all who are willing to take advantage of them. In order to explain this problem, Eugenia turns to the Romani "mind-frame" that she claims is permanently turned against the *gadje*, or non-Roma. To Eugenia, the choice is stark: one integrates and relaxes one's Romani identity, or one rejects the *gadjekane* world and remains stuck in a life of marginality. It is a zero sum game the stakes of which Eugenia continues to weigh for herself.

> *My ex-husband, he moved out of [location withheld] because he beat me up ... it's okay, it's covered under the table and you know, in the Roma culture because the woman, it's like if we abused, then we are not saying....* *So I decide I don't want to live that way anymore because I already have been in [location] nine months I think ... he is [pause] put me in depression and all this caring of him, because, not because he is a bad person, not because he was a bad husband, because he had a lot of problems back home. So I really, really miss that too. My marriage is really broke up and went down because we came [to] this country from a country where we have a lot of discrimination, a lot of beat up from the police and the [details withheld] person. So when we came here we had too much peace [laughs] and relax, and that time, I think, the stress was on him and on me and we started fighting with each other. We had this problem in back home with the marriage, in the marriage, but that time we was, um, really strong together because we was really helped each other back home ... he doesn't have to protect me, I don't have to protect him from the people on the street or from the police, so we always together. But in a last few*

years in [country of origin] ... we decide that we are not going all the time together shopping back home I mean or somewhere because he has dark skin, and I always had trouble. So that's why, it's so bad ... it's easier for you to go by yourself shopping because you're, you don't have dark skin so much than he. (Eszter)

Eszter recounts the impact of anti-Roma racism in her country of origin, and the effects it had on her and her then-husband once they migrated to Canada. Evocative in its candor, Eszter's story describes the police brutality and chronic discrimination they faced, and perhaps ironically, how it worked as a force against which the couple united. Without the backdrop of overt racism, the stitches of the marriage ripped open, and Eszter became the husband's target of abuse, driving her away. Despite her experiences of domestic violence and systemic racism, Eszter has been able to embrace what Lalai Manjikian calls the refugee's "proactive existence" (50). In Eszter's case, she overcame oppression through active community work, the church, and her family:

So [my grandfather] made a conscious effort to move away from [name of village withheld], and to instill those values of don't steal, don't...and also education and all of those things. But my grandmother wanted nothing to do with Roma as well. So they both kind of said let's separate ourselves from those kinds of people. So my grandmother wouldn't allow.... My mom wasn't allowed to wear long skirts or bright colours, like everything you could think of. My grandfather in his later life ... there was something in him still that he wanted to still help his people. He was a good businessman ... he was respected by non-Roma and Roma as well. He ... was the go-to Roma guy and he helped his community.... My grandmother use to always put him down for helping those people, but she was Roma. But she gets the racism now in the nursing home too, but she takes offense because she says I'm not one of those people.... My mom ... moved away from the little village, to get away from them.... She was in medical school and all of that, and my mom, she was detecting cancer, she was in the sector of technology. So she always made a point of denying, and she said there was another girl she was sure, in the clinic in the hospital who was Roma, but the two of them never talked, and the two of them never wanted anything to do with it. She believed that there is a lot of Roma here probably, and a lot of the intelligent people and the role models, are not going to come out because they're smart and they don't want anything to do with it. So she says the only ones who want to come out are the ones who are the stereotype, or the label or whatever. Because I said like is there no one else like me? She said there probably are but they don't want to risk that. So, I feel like there's that conflict of helping and unifying, yes but no at the same time. You went from my grandfather to my mom now, to me. So I feel like there is that collective, and what she says is there are people who are intelligent and Roma and whatever?....Some of the dysfunction had been passed on as well.... So there's such an identity that's not letting people to identify somehow. (Gail)

Gail traces her ethnic heritage back two generations, where she recognizes the roots of her own community engagement with the Roma. But alienation and shame run like a theme through all the characters in her story, and Gail remains poignantly affected by it. Romani identity was actively suppressed by her grandparents and then denied altogether by her mother, but it refuses to disappear entirely. Gail's pride in her grandfather is evident. His dedication to "helping his community" inspires her own work, as does the bitter distinction between "those" kind of Roma and "ours"—those with potential and success. When educated Roma repudiate their identity, they are lost not only to Gail in her quest for others like her, but also to the Roma community at large.

I know women who take care of their children and they study at the same time, like many Canadian women

But there are some men who don't want their wife to go out because they feel that she will be the leader of the family.... And I think men shouldn't worry about that. If they have a good marriage, then that's not going to be a problem.... People should understand that here [Canada] is different. And your culture is okay until you are in your family. But if you want to do something out in the world, then you have to accept the rules ... we shouldn't concentrate on culture, we shouldn't concentrate on the ... differences between this tribe and that tribe.... It's not good if they concentrate on the cultural things, it's not going to get better. They will not be able to integrate ... like I personally want to go to study. Maybe college or university, maybe study social work or maybe something else I didn't think about yet. But I still want to be a good wife too later on, when the time comes and I would let my husband be the head at home and that's what I think. Like it's not a traditional thing for a woman to go to university but it can work together at the same time. Because I don't like the Roma culture. I don't want to follow the culture.... I follow whatever.... It's a personal opinion and I don't think other people will agree.... Cultural things are okay at home, but if they want to integrate, they have to let go of some things. (Marta)

Marta's narrative reveals a curious blend of traditional gender roles in the private sphere and desire for women's freedoms in the public sphere. She is hoping that the latter needn't be sacrificed to the former, but the way forward sounds like that of a pioneer. Whether she will be able to straddle the conservatism of traditional Romani culture and the possibilities in education and work that appeal to her remains to be seen. When Marta soundly rejects "Roma culture," and lauds "integration," she seems hopeful that her self-respect will not be among the things that must be "let go." That her earlier engagement to a young Romani man came to an end may very well tell something about Marta's self-determination.

My parents ... had this thing about pollution and filth, and they used certain terminology.... I started to feel comfortable [laughs] when I noticed a lot of people saw this as normal in the Roma community.... When I said we should think about long-term planning I was laughed at by somebody who is not Romani but involved in the organization, who said, "You don't know Roma. Roma have to survive day-to-day." You know? "And if you're surviving day-to-day, you can't plan for the future." Which I took real exception to because I, that Roma part of me did not like that, and said, "Yes and you're going to have to accept that some Roma can plan ahead, and you know, can plan in the long-term and perhaps we should be recruiting people who identify as mixed Roma." To which this person immediately said, "If you are mixed you're not Roma, you should know that." And I said, "You know things are changing, this is Canada, this is Toronto, and last I checked, you know, we're in the year 2000 something. So we have to start to expand our consciousness and our awareness and allow Roma, mixed Roma, and allies to all work together for the same cause and be cause-driven, not blood quantum-driven." [laughs] (Rose)

In her interview, Rose identified many orthodox Romani customs, for example, standards of cleanliness in food preparation and bathroom rituals that she came to appreciate lay deeply in herself. The discovery came only after a long journey during which she had come to accept her virtual isolation from others like her. Yet Rose's hard-won knowledge of her heritage was rejected by a non-Romani community member. Rose's desire to encourage outreach to people of mixed Romani heritage implies an abandonment of the conventional and highly exclusionary designation of Romani authenticity. In her analysis, Rose deliberately adopts the harsh language of race—blood quantum—that was used to rationalize the murder of the Roma during the Holocaust. That Rose's constructive recommendation of long-term planning was excluded on such a basis flags the operative fractures that the local Roma community sustains to this day. It also evinces Rose's difficult experience in finding a place for herself, a theme that runs through the words of all of the women quoted in this chapter.

THEORIZING SUBJECTIVITIES

Postmodern approaches to identity emphasize themes of complexity, intersectionality, and subjectivity. One paradigmatic expression of subjectivity originates with French social theorist Chantal Mouffe who discusses the human subject as a "multiplicity of subject positions" (37). Rejecting the idea that individuals belong to only one community, she claims that "we are in fact always multiple and contradictory subjects, inhabitants of a diversity of communities (as many … as the social relations in which we participate and the subject-positions they define)" (Mouffe 44). Identities are not rooted in the primordial characteristics of a group or in the interactions between ethnocultural groups. Identity is better understood as a dynamic force that changes over time, giving rise to meanings of sameness and difference, inclusion and exclusion. Human subjects differentiate themselves within sanctioned categories of knowledge, which are always subject to the continuous impact of history, culture, and power. Identities emerge, therefore, through structures of authority and in relation to the compromises, conflicts, or contradictions produced by such encounters (Rattansi 2007).

Romani women, like those who speak here, cannot be reduced to their ethnicity alone. Like all Canadians, they are much more than occupants of an ethnic category, even more than subjects in what Brubaker might call a process of group making. Their subjectivities intertwine with others, in contexts that can evoke ethnicity, but are just as likely to evoke other categories of selfhood. Members vary widely in the way they recognize and identify themselves. Such identifications can involve intersecting dimensions of gender, social class, sexuality, family status, and citizenship status, but to different degrees at different times that change in relation to the local milieu. The premise is that "everyone relates to a plurality of social groups; every social group has other social groups cutting across it" (Young qtd. in Vermeersch 455). How do these dynamics emerge for Pam, Eugenia, Eszter, Gail, Marta, and Rose?

While respecting the women's confidentiality, it is possible to provide some general analysis of subjectivities and intersectionality. Some tensions are apparent in Pam's narrative—specifically between the continuous connectedness to her father's memory versus his detachment from Roma identification. Pam has developed a positive Romani identity despite the weak tie to the substance of her father's life, attesting to a unique and dynamic subject position. Her involvement with multiple groups, Romani and not, finds its inspiration in her complex subjectivity interpreted anew. Revealing simultaneous intersections of gender, ethnicity, and social class mobility, Pam's narrative engages the Romani diaspora. The theme of contradiction in Eugenia's account is signalled by her ongoing desire to help local Roma and her criticisms of them. Equally engaged with non-Roma, she cannot turn her back on the Roma despite her misgivings about their potential to "integrate." Eugenia's subjectivity reflects a particular immigration history and pluralistic social positioning. She negotiates intersections of gender, ethnicity, class, and religion elsewhere in her interview as these axes crosscut and produce meaning for her. The theme of differentiation and its effects is heard in Eszter's words as she tells of abuse and resilience. Oppressed as a Romani woman in her original country and as a wife and asylum-seeker in Canada (as she discusses elsewhere in her interview), these factors and others bear upon her complex subjectivity. These experiences, together with the power relations for Roma in Europe and the treatment of the Roma in the Canadian refugee system, substantiate synchronous intersections of gender, ethnicity, and immigrant status.

The themes of contradiction and complexity are evident in Gail's narration of attachment and detachment from family stories. Emulation of her grandfather co-exists with her dismay over her isolation from Roma like her. Yet her family's denial of their heritage is a dramatic testament to the effects of living within dominant cultures that are resolutely hostile. History and belonging are key themes in Gail's subjectivity, and concurrent intersections of ethnicity and class are equally salient. Multiple subject positionings are also found in Marta's remarks, specifically in her shift between respect for and rejection of traditional gender roles for Romani women. Marta differentiates herself not only as a Romani woman, but also as a young woman seeking her own possibilities in a new place where some can express social pluralities more easily than others. Her account affirms a dynamic yet indivisible convergence of gender, ethnicity, immigrant status, and family status. The theme of differentiation and its complex impacts on subjectivity is communicated in Rose's remarks about her efforts to participate in community development. Her embrace of multiple ethnic and other social groups leads to a confrontation with the power vested in primordial notions of Romani authenticity. This vigorous and enduring idea clashes with Rose's knowledge that such categories are of limited value when seeking ways to strengthen the diverse Romani community. Rose animates her own complexity to her personal satisfaction, but she suffers when it is the object of rebuke by other Roma. Simultaneous intersections of gender, culture, and ethnicity are manifest in her biography as she defends her experience as a middle-class Romani woman.

No consolidation may be made of the six women's voices. They are not representative of a mode of adaptation or a form of resistance, subjugation, or power. They embody all of these moments. No generalization is possible other than to highlight the tension between subjectivities and its contexts sculpted by experiences particular to the Roma. There is no expectation of congruence between members of a group, and indeed within individuals. Their narrative opens up the interpretive space in which enormous divergences in subjectivities can be played out. Romani women's subjectivities are complex, since they, like everyone else, participate in multiple cultures. Romani women's identities are not bounded or singularly apprehensible. They are dynamic, nuanced, multiple, complex, differentiated. In the postmodern identity, Ali Rattansi sees "the astonishingly complex manner in which populations appear to draw and redraw, and maintain and breach, and narrow and widen the boundaries around themselves and others" (1995: 253). Complexity is paramount. In his field research on Romani refugees in Toronto, Esteban Acuña shows that personal narratives indicate no "evidence, generalizations, or reductions of Roma movement to culturally specific perceived practices" (5). No monolithic pattern emerges for identity formation or for collectivity. Such categories take on meanings forged by the Roma themselves. In listening to Romani women's subjectivities, we hear them working out their own balances of beloved characteristics and shameful stereotypes, permanence and change, differentiation and sameness. Diverse acts of self-identification, meaning-making, regard for other Roma, and personal trajectories of love and attachment are heard. In the end, there is nothing more than a multiplicity. An assemblage without congruity, this "nothing more" is inclusive of all.

WORKS CITED

Acuña, Esteban C. "Romani Mobilities as Resilience Strategies: Trans-Atlantic Expectations, Lives and Journeys." Paper presented to the Second World Congress on Resilience: From Person to Society. Timisoara, Romania, 2014. Print.

Ayed, Nahlah. "Seeking Safety." CBC *The National*. December 12, 2012. Web. Accessed 24 December 2012.

Beranek, Natasha. "Romani Individuality? Ethnographic Examples of Distinctive Social Action Within a Local Czech Romani Population." *Acta Ethnographica Hungarica*. 59.1 (2014): 145-195. Print.

Bergo, Bettina G. "Circulez! Il N'y a Rien á Voir, or, Seeing White: From Phenomenology to Psychoanalysis and Back." *White on White/Black on Black*. Ed. G. Yancy. Lanham, MD: Rowman & Littlefield Publishers, 2005. Print.

Boesveld, Sarah. "Efforts to Keep Bogus Roma Refugees Out Have Failed: Jason Kenney." *National Post* 22 April 2012. Web. Accessed 22 April 2012.

Bogdal, Klaus-Michael. "Europe invents the Gypsies." *Eurozine* 24 February 2012. Web.

Brah, Avtar, and Phoenix, Ann. "Ain't I a Woman? Revisiting Intersectionality." *Journal of International Women's Studies* 5.3 (2004): 75-86. Print.

Brooks, Ethel C. "The Possibilities of Romani Feminism." *Signs* 38.1 (2012): 1-11. Print.

Brosnahan, Maureen. "Deported Roma refugee family receives permission to return to Canada." *CBC News* February 8, 2016. Web. Accessed 10 February 2016.

Brown, Louise. "Parkdale Schools Mourn Deported Roma Students." *The Star* 7 October 2013. Web.

Brubaker, Rogers. *Ethnicity Without Groups*. Cambridge: Harvard University Press, 2004. Print.

Brubaker, Rogers, Margit Feischmidt, Jon Fox, and Liana Grancea. *Nationalist Politics and Everyday Ethnicity in a Transylvania Town*. Princeton, NJ: Princeton University Press, 2006. Print.

Cameron, Jenny and Katherine Gibson. "Participatory Action Research in a Poststructuralist Vein." *Geoforum* 36 (2005): 315-331. Print.

Catalano, Theresa. "The Roma and Wall Street/CEOs: Linguistic Construction of Identity in U.S. and Canadian Crime Reports." Faculty publications, paper 133: Department of Teaching, Learning and Teacher Education. University of Nebraska-Lincoln, 2012. Web. Accessed 12 November 2012.

Ciampini, Giordano. "New Exhibit Sheds Light on Canada's Roma Community. *Torontoist* 21 April 2015. Web. Accessed 21 April 2015.

Cohn, Martin R. "Canada's Splendid Isolation from the Realities of Human Smuggling." *The Star* 25 December 2012. Web. Accessed 25 December 2012.

Connor, Kevin. "Durham Region Cops Bust Gypsy Crime Ring." *Toronto Sun* 5 September 2012. Web. Accessed 21 December 2012.

Council of Europe. "International Review Conference of Romani Women: Advancing Despite Everything." Skopje, 6-7 October 2015. Web. Accessed 11 June 2016.

Council of Europe. "Final Report of the Fourth International Romani Women's Conference." 17-18 September 2013,

Helsinki. Strasbourg, 2013. Web. Accessed 11 June 2016.

Council of Europe. "Human Rights of Roma and Travellers in Europe." Commissioner of Human Rights. Strasbourg: Council of Europe Publishing, 2012. Web. Accessed 28 November 2014.

Crenshaw, Kimberlé. "Mapping the Margins: Intersectionality, Identity Politics, and Violence against Women of Color." *Stanford Law Review* 43 (1991): 1241–1299. Print.

Csepeli, György, and Dávid Simon. "Construction of Roma Identity in Eastern and Central Europe: Perception and Self-Identification." *Journal of Ethnic and Migration Studies* 30.1 (2004): 129-150. Print.

Do, Eric M. "Hate Crime Investigation Launched Surrounding Ezra Levant's Roma Broadcast." 24 October 2012. *J-Source. ca.* Web. Accessed 15 December 2012.

Durst, Judit. "What Makes Us Gypsies, Who Knows...?!" Ethnicity and Reproduction. *Multi-Disciplinary Approaches to Romani Studies: Selected Papers from Participants of Central European University's Summer Courses 2007-2009.* Ed. M. Stewart and M. Rövid. Budapest: Central European University Press, 2010. 13-34. Print.

Elliott, Louise. "Hungarian Roma Refugee Claimants Targeted in CBSA Report." *CBC News* 17 October 2012. Web. Accessed 17 October 2012.

European Roma and Travellers Forum. "The Life of the Roma in Europe: Discrimination, Aggressions, Intimidations, Evictions, Deportations, Hate Speech and Positive Measures Taken by Governments." 2015. Web. Accessed 24 October 2015.

European Union Agency for Fundamental Rights. "Roma Survey: Data in Focus: Discrimination Against and Living Conditions of Roma Women in 11 EU Member States." 2014. Web. Accessed 24 November 2014.

Fekete, Liz. "Europe Against the Roma." *Race and Class* 55.3 (2014): 60-70. Print.

Fiorito, Joe. "Fiorito: Roma in Parkdale Schools." *The Star* 27 December 2012a. Web. Accessed 27 December 2012.

Fiorito, Joe. "Roma Health Forum Takes Aim At Fallout From Misinformation And Ignorance." *The Star* 26 December 2012b. Web. Accessed 26 December 2012.

Fiorito, Joe. "Roma Women Go On Strike." *The Star* 18 September 2013. Web.

Gay y Blasco, Paloma. "The Fragility Of Cosmopolitanism: A Biographical Approach." *Social Anthropology* 18.4 (2010): 403-409. Print.

Gelbart, Petra. "Either Sing Or Go Get the Beer: Contradictions of (Romani) Female Power in Central Europe." *Signs* 38.1 (2012): 22-29. Print.

Green, Jeff. "Roma Group's Complaint Against Ezra Levant Prompts Toronto Police Investigation." *The Star* 24 October 2012. Web. Accessed 26 December 2012.

Hatfield, Erin. "Students Win Anti-Racism Contest." *InsideToronto.com* 22 March 2011. Web. Accessed 2 June 2013.

Jovanović, Jelena, Angéla Kóczé, and Lidia Balogh. "Intersections of Gender, Ethnicity, and Class: History and Future of the Romani Women's Movement." Centre for Policy Studies. Budapest: CEU Press, 2015. Print.

Keung, Nicholas. "Ottawa Accused of Racial Profiling of Roma Travellers." *The Star* July 13, 2015. Web. Accessed July 13, 2013.

Kóczé, Angéla. "Missing Intersectionality: Race/Ethnicity, Gender, and Class in Current Research and Policies on Romani Women in Europe." Central European University Center for Policy Studies. Budapest: CEU Press, 2009. Web. Accessed 8 June 2016.

Kóczé, Angéla and Julija Sardelic. "Contesting Myths and Struggling Realities." 2016. Web. Accessed 8 June 2016.

Levine-Rasky, Cynthia. "Research For/About/With the Community: A Montage." *Cultural Studies <–> Critical Methodologies.* 15.6 (2015): 455-467. Print.

Levine-Rasky, Cynthia. *Writing the Roma.* Halifax: Fernwood Publishing, 2016. Print.

Manjikian, Lalai. "Refugee "In-Betweenness": A Proactive Existence." *Refuge* 27.1 (2010): 50-58. Print.

Marmur, Dow. "Roma refugees should be welcomed, not rebuffed: Marmur." *The Star* 24 June 2013. Web. Accessed 24 June 2013.

Matras, Yaron. *The Romani Gypsies*. Cambridge, MA: Belknap Press/Harvard University Press, 2015. Print.

Matras, Yaron. "Scholarship and the Politics of Romani Identity: Strategic and Conceptual Issues." *European Yearbook on Minority Issues*, Vol. 10. Ed. European Centre for Minority Issues. Leiden and Boston: Martinus Nijhoff Publishers, 2011. 211-247. Print.

Mouffe, Chantal. "Radical Democracy: Modern or Postmodern?" *Universal Abandon? The Politics of Postmodernism*. Ed. A. Ross, Minneapolis: University of Minnesota Press, 1988. 31-45. Print.

Murphy, Jessica. "Roma People Not 'Bogus' Refugees: Advocates." *Toronto Sun* 3 May 2012. Web. Accessed 19 April 2013.

Narayan, Uma. Working Together Across Difference: Some Considerations on Emotions and Political Practice. *Hypatia*. 3.2 (1988): 31-47. Print.

Oleson, V. "Early Millennial Feminist Qualitative Research: Challenges and Contours." *The Sage Handbook Of Qualitative Research*, 3rd ed. Ed. by N. K. Denzin and Y. S. Lincoln, Thousand Oaks, CA: Sage Publications, 2005. 235-278. Print.

Oprea, Alexandra. "Romani Feminism in Reactionary Times." *Signs* 38.1 (2012): 11-21. Print.

Patterson, Brent. "Canada Blocks Roma Refugees, Visa Tensions Threaten CETA." The Council of Canadians, 19 May 2016. Web. Accessed 5 August 2016.

Rattansi, Ali. *Racism: A Very Short Introduction*. Oxford: Oxford University Press, 2007.

Rattansi, Ali. "Just Framing: Ethnicities and Racisms in a 'Postmodern' Framework." *Social Postmodernism*. Eds. L. Nicholson and S. Seidman. Cambridge: Cambridge University Press, 1995. 250-286. Print.

Roffe, Jonathan. "Multiplicity." *The Deleuze Dictionary*. Revised edition. Ed. A. Parr. Edinburgh: Edinburgh University Press, 2010. 181. Print.

Sachdev, Poonam. *The "Gypsy" as Muse and Metaphor: Modernity, Mobility and a People's Struggle for Subjectivity*. Unpublished PhD dissertation. University of California, Davis,

2008. UMI Microform 3317968.

Silverman, Carol. "Education, Agency, and Power among Macedonian Muslim Romani Women in New York City." *Signs* 38.1 (2012): 30-36. Print.

Szalai, Júlia, and Violetta Zentai, eds. "Faces and Causes of Roma Marginalization in Local Contexts." Hungary: Centre for Policy Studies, Central European University, 2014. Print.

Tremlett, Annabel. "Demotic or Demonic? Race, Class and Gender in 'Gypsy' Reality TV." *The Sociological Review* 62 (2014): 316-334. Print.

United Nations Development Program (UNDP) in the former Yugoslav Republic of Macedonia. "Opening Remarks by UN Resident Coordinator and UNDP Resident Representative Louisa Vinton at the Fifth International Review Conference of Romani Women 'Advancing Despite Everything'." 6 October 2015. Web. Accessed 11 June 2016.

Vermeersch, Peter. "Marginality, Advocacy, and the Ambiguities of Multiculturalism: Notes on Romani Activism in Central Europe." *Identities* 12.4 (2005): 451-478. Print.

Wing, A. K. "Brief Reflections Toward a Multiplicative Theory and Praxis of Being." *Berkeley Women's Law Journal* (1990-1991): 181-202. Print.

SEEKING JUSTICE FOR ROMA REFUGEES

How I Became a Leader in My Community

GINA CSANYI-ROBAH

INVITATION TO THE UNITED NATIONS

ON FEBRUARY 26 of 2014, I opened an email with the subject line "Romani Day." I noticed it among the countless emails I received daily for years, pertaining to all things related to the Roma community in Canada, especially in Toronto. This particular email was special, indeed. First, it was from the Office of the United Nations High Commissioner for Human Rights (UNHCHR) in Geneva, Switzerland. Second, it was inviting me to be a panel speaker at an OHCHR "high-level event" to mark International Roma Day at the United Nations for the first time! This international audience wished to hear my remarkable story of community development, capacity building, solidarity, leadership, and fighting anti-Gypsy discrimination that had received so much public attention and that had propelled the Roma community and its leadership to the foreground.

This extraordinary recognition from the United Nations was a wonderful acknowledgement of my years of sacrifice and ten years of hard work on behalf of my community, work that continues today. My journey to this pinnacle began in 2003, but it was inspired by questions I had posed all of my life. Luckily, I discovered the answers with the help of a great many teachers, friends, allies, and, paradoxically, a few adversaries. But the story begins with my childhood.

MY EARLY DAYS

My mother is Canadian Hungarian Roma. My father was born in Hungary and identified himself as ethnically Hungarian. In Hungary, people who identify as Roma are referred to as Ciganys. Both my father and my maternal grandparents, Rudolf and Klara Csanyi, arrived in Canada in 1956 as Geneva Convention refugees escaping the Hungarian Revolution. My grandparents' families were well-known musicians in Hungary, especially the multiple generations of violin players from the Csanyi family. Like so many other European Roma, music is a form of enjoyment but also an important means of subsistence. By 1968, my grandfather had become a well-known violinist in the bustling Hungarian restaurants in the downtown Toronto neighbourhood of Bathurst Street and Bloor Street West, where many of the 100,000 Hungarian refugees settled after arriving in Canada in 1956 and 1957. It was at one of these vibrant and popular Hungarian restaurants with delicious cuisine and fine Hungarian Gypsy violinists that my parents met in 1972.

Ultimately, institutionalized racism is to blame for the destruction of my mother's family in 1964. The fact that they were a "Gypsy family" was referenced countless times in the records of what took place. Apparently, saving "Gypsy" children and "Indian" children was commonplace in the 1960s in Ontario. In what is now referred to as the "Sixties Scoop," the Catholic Children's Aid Society engaged in the large-scale practice of systematically removing Aboriginal children and other non-white children from their families and placing them into white foster families. The same thing happened to my family. The Catholic Children's Aid Society removed all six children, all under the age of ten, from my grandparents' home in Hamilton, Ontario, and placed them into separate foster homes. Although not regularly attending school was cited as the reason for removal, my grandparents likely did not understand why their children were being taken because they had not been informed of the expectations in this new country they were in, nor did they have the knowledge or capacity to fight to have their children returned to them before they were declared crown wards and kept until they reached adulthood.

Grandpa Rudolf was broken-hearted after losing all of his children, including the one daughter that had been left behind in Hungary during the escape across the Austrian border during the revolution. He turned to alcohol and died in 1976, two years after I was born. I was the only grandchild that he'd had the opportunity to meet. Eventually, there ended up being twenty-nine of us. I still have one unbelievable memory of him walking around Centre Island with me sitting up high on his shoulders. The joy he felt and the laughter I heard remains with me today.

MY INTIMATE FAMILIARITY WITH HATRED

Many of the Central and Eastern European Romani people whom I have encountered through my work have often been unable to imagine how I could have experienced the same discrimination or hatred as they have, especially considering that I was born and raised in Canada. There is this common perception among them that Canada is a Mecca for the protection of human rights and equality for all. What people do not know is that my father imported his big baggage of "Gypsy-hate," which is commonplace in Hungary, when he came to Canada at the young age of twelve. My father was separated from his family during the Revolution and crossed the Austrian border alone. He grew up alone on the streets of Toronto, and had become somewhat of a celebrity in the Hungarian Canadian community due to his short career as a professional heavy-weight boxer and his involvement with organized Mafia crime.

As a child, my father would pick me up for weekend visits during his prison passes and take me to the Hungarian restaurants that his friends owned on Bloor Street West. There they would sit and talk for hours about many things, including how disgusted they were with the low-life *Magyar Ciganys* (Hungarian Gypsies) in Toronto. My father continuously reminded me that I was dangerously close to becoming a low life like the rest of the Gypsies in my family. He strongly encouraged me to lie to people and hide the fact that I was half-Gypsy. This always made me feel like there was something inherently wrong with me, and certainly marginalized me from other Hungarians who were non-Roma.

It wasn't until 2012 that I publicly revealed the nature of my father's racist abuse.

On September 17, 2012, I was invited for a second time to *The Agenda with Steve Paiken* on TV Ontario (TVO). The topic for the show was "The Rise of Ethnic Hate in the West," and I was to discuss then recent racist anti-Roma rant given by commentator Ezra Levant, which was broadcast live across Canada on September 5, 2012 on the Sun TV network. It fell within the description of a hate crime according to Section 319, sub-section 2 of the Criminal Code of Canada. In response to a request by the producer of the Steve Paiken show, I submitted a short essay for the show's online blog. I called it "A Childhood Lesson in Hate":

> By the age of three, I can remember the terror instilled in me by my father's diatribes during his occasional visits when he was released from prison or on a weekend pass. He would burst into our front door without knocking and begin verbally and psychologically abusing my mother, and any of her siblings if they were present. He would spit on them and scream, "Gypsies are the parasites and disgusting scum of the earth." If challenged by any of my uncles, he would delight in physically abusing them. No one was safe from his terror. Once, he even kicked my grandmother's back when she was defending me from one of his attacks due to me having Black friends. Needless to say, my entire family lived in utter terror of this man. I have learned that Roma in Europe, particularly in Hungary, are subjected to physical, psychological, and verbal abuse just like this every day. I have also learned that when people regard you as an inherently inferior human being, there is no limit to how justified they feel in degrading, humiliating, and abusing you. Certainly, this hate is learned and passed from generation to generation by way of the family, and often condoned by the broader society that one lives in.

My early experiences with discrimination and hate while growing up placed me at the periphery of society. I always felt like an outsider looking in, and carefully concealed my identity and shame. School became my safe haven. I was able to overcome my insecurity whenever I was acknowledged for my academic ability. I loved learning, and it was also a great distraction from my home life where I often witnessed alcohol abuse and domestic violence. My mother often allowed me to miss weeks of school, sometimes even for an entire month, but I always went back because I eventually wanted to. School was the only thing that I was certain was not a mistake in life, and I deeply desired to be a good role model for my younger siblings and cousins by being the first person in our family to graduate from high school, and eventually from university. We all deserved better, and education was the ladder that I used to climb out of the gutter of poverty and shame.

THE INSPIRATION

In 2001, a friend of mine in Toronto, one who was aware of my Romani identity, recorded a documentary for the National Film Board of Canada that was broadcast on a Canadian television channel. *Opre Roma: Gypsies in Canada* was my first exposure to Romani rights activism. In the film, Ronald Lee, who I learned was an elder in the Canadian Roma community and co-founded the Roma Community Centre in Toronto in 1998, spoke passionately from a podium about his autobiographical novel *Goddam Gypsy*. I was fascinated by his historical knowledge of our community and immediately felt connected to him. We shared the anger and frustration that came from having to live our lives confronting either negative or romantically ridiculous Gypsy stereotypes, together with the prejudice and discrimination that these pernicious beliefs sustained. I was deeply moved by his conviction and anger about how we have been historically mistreated. It is a massive tragedy that our history has almost been entirely omitted from accounts of world history. Certainly, the millions of European Roma systematically imprisoned and murdered during the Holocaust is a prime example of this omission. It is incredible that I never encountered a single textbook that included this information. I only became aware of the Romani victims of the Holocaust from listening to my grandmother's stories. Her eldest sister, Marika, had survived Auschwitz doctor Josef Mengele's medical experimentation on her reproductive organs. After World War II ended, Marika's first baby, a little girl, was born severely deformed and only lived until she was nine years old. Throughout all of my years of education, not a single textbook or teacher shared that Gypsies were also targeted by the Nazis. I was enraged to learn that 500 years of our enslavement, in what is now Romania, ended at the same time as the emancipation of African American slaves.

Since seeing the film, I have spent countless hours with Kako (Uncle) Ron who, in 2014, received an honourary doctorate degree from Queen's University. Now well into his eighties, he continues to be a pillar in our community. Little did he know that the documentary in which he was featured would have so much impact on my life, and subsequently on those of so many other Romani in Canada and in Central Europe.

The co-producer of the film, Julia Lovell Mohammed, founded the very first Romani organization in Canada, the Western Canadian Romani Alliance, in 1996. Many years of her life were dedicated to helping the first very large group of Roma refugees who arrived in Canada. In one of our many conversations, she shared the struggle she had with persuading the National Film Board to avoid all Gypsy stereotypes. When she told me that the film director wanted a shot of Gypsies on horseback, their necks draped with flowing red scarves, we laughed until we were in tears. Imagine how challenging it is to convince Canadian officials that Roma people need refugee asylum when ridiculous images like this one are so prevalent. It is not uncommon to encounter either romanticized or derogatory Gypsy stereotypes: Gypsies are wild and free; they do not like to conform to mainstream society; they have an inability to live in one place for long due to their untamed, wandering Gypsy spirit; they do not value education or steady work; and criminality is normative and a "way of life." To borrow a phrase from the famous 1960s singing duo, Sonny and Cher, we are often referred to as "Gypsies, Tramps & Thieves." Deconstructing the plethora of Gypsy stereotypes is a part of the public education mandate of the Canadian Romani Alliance, the organization that Julia and I co-founded in 2014 after I moved to Vancouver.

Growing up, the stereotypes, both negative and romanticized, were not things with which I wanted to be associated. At times, when the truth of my Gypsy identity was publicly revealed, I was perceived as either a thieving criminal (and, oh! Hang on to your wallets!) or a crystal ball-reading fortune teller with esoteric abilities to cast spells, and a Gypsy caravan parked in the driveway. During that time, what made things worse is that I was still learning who we were, and where we came from, and I often struggled with answering even simple questions about our history and identity. The fracture of our family that happened during the Revolution and the subsequent destruction of my mother's family in Canada, resulted in a loss of language, culture, and ancestral history. I turned to outside sources for knowledge, but it was virtually impossible to find books in libraries or bookstores that had any accurate information about our people. I never did come across any information or role models to counter-balance the lies until the film *Opre Roma*. How appropriate that its title translates to *Rise up Roma*.

THE ROOTS OF MY ACTIVISM:
MY TIME AT THE EUROPEAN ROMA RIGHTS CENTRE

My journey as a Romani rights activist began in 2003 when I completed my Honours BA with a double major in Political Science and Sociology at the University of Toronto. Thankfully, while I was still in university, the internet became a pervasive medium for research and education and I was able to learn a tremendous amount about our history and about the human rights abuses of Romani peoples in Europe. After graduation, I was ready to become a human rights activist in order to help my community. I would use the privilege of my education for something about which I had become deeply passionate: human rights, social and economic justice, equity and equality, anti-racism, and addressing the roots of oppression faced by many. Being born and raised in a country like Canada that emphasized multiculturalism, inclusion, equality, and human rights, it felt like a natural inclination for me to advocate for these values. In 2004, I found the perfect opportunity at the European Roma Rights Centre (ERRC), based in Budapest.

In March 2004, I discovered that, in collaboration with the Canadian Human Rights Foundation, the ERRC, located in Budapest, offered a four-week-long intensive training program in human rights advocacy. I applied immediately and was accepted. I was tremendously excited to meet other university-educated Romani people for the first time in my life. The experience was amazing; we bonded like family during those four weeks we spent together in a Budapest hotel. Six days a week, ten hours a day, we studied many things: European and international human rights law, how to utilize anti-discrimination laws to fight for our rights, effective tools for advocacy, and how to work in solidarity with different stakeholders.

We were a special group of educated Roma from at least eight countries who were all intending to use this experience to help our respective communities. Yet, despite our combined twenty-one university degrees, we were still treated in an inferior manner. The waiters in the hotel restaurant greeted us daily with a look of disgust and would consistently serve our table last. When they finally made it to our table, the waiters often refused to make eye contact with us. At times, it became so emotionally challenging that I considered skipping meals. Unfortunately, this was nothing new to my new friends, who would share stories of being randomly asked for identification by Hungarian police officers while walking down the street, or being refused entry to restaurants and dance clubs. My lighter skin and Canadian English accent exempted me from this racial profiling and discriminatory treatment when I was alone. However, when I visited with my mother's sister who had grown up in Hungary and who was darker skinned like my mother, I too witnessed hatred and received the same looks of disgust.

Until I became part of the beautifully diverse family for four weeks at the ERRC, it seemed that fighting for our human rights as a unified group was simply a pipe dream, due also to the linguistic, religious, cultural, and socio-economic differences that polarize us as a community. I returned to Canada where I was again without a Roma community outside of my immediate family, but where, to the best of my knowledge, we did not suffer human rights abuses. But ironically, it was in Budapest that I learned about the Roma Community Centre in Toronto. I also learned that a large group of European Roma refugees were in Canada seeking asylum from racially motivated hate crimes and, discriminatory practices so entrenched that they amounted to persecution.

A couple of years passed and I could not stop thinking about my deep desire to return to the ERRC in Hungary and to join the Romani Human Rights movement. In September of 2006, I returned to the ERRC as an intern. During my first day at the ERRC office, I was informed that, as an ERRC representative, I would attend a roundtable discussion held at the Central European University in Budapest and hosted by the Canadian government. The topic of the meeting was, "The Socio-Economic Status for Roma in Hungary." It was set up to respond to a plan by the Canadian government to remove the travel visa restriction for Hungarians without opening the door to too many Hungarian Roma who might want to seek refugee status. This is what had happened the last time the visa was lifted in the 1990s and nearly 3000 Roma applied for asylum. As the only person in the room who was Canadian, Hungarian, and Romani, I suddenly realized the significant role I could play in this dialogue. I knew then that I was exactly where I was meant to be in my life.

The Canadian Ambassador to Hungary, the Honourable Robert Hage, and his embassy colleagues, sat and listened carefully to the numerous presentations by Hungarian academics and journalists. They made it abundantly clear to the Canadian officials that Hungary's Roma suffer from endemic racism and serious impediments in housing, education, employment, and healthcare. Since I had begun teaching children while still in university, the appalling education statistics stood out in my mind: by 2006, only fifty percent of Romani children managed to finish elementary school, ten percent obtained a secondary school education, and fewer than one percent had a university education.

During the discussion period, I raised my voice. I wanted to know why the Canadian government did not want to accept

Roma refugees in Canada in the 1990s and early 2000s. I wanted to know why a Canadian politician had said to the media that Canada did not want these "Gypsy pimps and drug dealers." I wanted to know why neo-Nazi skinheads protesting the Roma refugees were not charged with a hate-crime for their signs that said "Honk If You Hate Gypsies." Ambassador Hage and his colleagues looked uncomfortable, perhaps dumbfounded. They did not have a response.

During the break, Ambassador Hage approached me and asked if I would like to attend the upcoming special celebration at the Budapest Theatre, hosted by the Canadian Embassy and the ultra-wealthy Hungarian Canadian businessman, Peter Munk, in commemoration of the fiftieth Anniversary of the Hungarian Revolution. My dear friend, Ostalinda Maya Ovalle, who had been my hotel roommate during the 2004 human rights training, and who had subsequently become the first Women's Rights Officer at the ERRC, accompanied me to the theatre. The architecture of the Budapest Theatre was fantastically lavish, and we could hardly believe it when we discovered that our seats were in the centre of the very front row. The Canadian jazz performers, the Holly Cole Trio, were fantastic, and although I appreciated the event, the best seats in the house would not buy my silence.

During my internship at the ERRC, I had another work experience that deeply enriched my knowledge and Romani rights activism skills. In October 2006, I served as an election monitor in Jaszladany, a village in North Eastern Hungary where an election was taking place for the Minority Self-Government (MSG) leader. The political climate for the Roma, the largest minority, was very poor. In the previous election in October 2002, a scandal had taken place that had made national headlines. Jászladány mayor, István Dankó, had horribly slandered the local Gypsy MSG leader, Laszlo Kallai. He had incited racially-motivated violence toward the Roma community, bought off voters, and ultimately had his non-Romani wife, Gabriella Makai Dankóné, run in the Gypsy MSG elections. She won the October 2002 election and, by September 2003, the mayor achieved his goal to segregate Roma children at school from the "ethnic Hungarian" children through the founding of a private school called the Zana Sándor Imre

Foundation School. According to the then-president of the Gypsy MSG, László Kállai, the private school signified a "milestone in a larger segregation process." The new Gypsy MSG of Jászladány, composed of one Roma and four non-Roma, among them the wife of Dankó, did not exercise its veto right on the private school issue as Kallai so fervently did (Danka and Pallai).

Imagine, that this is taking place fifty years after African Americans won the right to integrated schools. The European Court of Human Rights has found Hungary in violation three times now for its practice of allowing segregated education for Roma children.

October 2006 was the first Gypsy MSG Election since the 2002 scandal and the subsequent school segregation that took place. I was one of three ERRC monitors present. Since the previous election, the National Government in Hungary had made changes to the Gyspy MSG election process. Now, only minorities were supposed to vote and voting cards were required by each person.

When we arrived at the elementary school in Jászladány, the five non-Roma election administrators gave us that familiar look of disgust when we entered the room where the voting was taking place. They did, however, reserve better behaviour for me since I was older, wore a suit, had lighter skin, and spoke English as my first language. They likely were quite uncertain about my Roma ethnicity. As for my two ERRC colleagues, I feared that they would have been run out of the room had I not been there.

Immediately, it was obvious that there were many barriers for the Roma to vote for their Gypsy MSG leadership. Due to the long distance of the election venue from the segregated Roma housing settlement, less than one hundred Romani people managed to make it to vote at the elementary school. Those who did were treated with overt hostility and spoken to in a condescending tone. Often, they weren't allowed to cast a ballot if there was even a slight discrepancy with their identification. The vast bulk of the voters were ethnic Hungarians who had brought a voting card with them. It was an overt violation of the new national rules that had been established. In the end, it was no surprise when, after all of the votes were counted, the Gypsy Minority Self-Government leadership was usurped by a non-Roma, once again. Despite the obvious elections violations that occurred, no reprimands were issued by the Hungarian government.

I was very sad to leave the ERRC, but at the end of 2006 I returned to Toronto. Certainly, I wanted to stay and continue the work I was engaged in, but I missed my family and the diversity of Canada that is my home. The most important thing I learned was that, although a country such as Hungary was a signatory to international human rights agreements, it did not mean that they were being implemented. Even if the will to ensure human rights did exist, there was no mechanism for enforcement and accountability. From my experience, human rights in Hungary existed only on paper. This knowledge stayed with me during the struggle to raise awareness of the plight of European Roma refugees in Canada. Many people imagine Europe as a just, progressive, and humane place. From my experiences, however, the vast majority has very little awareness of the reality for Europe's largest minority group, the Roma.

MY START AT THE TORONTO ROMA COMMUNITY CENTRE

By International Roma Day, April 8, 2007, I was on a mission to find the Roma Community Centre in Toronto. It did have a website indicating a phone number. But no one returned my calls or responded to my voicemails for some time. Paul St. Clair, the Executive Director of the RCC, eventually called and invited me to attend the upcoming Board of Directors meeting later that month.

I found the RCC in a decrepit office building on Springhurst Street in the Parkdale neighbourhood. I went up to the third floor where CultureLink, one of Toronto's largest immigration and settlement organizations and host to RCC, was located. Paul brought me to the meeting room and introduced me to about eight people, half of whom were non-Roma, and several of whom were not native English-speakers. Since I was there to listen and learn about what they were doing, I did not say much. It quickly became evident to me that the board was dysfunctional. Their diversity divided them, and they used their time to argue and aggressively attack each other rather than to work together. The agenda that Paul had prepared was useless in this environment. Despite the lack of professionalism that I observed among most of the Board members, I expressed interest in joining the Board because I wanted to get to know the Roma community in my home city, and I wanted to utilize my education and skills while gaining valuable experience.

The Annual General Meeting took place the following month, and in May 2007, I was voted onto the RCC Board of Directors. I was on a mission to learn and understand as much as possible. In addition to learning about refugee protection, I became busy with finding ways to make the small RCC space a more welcoming and inclusive place for the diverse Romani people who came to seek help for a variety of settlement, social service, and legal needs. I created welcome signs in eight different languages and attached them to a large bulletin board that I purchased and placed outside of Paul's office. For the remainder of the year, I made it my full-time job to learn as much as possible about what a Board of Directors is supposed to do and how it should operate, and how to develop the capacity of a not-for-profit organization.

In January 2008, despite huge resistance due to my gender, I was nominated for and elected as President of the Board of Directors. During the next year, I worked to build the RCC, unify the community, create community partnerships, and look for professional development opportunities for myself. I created a number of public education materials, including RCC information pamphlets. I tried to hold cultural events as often as possible. At that point, our budget was approximately $6000. I did my best to model unity and peaceful collaboration for the Board, to learn and implement Canadian not-for-profit organization standards, to build the RCC membership, to recruit new members to the Board of Directors, and to develop my leadership skills. Ultimately, I knew that the RCC needed a Romani Executive Director to unify and lead the community.

The following year, 2009, was one of change for me. I gave birth to my son, and I took a leave of absence to begin my Bachelor of Education degree at the Ontario Institute of Education at the University of Toronto. Although I was gaining amazing skills and incredible experience at the RCC, it was volunteer work. The only paid position was the Executive Director, and Paul was only earning $350 per month. I returned to school to pursue my dream of being a professional teacher working with at-risk students in the inner-city. I have always had a passion for teaching, and I needed to pursue a career that would enable me to be financially independent and provide a good life for my son.

During 2009 and 2010, when I was studying to become a professional teacher, the Canadian government finally lifted the travel visa restriction, and many thousands of Roma refugees began arriving in Canada seeking refugee status. Amnesty International had begun to document the increased attacks against the Roma communities in the Czech Republic and Hungary where neo-Nazism was undergoing a revival. Paramilitary groups regularly fire-bombed homes and attacked people on the streets. The police refused to intervene in what became a wave of racially-motivated violence. In a June 2010 incident, Natalka Kudrikova, a three-year-old Czech Romani child, suffered third-degree burns when a white extremist threw a Molotov cocktail into her home in the village of Vitkov. The little girl spent months lying in an induced coma following the attack, and needed fourteen major surgeries while recuperating. The police in her town were quick to place the blame on Natalka's parents, claiming that they were responsible for the fire. Czech Roma fled to places like Canada, and, at first, our Immigration and Refugee Board acknowledged their persecution. In 2009, their acceptance rate was eighty percent.

By 2010, Hungarian Roma refugee seekers began to arrive, but the acceptance rate was nearly zero percent. Jason Kenney, then Canadian Immigration and Citizenship Minister, began referring to "bogus refugees" from the Czech Republic and Hungary. It was obvious that he was making reference to Roma refugee claimants (Levine-Rasky). In the House of Commons and in the media, Kenney declared countless times that Roma had come to Canada to commit crimes and to take advantage of our welfare and health care (Cohen). What neither Kenney nor the mainstream Canadian media acknowledged was the well-documented serial murder spree that was taking place in

Hungarian Roma communities (Amnesty International). As Amnesty International had documented, the Hungarian police were reluctant to investigate ("Amnesty Accuses Hungary"). I felt strongly, that the wave of racially-motivated violence and the lack of state protection, in addition to the endemic racism that already exists in these countries, provided credible reasons for people to seek refugee status in my country. In fact, a well-known Hungarian Romani politician, once a European Union parliamentarian, also sought refuge in Canada after many threats to her life for investigating and exposing the terrible violence toward Roma that takes place throughout Hungary.

On behalf of the Roma community in Canada, I spent the next three years of my life advocating for Roma refugee claimants and addressing the institutionalized discrimination of the Canadian government and specifically of Stephen Harper's Conservatives.[1] I knew the truth about the hate and violence that European Roma are subjected to—especially in Hungary—and I shared it at every opportunity I had. Due to my own personal experiences, I felt an immediate and emotional connection to the refugees. Moreover, from my time at the ERRC, I strongly believed that there were legitimate reasons propelling Romani people to leave Hungary and seek refuge in Canada. At the Roma Community Centre, I heard firsthand accounts daily of the trauma that people had endured. Yet Minister Kenney fanned the flames of Gypsy fiction.

I completed my B.Ed. degree in June 2010, and, by September of that year, I began contributing almost forty volunteer hours a week to the Roma Community Centre at the same time as I started to work as a teacher for the Toronto District School Board. I was quickly propelled to the front of the storm and found myself explaining to a vast number of stakeholders and to the media who the Roma refugees were, and the real reasons they were coming to Canada. Speaking truth to power was no easy task, and learning to be a leader and spokesperson for my community almost overnight was extraordinarily challenging for me both emotionally and physically. My faith in God strengthened me and I felt that I was doing the work that I was meant to do despite the fact that I was alone in my role as community leader. Quite divinely, crucial people were placed in my life that truly helped me along the journey.

I could not have accomplished all that I did on my own. There were a number of excellent people who joined the RCC Board of Directors and helped to build the organization and support my efforts at developing its capacity to help the refugee claimants. In addition, the RCC had an exceptional network of supportive community partnerships not only in the Parkdale-High Park area where the office was located, but also in surrounding areas and cities. These included individuals, not-for-profit organizations, social service agencies, colleges and universities, broadcast and print news journalists, and multiple levels of elected government officials from both the Liberal and the New Democratic parties. One amazing person in particular, Mary Jo Leddy, founder of the Romero House for Refugees, has supported me and my community at every juncture.

The blatant and pervasive injustices stemming from the top echelon of Canada's government toward the European Roma refugees were counterbalanced by an equally huge dose of Canadian love that manifested in countless ways. It was this support that sustained my own efforts to help thousands of people from my community. Over the next few years, I met with Hungarian and Canadian government officials and diplomats,; circulated petitions; learned how to lead demonstrations and protests with my community; participated in many television, newspaper, and radio interviews; and hundreds of public education presentations in universities, classrooms, school boards, social service agencies, symposiums, and conferences where I was invited to speak. Each invitation to speak publicly, was a sign of allyship and also an important opportunity to speak truth to power.

IN THE EYE OF THE STORM

In November 2010, I became the Executive Director of the Roma Community Centre. By that time, CultureLink had moved offices and completed a huge upgrade to its facilities. Despite that, my goal was to create an independent office for RCC so that we could help the community more effectively. It took me almost one full year to make that a reality, and in October 2011 we opened our new office space.

I raised funding for the space through fundraising events that I coordinated every few months. Canadian Hungarian Romani musicians such as Robi Botos, the Juno award-winning jazz artist, often helped with benefit concerts for the RCC. The lineup of clients was never ending, and we needed more office staff to accommodate the workload. I had to coordinate and manage a workforce that was ninety percent volunteers. Entering into partnerships with educational institutions was tremendously beneficial. We provided a space for student interns to learn while they completed their practicum placements and they gained experience in a community setting. They came from the Faculties of Social Work at the University of Toronto and Ryerson University, and the Settlement Worker Programs at Seneca College and Sheridan College. Some of the RCC volunteers were lawyers and university professors. They made vital contributions to the community by helping as advisors to the Board, providing *pro bono* legal help, and writing grant applications for programs and services that our small organization could offer. Lastly, many of our frontline staff were Romani volunteers who wanted to learn skills and improve their English, while helping their community. I took on the bulk of this massive workload as a volunteer because of my passion for justice and my deep desire to help my community. While directing the RCC, I was also doing paid work as a teacher and an education program manager for Toronto's Mosaic Institute.

Citizenship and Immigration Canada had requested a meeting with me to discuss some "issues" and, on October 29, 2011, during the same month that we opened our own Roma Community Center office, Minister Kenney paid us a surprise visit. I carefully used the opportunity to create an information package for the government officials that included a number of human rights reports on Hungarian and Czech Roma. I invited human rights and refugee advocates to participate in the discussion, and also Roma refugees from Hungary who could share firsthand accounts of what happened to them and their families. As a result, I was prepared when the Minister unexpectedly walked into the room. Despite all he heard and was presented with, he insisted on continuing to refer to Roma as "bogus refugees," right there in our office!

In response to Minister Kenney's explicitly racist attacks on our community, in February 2012, I reached out to the United Nations Committee for Elimination of Racial Discrimination (CERD), who was hearing submissions from Canada. Professor Julianna Beaudoin and I submitted a report to CERD entitled, "Delegitimizing Roma Refugees in Canada." We carefully described the Minister's efforts to destroy the credibility of those seeking refuge here, writing:

> "Gypsy" stereotypes persist in Canada, in no small measure reinforced by Minister Kenney and Canadian media who persist in labelling Roma as thieves, criminals, bogus, and undeserving refugee claimants who only clog up the IRB system. Kenney's allegations towards Roma have actually had a direct impact on the acceptance rates of Roma; his statements are unprecedented in Canadian history—never has a Minister (much less the Citizenship, Immigration, and Multiculturalism one) so blatantly denounced an entire ethnic group and called them criminal. (Brosnahan)

One of the most memorable things I organized for my community was a candlelight vigil in remembrance of Romani victims of hate crimes, which was held on February 23, 2012, in front of Parkdale Collegiate Institute. I was honoured to stand side by side with Aladar Horvath, a well-known Hungarian Romani politician and community leader, who was visiting Canada at the time. I was inspired by the huge community turnout and awed to witness the solidarity among the Romani diaspora from so many different European countries. Lastly, I was humbled by the support of the Canadian community. The Member of Provincial Parliament for Parkdale-High Park, Cheri Di Novo, who attended the vigil, made the following statement to the Legislative Assembly in Queen's Park the next day:

> Mr. Speaker, last night in my riding, we had a powerful and moving event. It was a candlelight vigil for the Roma refugees and immigrants in my riding. There were about 300 people there, and when asked if they had ever experienced violence in their home countries, many of them coming from European Union countries such as Hungary and the former Czechoslovakia, all of them put their hands up. We asked them if they had ever experienced oppression or racism. All of them, including the children, put their hands up.

Everything that I was doing, I was doing for the first time, often with the generous support of more experienced human rights advocates to help guide some of my work. Learning how to advocate for my community on a provincial, national, and international level required me to exemplify confidence that I did not always have. But I persevered with the conviction that I would learn with experience. By far the biggest test of my confidence came in May 2012, and again in July 2013, when I went to Ottawa to testify in front of the Canadian government.

At the time, Minister Kenney had proposed Bill C-31, a discriminatory piece of legislation that while targeting the Roma community, also affected countless other refugees who would suffer as a result of the new list of "designated countries of origin," or DCOs. This policy would ultimately create a two-tier refugee determination system in Canada. To make matters worse, DCOs, or "safe" countries, would be determined solely by the Minister rather than by an independent panel of human rights experts. There would also be a change in the possibilities for challenging a negative decision on a refugee claim for claimants from DCO countries. The timeframe for submitting pre-removal risk assessments (PRRA) would require a three-year waiting period, and people could now be removed from the country while waiting for a federal court judicial review of their refugee claims. These reforms ultimately had disastrous repercussions when people were deported in the thousands.

I tried to stop these changes from happening. A few days before my trip to Ottawa, I organized a huge rally at Dundas Square in downtown Toronto on April 30, 2012. The slogan was "Rally for Roma, not Bill C-31." Hundreds of Roma came from around Toronto and Hamilton, and the interim Executive Director at the Canadian Council for Refugees came to support us and speak at the event. It was inspiring.

A few days later, I flew to Ottawa with Maureen Silcoff, a remarkable human rights advocate and immigration lawyer who had helped facilitate my testimony at the Parliamentary Standing Committee on Citizenship and Immigration on May 3, 2012. To say that I was nervous that day is an enormous understatement. I felt like I was carrying my entire community on my shoulders at that moment, and that it was essential for me to say the right thing to save them from deportation back to their threatened existence. Here I was, a woman from a dysfunctional family who had always felt like an outsider in society, a woman who was once ashamed to reveal her Gypsy identity. I worked hard to fight those negative voices. I reminded myself that I was capable of doing it; my community depended on me. I naively believed that if I said the right things to our parliamentarians, it would make a difference. Maureen and I each had five minutes to speak. Although I had prepared numerous written notes, I was too nervous to read from them. Instead, I opted to maintain eye contact with the hope that the truth would be conveyed more effectively and that I would be more compelling.

Maureen and I were a team. Despite my nervousness, I tried my very best to speak well, as I described why Roma refugees have justifiable reasons to flee counties like the Czech Republic, Hungary, and Slovakia. Maureen did an outstanding job describing the negative repercussions that the changes in the refugee determination would have. She also spoke about the impact of the removal of healthcare services for refugee claimants. I felt hopeful about our presentation. Afterwards, we received many positive comments from people and from the press.

A month later, on June 20, 2012, I was back in Ottawa, this time with another brilliant human rights advocate, co-founder of the FCJ Refugee Centre in Toronto, Mr. Francisco Rico-Martinez. This time, as representatives of the Canadian Council for Refugees, we addressed the Canadian Senate Committee for

Social Affairs, Science and Technology. My testimony this time around was very different. I was not as nervous as I had been for the Standing Committee on Immigration and Citizenship in the House of Commons. And I had lost much of my naïveté and hope. I realized that having my voice heard was simply part of the democratic process that requires the government to listen to members of society, but that it unfortunately would not necessarily change a single thing. But, my confidence had recently received a tremendous boost on June 13, 2012, when I received the Queen Elizabeth Diamond Jubilee Medal from MPP Cheri Di Novo in Parkdale-High Park, for my community service. Without worry of offending anyone or feeling intimidated by the power in the room, I proceeded to methodically describe how Prime Minister Stephen Harper's Conservative government, specifically Minister Kenney, discriminated against the Roma community. As I had anticipated, my statement did not make any difference whatsoever, but at least it is on record.

A short while later, on September 14, 2012, I was honoured again by an award, this time by the Canadian Association of Refugee Lawyers, who presented me with their Advocacy Award. Not long afterwards, in spring 2013, I was nominated as a Toronto Public Health Champion. By this time, the RCC had a budget of $135,000 and was successfully running a number of important programs, projects, and services out of our independent office.

THE HEART-WORK MUST CONTINUE

The work I do on behalf of my community continues to be service from my heart, arising from my passionate belief in justice and human rights. Since 2013, I have been a member of the Canadian delegation to the International Holocaust Remembrance Alliance (IHRA) and an active participant in the Roma Genocide Working Group. It is here, on an international level, that I am now able to share and educate about the Romani victims of the Holocaust. In 2014, I co-founded the Canadian Romani Alliance to continue public education, to deconstruct Gypsy stereotypes and myths, to continue capacity building and community development, and to continue the important advocacy work on behalf of Roma refugees in solidarity with Canadian human rights and refugee rights groups. Our biggest collaborative success to date has been at the Law Society of Upper Canada where three lawyers who mishandled two-thirds of the Hungarian Roma refugee claims— acts affecting thousands of vulnerable clients—were all recently found guilty of professional misconduct (Keung). When not volunteering my time for my Roma rights activities, I continue to work as an educator. The project I manage at the Mosaic Institute, "Next Generation: Canadian Global Citizenship," won the Canadian Race Relations Award of Excellence for 2012. I embody what I teach and I encourage young people to make a positive difference in their communities, as well as in the world we share. I continue to be optimistic that each and every one of us has the power to overcome barriers in our lives, and to push for change that makes social, environmental, and economic justice a possibility.

[1]Stephen Harper served as the 22nd Prime Minister of Canada from February 6, 2006 to November 4, 2015.

WORKS CITED

"Amnesty accuses Hungary of failing to protect Roma." BBC News, 10 November 2010. Web.

Amnesty International. *Violent Attacks Against Roma in Hungary: Time to Investigate Racial Motivation*. London, UK: Amnesty International Publications, 2010. Web.

Brosnahan, Maureen. "Roman refugees victims of systemic discrimination in Canada, newreport finds. Many claimants faced bias and unfair treatment." CBC News 2 April 2015. Web.

Cohen, Tobi. "Controversial refugee bill set to clear House of Commons Monday." *National Post* 10 June 2012. Web.

Danka, Anita and Nicole Pallai. "Legal but Illegitimate: The Gypsy Minority Self-Government in Jászladány." European Roma Rights Centre (ERRC), 7 February 2004. Web.

Keung, Nicholas. "Lawyer guilty of professional misconduct in handling of Roma refugees." *Toronto Star* 11 October 2016. Web.

Levine-Rasky, Cynthia. "Who Are You Calling Bogus? Saying No to Roma Refugees." *Canadian Dimension* 25 September 2012. Web.

ROMA

JULIA LOVELL

How strong is that name to me.
Our struggle to survive brings tears
To my eyes with all we endure to
Stay alive.

Chains around our feet,
Tongues denied to speak,
Mothers sterilized,
Myths paralyze

Hitler's blackbird of death flew down
To terrorize; we still survive, Roma
People, strong Roma people.

Generations now arise, a nation
With pride for our own ancestors kept
It alive; we carry their will to
Survive. Roma people, strong Roma
People, shine on. Live on...
Stay Rom.

ACTIVIST IN HUNGARY / ASYLUM-SEEKER
IN TORONTO

Five Years in Transition

VIKTORIA MOHACSI

M Y FIVE SIBLINGS and I—one brother and four sisters—grew up in the Hungarian village of Berettyóújfalu, a shantytown beside the Romanian border. Not everyone in the village was Roma. Most of those who were Roma were unemployed and, because they were unemployed, they were targeted by communist officials. Childcare officials often pursued entire Romani families. I witnessed four of my six cousins being taken away and placed in children's institutions. I never saw two of them again. They had lived only a couple of houses away from my family. Their parents did not have jobs, so in compliance with the *Child Care Act* of 1985, children had to be removed from their homes. Parents were told they were not providing enough food for their children, thus putting them at risk. The children therefore became wards of the state.

I have another terrible memory. It was of the forced bathing of the Roma. We were put in a big tent, open to the outside. Everybody had to enter the tent naked. Inside the tent, they shaved our hair, even adults' pubic hair. Then they sprayed us with DDT, a chemical that later caused cancer in many of the people. Officials went though the whole country, including all of the Romani ghettos. They believed that Gypsies were dirty and that they were a danger to public health, so everybody had to be washed by force. I experienced this with my mother. I remember going to a separate tent, and it was horrible. I cannot even tell you how I felt. I saw my cousins there, too, and I was so mortified that I felt that it was no longer possible to live. But I was the only one to ask my mother, why, why, why did this happen? She said it was God's will. For me, that was no real answer. If this was done to us just because we are Roma, that was not an answer! As a child, I could not accept that answer. This incident was probably the biggest push for me to become an activist and to dedicate my life to the improvement of Romani peoples' rights.

That was many years ago, but Roma are still the victims of widespread discriminatory practices in nearly every area of life. According to the *European Union Minorities and Discrimination Survey* published by the European Union Agency for Fundamental Rights, 62 percent of Hungarian Roma surveyed in 2008 felt that they were the victims of discrimination based on their ethnicity in the previous twelve months—whether when looking for work, entering a store, or trying to open a bank account. This research and more like it by the Council of Europe, the European Roma Rights Centre, and Amnesty International reveal patterns of discrimination in housing, healthcare, and education services. In a 2008 survey of 3500 Roma across seven European countries (Bulgaria, Czech Republic, Greece, Hungary, Poland, Romania, and Slovakia), Human Rights First found that 624 (18 percent) claimed to be victimized by a racially motivated assault, threat, or serious harassment in the last twelve months. When respondents were asked to identify experiences of discriminatory treatment by the police, 41 percent of Hungarian Roma reported that Hungarian law enforcement authorities stopped them in the past year. Of these, 58 percent believed that they were stopped on the basis of their ethnicity (4).

The idea of "Gypsy criminality" (*cigánybűnözés*) pervades Hungarian society. It stems from the racist stereotyping of the Roma as a people prone to criminality—a view that continues to permeate Hungarian media and is heard everywhere, whether in public debate or in local pubs. Extremist groups, especially the xenophobic Jobbik Party, nurture such anti-Roma prejudice. When they were voted in as the third largest party in the country's 2010 parliamentary elections, they had campaigned on the idea of "restoring order" and fighting "Gypsy crime" (Human Rights First 2016)

When citizens perceive that petty crimes are growing in number, the government is placed under heavy pressure to restore law and order. Clearly, those who transgress the law should be punished. The challenge is to collect crime data that is not only accurate but is also disaggregated by ethnicity. This way, authorities can identify trends in criminal justice that avoid the kind of racism found in many discussions of "Gypsy crime." When asked why there is no data on the actual extent of crimes carried out by Roma, officials respond that the collection of such ethnic data violates constitutional norms. Amnesty International has noted that this prohibition is a barrier to investigating hate crime in Hungary (21). Prohibitions against identifying people by ethnicity may be a constitutional protection that non-Roma Hungarians enjoy, but it does not apply to the Roma, especially when they are alleged to have perpetrated a crime. Elected politicians and state officials receive a lot of populist support when they publicly link the Roma community with criminality.

Another area in which the Roma experience systematic discrimination is school segregation. When I was a child, my skills as a student were about average. There is a word for Romani students like me in Hungary. Translated it means, "coming from the back row," because all the Gypsy kids were forced to sit in the back row of the classroom like I was. On the first day of school, the teacher told everyone that we could sit wherever we like in the order in which we entered the classroom. I wanted to sit in the front row, so I appeared at seven in the morning and took my seat. No one else was in the classroom at that time. When the teacher came in, she told me that this seat was not for me, but for the children who use eyeglasses to see the board. Every year, I ended up in the last row.

Educational discrimination is very much alive in Hungary today. The European Roma Rights Centre (2014) has documented a long pattern of segregating Romani children in schools for children with mental disabilities. For example, in Heves and Tolna Counties, almost all of the children in special education are Roma (8). In 2013, the European Court of Human Rights recognized a long history of this practice and ruled that it violated the European Convention on Human Rights. Fifty-one percent of Romani children drop out of school before age 18, and only 20 percent take secondary school final exams (ECRI). In a 2014 report, the Council of Europe Commissioner for Human Rights confirmed that a "significantly low" number of Roma attend university. When I worked for the Hungarian Ministry of Education, we were successful in drafting legislation for combating educational segregation—the *Public Educational Act* and the *Equal Treatment Act*—and in changing the Constitution to reflect this new formal equality for the Roma. Romani children who had been forced to attend special schools for the mentally disabled were re-examined. We won new per-capita funding for re-integrating children into mainstream education, as well as for new culture-independent testing methods, and we established a National Education Integration Network.

Despite these efforts, in general, conditions are so bad for Roma in Hungary that they really amount to persecution on the basis of ethnicity. This is why we fled the country.

I wish to describe how I have been surviving as a European Roma refugee in Canada. Today my daughter, my son, and I live in a two-bedroom basement apartment in the north end of Toronto. This is the eleventh apartment we have lived in since our arrival in Canada on November 27, 2011. On that date, I travelled with my three children who were thirteen, eleven, and six years of age at the time. As I write this, my eldest daughter is turning eighteen years old. She has had to go back to Hungary, to live with her father.

When you think your life is in danger, planning a trip to Canada is not an easy thing. I had to make the decision to never return to the place I came from. And I had to bring the most important things in my life: my three children. Everything we would need we packed into four suitcases, each of which weighed less than twenty-five kilograms: some clothes, favourite toys, books, and photographs. I did not know what would happen at the airport, how long the border service agency would keep us there, and where we would spend our first night. So I packed everybody's pillows and blankets. We are still using them.

My oldest daughter did not have her father's consent to leave the country. When I mentioned to him earlier that I was thinking about moving to another country, he was not happy at all. So I decided not to share with my children my plan to seek asylum in Canada. Children cannot keep a secret so, instead, I told them that we were going for a long trip and that our destination was a big surprise. I told them the truth about why we were travelling only once we were on the plane. Everyone was crying. They did not like the idea of never returning to our house, and never seeing their family, friends, classmates, and teachers again.

I found a Romani person I knew on Facebook. He had moved to Toronto a couple of years earlier with his family. He offered us a place to sleep on our first night. We ended up staying only briefly because I had to leave to testify to the immigration officers about our reasons for fleeing Hungary. After that, I was able to contact a former employee of mine when I was a member of the European Parliament. His family offered us a room while I looked for an apartment. But after one month, his family was threatened with deportation. They were afraid to go back to Hungary, so they moved to a church to seek sanctuary. Eventually, they were able to remain in Canada.

In the middle of December of 2011, we moved to a third place, where another family accommodated us for one and a half months. It was not easy to find a rental unit since most landlords preferred a tenant who was settled down and had a job. We did not fulfill those criteria. The first property manager explained to me that I was a "newcomer," and that was why finding somewhere to live was so challenging. I was very upset since I felt discriminated against. In Hungary, people do not want to rent apartments to a Romani person or a Romani family. I experienced a lot of rejection by Hungarian landlords until I bought my own house. I did not want to believe that Toronto was the same. The thought of it made me cry.

I had asked many members of the Romani community in Toronto what they thought were the most crucial risks for children in schools here. Everybody said that our language created such tremendous difficulties for children that they were not learning anything in the schools. Many Romani children did not speak

English even after attending school for two years. I did not want to believe that. But to be safe, when I asked the staff at a rental agency to help us find an apartment for my family, I requested a location where there were no Hungarian-Romani families. Within one week, she had found one. On February 1, 2012, we moved for the fourth time.

This time we moved into a cozy house in a very nice Portuguese neighborhood only a few minutes' walk to the school that all three of my children attended. Just like our neighbours, no one in the school had heard about us. So many people in Toronto do not know about Romani people, even that we exist. It is very hard to imagine a group of people arriving from Europe but who do not have a country. When asked if I was Hungarian, the answer was complex. I was born into a country where White Hungarians create differences between themselves and us. Even if I had wanted to be a Hungarian-Romani woman and feel that I had a home country, I had difficulty doing so.

On the first of July of 2012, we had to move to a one-bedroom apartment just down the street. Since my ex-husband had initiated a Hague Convention case against me on the basis of child abduction, I was very afraid that I would be served with a notice from Family Court. I was hoping that my refugee case would be dealt with before the Family Court case, but this did not happen. When I was packing our things for moving, a car stopped in front of our apartment. A woman stepped out and asked me if I was Viktoria Mohacsi. She handed me an envelope. She was my ex-husband's lawyer. As a result of the Family Court case, my eldest daughter was forced to return to Hungary. Now only two of my children live with me instead of three.

The last apartment we lived in was located in the Weston Road area in Toronto. Most people there are from Caribbean countries. They tend to settle as permanent residents or citizens after only a few years in Canada. Like our family, most of them depend on social assistance. Unfortunately, we had to move from that apartment, too. The reason—among others—was because I called the police after witnessing a fight between two men in the middle of the street. Two days before that incident, the same two men were fighting and one of them pulled out a gun and fired it.

Someone else called the police. No one died. I learned that in this society, it is best not to report crimes to the police. A cannabis dealer on the street told my ten-year-old daughter that even if her aunt was beaten up, if the police asked for witnesses, she should say that she saw nothing. This turned out to be good advice, but we received it too late.

As bad as things are sometimes in Canada for groups like Roma and people from the Caribbean, there is nothing like the hate crime that occurs in Hungary. A hate crime is a crime that is motivated by intolerance towards a certain group within society who share characteristics such as race, religion, ethnicity, language, or sexual orientation. Since there are no official statistics on the number of cases of targeted violence against Roma in Hungary, I will describe a serious pattern of violent attacks that occurred in 2007-2010. These involved beatings in daylight, murders by arson, shootings, and throwing of Molotov cocktails into houses where Romani families lived (Amnesty International 2010). There was a series of these violent acts against the Roma in 2008-2009 that became known as the "Roma Murders" (ECRI). I travelled to these sites and documented many of these attacks on Romani families that often resulted in death. Since I recorded only those cases in which the survivors were able to contact me, I believe that many hate crimes go unreported. When I was a member of the European Parliament, I travelled to many countries and recorded incidents like these. They are similar all over Europe. It is the same for Roma everywhere.

As a former member of the European Parliament, I founded the Movement for Desegregation. Between January 2008 and June 2010, we mostly monitored anti-Roma attacks and hate crimes, and documented sixty-eight attacks, twelve of which led to death. I recently received notification from the current director that the organization was closed down since our activities ended after I left the country. But when the organization was active, we documented many incidents of anti-Roma violence. This is just a selection in chronological order that was later published by Amnesty International:

Fadd: On April 13, 2008, Molotov cocktails were thrown at a house into which a Romani family was about to move. The family was forced to look for a new home after the fire destroyed all of their belongings. A woman who was going to sell the family a new home was allegedly told by a member of the local government not to sell the home to the family, and was also verbally threatened. She ignored the threat and sold the home to the family. A few days later on April 18, 2008, the family's new home was set on fire with Molotov cocktails. Closely following this attack, a demonstration against "Gypsy criminality" was held in the village on June 21, 2008. It was organized by the local self-government, a motorcycle gang known as the Goy Bikers, and the Hungarian Guard.

Fényeslitke: On June 15, 2008, a fourteen-year-old Romani boy was stabbed to death by a drunk neo-Nazi. The man reportedly expressed anti-Roma threats. The boy's sixteen-year-old brother was also seriously injured.

Nagycsécs: A forty-three-year-old Romani man and a forty-year-old Romani woman were shot dead by neo-Nazis on November 3, 2008. Their home was set on fire by a Molotov cocktail and the two were killed while they were trying to flee the burning house. A firebomb thrown across the street at another Romani home failed to explode.

Alsózsolca: On December 15, 2008, a nineteen-year old Romani man was chopping wood in his yard when he was shot twice by neo-Nazis. His injuries were life-threatening. His partner was also shot.

Tatárszentgyörgy: On February 23, 2009, the house of a Romani family was set on fire by a Molotov cocktail. The neo-Nazi perpetrators shot and killed a twenty-seven-year-old man and his five-year-old son while they were fleeing from their burning home. The man's six-year-old daughter, three-year-old child, and wife were also injured in the attack.

Tiszalök: On April 22, 2009, a fifty-four-year-old Romani man was shot as he was leaving for work. The man was killed instantly.

Abádszalók: On May 27, 2009, a man broke into a house at three am and attacked the Romani family inside with a razor blade. The man, who was known to have had connections to the neo-Nazi organization known as the Hungarian Guard, entered the house through a window and injured the father by cutting into his neck and chest and harmed the mother by cutting into her legs. The family managed to overtake the perpetrator, who was also armed with a gun. The couple was taken to the hospital.

Kisléta: On the night of August 3, 2009, a forty-five-year-old woman and her daughter were attacked by neo-Nazis in their home. The mother died after being shot while still in bed. Her daughter survived but was badly injured.

Bringing about social and political change in Hungary became my life's mission. When I arrived in Canada, it felt like a kind of death because I had to abandon that mission. It is bad enough to lose your home and everything you have collected in your life. I had to leave everything behind, including my mission. If I am able to obtain legal status in Canada, I hope I can use that as a safe position from which to continue my human rights work in Hungary, and to solve the problems I left behind. I am afraid of what I see in Europe now—how governments treat our people, and how they are implementing so-called security measure against Roma. But I really do believe in change. I really believe that with some action and some power, good people can prevent what I fear will be a new Holocaust. This should be the most urgent thing.

In the meantime, my children and I wait in our little apartment in Toronto. We wait endlessly for word about whether we can remain in the country or whether we will be rejected. The word could come any day, or any year. I work hard at my job, and I dedicate countless volunteer hours to helping people in my community. I know what they are going through as asylum-seekers, and my activism in Hungary gave me the skills to advocate for them. After five years in transition, we share the same vulnerability.

WORKS CITED

Amnesty International. "Violent Attacks Against Roma in Hungary: Time to Investigate Racial Motivation." Amnesty International Publications: London, 2010. Web. Accessed 10 August 2016.

Council of Europe. Commissioner for Human Rights. Nils

Muižnieks. *Report by Nils Muižnieks Commissioner for Human Rights of the Council of Europe Following His Visit to Hungary from 1 to 4 July 2014*. 16 December 2014. Accessed 25 November 2014.

European Commission Against Racism and Intolerance (ECRI). *ECRI Report on Hungary. (Fifth Monitoring Cycle).* Council of Europe, ECRI, 9 June 2015. Web. Accessed 16 August 2016.

European Roma Rights Centre (ERRC). "Attacks against Roma in Hungary: January 2008-September 2012." 1 October 2012. Accessed 16 August 2016.

European Roma Rights Centre (ERRC). Written comments by the European Roma Rights Centre Concerning Hungary for Consideration by the European Commission on the Transposition and Application of the Race Directive and on the Legal Issues Relevant to Roma Integration, 2014. Web. Accessed 27 November 2014.

Human Rights First. "Combating Violence Against Roma in Hungary: Blueprint." October 2010. Web. Accessed 21 October 2011.

Human Rights First. "The Jobbik Party in Hungary: History and Background." December 2015. Web. Accessed on 12 August 2016.

TILLSONBURG

Strategies for Living

LYNN HUTCHINSON LEE

Erasure

(a process)

This is how we fade to mist
unless we're caught
by desperation
to reverse the process

HOUSES

IT WAS 1910 or thereabouts, near the end of the tobacco harvest. All summer the sun had burnt their skin. Their backs were bent over the leaves. They could not wash out the dark bitter juices that had been worked into the lines of their hands. They were dizzy from the nicotine and sometimes sick, especially the children, right there on the ground beside the plants.

Some weekends they travelled. They were entertainers, performing at the garden parties of rich farmers. My brother Willie told me about those days. The work, the travelling, the troubles. He was fifteen years older than I, and the politics of the family—for they were, ultimately, politics—had not been kept from him. We were sitting in my kitchen, drinking tea. We talked about our father who was long dead.

We always talked about our father. He was an enigma to us.

"Such fancy parties they were," Willie told me, parties held in Tillsonburg, Aylmer, Courtland, Delhi. "Dad wasn't much more than a kid," he said. Daddy had never spoken to me of this. If not for my brother I wouldn't have learned the old stories.

In October, after the tobacco harvest, they travelled again— my grandmother Lizzie Lee, her husband Anthony Hutchinson, and the four children, who at that time were anywhere between twelve and eighteen, Daddy being the youngest. Anthony, Daddy's father, although not by blood, made signs for small shops and businesses around Tillsonburg. Daddy, at his side, learned to paint in the style of the time, flourishing the brush across the wood, transforming swoops and swirls into letters. Such painting was done on the caravans back home.

They built houses too—plain, small wooden houses—kitchen, living room, two bedrooms at the back. They framed the windows and built a no-nonsense entrance, nothing like the doors of the rich farmers with their pilasters, transoms, and sidelights. As an old man Daddy would still make a doorframe and hang the door with his builder's intuition. No level was needed. He'd frown slightly, look into the emptiness within the perfectly made frame, and his hands would lift the door and slip it into place.

* * *

At the edge of town they built a house for Daddy's sister Ophelia. Ophelia was older, married. I never knew her, although as a child I once met her daughter. It was at my sister's, in a two-room log house she'd rented near Lake Ontario.

My sister Rose was a half-sister, twenty years older than I. Our father had left her mother and run off with mine. I was in love with Rose. She was like a movie star, sweeping through the door in long dresses and ropes of necklaces, bringing us gifts and stories of where she'd been. We rarely saw her. She'd show up for days or a week and then leave.

It was near the end of summer when we drove to her house along the back roads. After veering over ruts and stones in a series of diminishing dirt roads, we came to a narrow lane under the trees, with the little log house at the end. I remember its painted window frames and squared timbers dark with age, the white mortar between the logs. Rose stood in her doorway, waving, and came out to meet us, running through the shadows.

I don't remember the interior of the house. We mostly stayed outside under the tree canopy. Daddy wandered through the old abandoned orchard, gathering branches and kindling as he went. There were still some apples clinging to the branches, and we ate them off the tree. My sister got enough to make a pie. Later we went into the woods and found a puffball, which we sliced up and cooked in a frying pan over Daddy's fire.

Ophelia's daughter, Harmony, who had come to my sister's house from Tillsonburg, didn't speak. She ate very little. Her silence made her bigger than the rest of us. I thought she was haunted by a series of diminishing ghosts, like a Russian doll, the ghosts getting smaller and smaller until the last one was just a sip of air.

At night we sat around the fire, drowsy with too much bread, too much chicken, tomatoes, pie, tea, the puffball in pieces, fried in butter. I couldn't tell if Harmony was sleeping or in retreat. Her eyes were shut. I remember saying to Rose, who was much older than me, *please, will you live here always, and sometimes I can visit you?* and Rose laughing, because she never stayed anywhere very long. The embers were turning blue and sending out little sparks. I fell asleep, and opened my eyes for a second when Rose put a blanket over me, then went into the house to wash the dishes.

LANGUAGE

The English Romanichals, my father's people, called themselves Romanies or Gypsies. They didn't say *Roma*. (These days they refer to their sisters and brothers from Europe as Roma, but they themselves remain Romanies and Gypsies.) Many still speak Angloromani. Throughout these pages I use some of those words: a caravan is a *vardo*; children are *chavvies*; those who are not Romanies are *Gorgios*; a person of mixed blood is a *didikai*, a *poshrat*. Angloromani is unique in its use of Romani words in an English grammatical structure. Not that I knew many of those words, for I was consciously assimilated. I had two identities: the shy Canadian child who studied ballet and was taken to see the great Russian dancers, and the *didikai*, the *poshrat*, who learned to keep certain things inside—the ancestors, the caravan, a gnawing fear of the outer world—knowing they could not be revealed.

I sometimes reflect on the language embedded in identity. Ways of seeing, human relationships, the order of things, expressions of love, all encoded in the language. What were we—my brother, my sister, and I—without that unique way of seeing the world? How would we navigate terrain that was both familiar and strange?

STRATEGIES

Rose was too beautiful. Men and women, they ached for her. They filled her house while she held court. After a few days or weeks they were dismissed and new ones would appear. It was only her family that she tried to keep close, even though we were all scattered, and there was much discord.

A Consul General from Italy gave Rose his mother's gold-rimmed dishes. I saw them when she was living in Toronto. They were almost transparent. He gave her money, too, lots of it, and a collection of old hunting engravings that covered her walls for a time. He asked her to marry him. When I next visited, the dishes and engravings were gone. They'd been sold. What she got for them would carry her over the next two months.

Shortly after, she left for Sudbury, Halifax, various towns in British Columbia. She borrowed or cajoled money on the strength of her beauty, and moved on. Everywhere she went she was presented with jewellery, clothes, televisions, furniture, and they were all sold or traded. She found people to invest in her new freezer business, and cleared off with the money, leaving a warehouse of freezers that had been delivered and not paid for.

One night she appeared at our door. She was crying. It was about the freezers, and the people from whom she had gotten the money. They were looking for her. She said she was with a friend who was waiting for her outside in a car. They were on their way out of town. I gave her a two-dollar bill that had been given to me by my Scottish great-aunt. When Rose paid me back on the next visit, months later, my mother said that it would have been the first, and probably only, debt she honoured. My mother looked as if she was ready to laugh or cry.

Rose never stole a wallet or odds and ends of change from people's pockets. That was too simple. She planned. She set up situations in which money or jewellery or other possessions were willingly surrendered, as if she herself were bestowing a favour upon the person whose money she took or whose gifts she accepted. The police were sent for, many times. They followed my sister back and forth across the country. She was always one town ahead, and was never caught.

***

People may not think of the social context of theft, of scamming. If I tell people that Rose scams and steals her way across Canada, they say, *that's terrible*. If I tell people that Rose scams and steals and her father is a Gypsy, they connect the dots. The accusation is clear, even if politely left unsaid. Rose is pigeon-holed. She's branded. Easy to do if she's known to belong to an ethnicity singled out for such accusations.

> *I better watch my wallet around you.*
> said to me while installing an exhibition
> while at a gallery opening
> while talking about my father to a friend

When Rose died, we hadn't spoken in almost a year. We'd had a fight that started in the north of Scotland and continued down to London and back to Toronto. I turned my back, walked past her at the airport; she stormed home to Calgary. I didn't see her again. She called me up to say *I love you little sister*, and died weeks later in her sleep.

***

Our father's uncle was hanged for stealing a horse. The circumstance of the theft is unknown. At least to me. Was this uncle hanged because he was poor, a Romani, or both?

(A Scottish relative, a virtuous citizen on my mother's side, paid off a disabled woman whom he had severely injured in a car accident. He paid her hospital bills and supported her, generously, for life, with the understanding that she would not identify him as the man who ran her down. He then met with the police chief and the newspaper editor, both of whom he knew. The story did not appear in the paper, nor in any court record, for the relative was never charged.)

If a Gorgio steals a horse—a Gorgio protected by title, family, money, influence—is it the same crime? I weighed my great-uncle's horse against the crimes of an empire that plundered lands and resources, civilizations, languages, cultures. *The Rom steals the hen; the Gorgio steals the farm.*

* * *

At the restaurant on the Lido, beside the hotel, my husband laid down two confiscated signs. One had been printed in Italian, the other, awkwardly, in English. We were there—a small group of artists from six countries, with our films, photographs, drawings, and a sound installation— curated into the Roma Pavilion of the 2011 Venice Biennale. The signs read: "*Non pagate gli zingari*" and "Do not pay the gypsys." We took turns holding the signs, one by one, holding them up as our friend took our photographs.

OPHELIA

As an old woman, Ophelia shouted at strangers. She was known as a healer of birds. People would bring a sick parrot or finch to her door and a week later they'd return and the bird would be cured. My brother's wife, as a child, believed that Ophelia was a witch, and told me how she hid behind her mother when they went, with their sick budgie, to the door of Ophelia's house.

Ophelia died alone in her bedroom. Her body was not found for two weeks, for she was a recluse and never went into the town. The story of her death was told to me by my mother. My father did not talk about his family. He'd start to whistle, or leave the room.

My account of Ophelia, of them all, isn't meant to be chronological. Memory is differently constructed. I move around my sister, my brother, my father, around Ophelia and Harmony, not to pin down the events of their lives that line up behind each other, but to bring a light to them, and perhaps to see them as I would a diamond. Looking into each small surface, finding what is lit or hidden.

Did Ophelia ever think of her life back home? The travelling, the fairs? Did any of them think of that life? Anthony would have laughed that there was no time to dwell on the past, they worked so hard, bending to the tobacco leaves under the hot sun, the tobacco juice running down their hands. They were so tired at the end of the day, that their eyes were unable to stay open, and there was no wakeful moment left for thinking. Thinking was done by rich people. By those who had time to waste. A luxury, like owning two pairs of shoes or a field of tobacco.

We put one foot in front of the other, chavvies; we don't stop until the moon won't show us the path or our feet are burning in our boots. We don't think about the lateness of the night, about what is possible or what is not. We think about the tools we need for the next job, the money we'll count at the end of the next day.

TRAVELLING

Back in England, Anthony had carved and painted horses for merry-go-rounds and carousels, and repaired the *vardo* that, in later years, would continue to be used after he and my grandmother left for Canada. He was, for a time, chairman of the Showmen's Guild, which began life as the United Kingdom Van Dwellers Association. The guild was created as a protest against the *Moveable Dwellings Act,* which severely limited the right to travel.

The old family *vardo* was abandoned, finally, during the Second World War, by relatives who remained in England. After the war, work was harder to find, as were the stopping places that began to disappear when new laws were enacted against Romanies and Travellers. The family believed they had no choice but to leave the road and move into houses.

As an old man, the age I am now, Daddy would hitch a trailer onto the back of his car and drive around Ontario in the summer. A little canvas tent was nestled inside this trailer, and could be unfolded into a place for two people to sleep. He'd stay in campgrounds and cook his meals over a fire. When he was at home, the trailer would be parked in the back yard and he'd sleep in the tent during the hot summer nights. All he really wanted, he told me, was to be on the road. That's the way it was, in those days.

* * *

Do you refuse to be tied down, but prefer to live a life of freedom? says a website devoted to "soul-work." *You might be a Gypsy soul. Take the test!*

A travel site says you can *Live like a Gypsy without going broke.*

Wandering Gypsy is the name of a clothing boutique in Moose Jaw, Saskatchewan.

Was travelling in Daddy's blood? What about wandering? What was going on with his soul?

* * *

The people who would, in the diaspora, become Roma, were driven from northern India in the twelfth century by invaders from the Ghaznavid Empire. Reaching Europe some two hundred years later, they were shunned, hunted in Germany for sport, enslaved in Romania, evicted and driven from towns and villages universally.

In England to be a Gypsy was against the law. The European Roma Rights Centre, in its historical account, provides details: in 1530 Henry VIII's *Egyptians Act* banned Roma from entering the country. In 1547, Edward VI ordered them to be "seized and branded with a V upon their breasts, and enslaved for two years." Seven years later, Bloody Mary decreed that Roma and those who "shall become of the fellowship or company of Egyptians" were to be put to death. In 1562 "Vagabonds, calling themselves *Egyptians*" were to be executed or exiled. Over one hundred Roma were to be executed in 1596; nine of that company, who were unable to prove they had been born in England, were put to death. In all cases, the death penalty was imposed upon them because they were Roma, and for no other reason. Later, in 1714, Gypsies were taken from England to work as slaves in the Caribbean and the cotton plantations of Virginia.

And what is that word, *Gypsy*? As a little girl I thought it sounded light-hearted or frivolous, like a carnival ride or a kind of decoration. How can a people be taken seriously with a name like that? Which, as I came to understand later, is surely the point. "They thought we were from Egypt," said Daddy when I was ten, "that's why they called us Gypsies." Daddy never said *Roma*, only *Gypsy*. Their word, not his. That's how deeply embedded it was.

EVICTIONS

Many Roma have not always travelled, but lived for generations—frequently over five hundred years—in cities and towns across Europe. The European Roma Rights Centre tells of the thousand-year-old quarter of Sulukule in Istanbul, Turkey, where Roma built a thriving society from the time of the Byzantine Empire. In 2007, their world came to an end. The private sector and Fatih Municipality of Istanbul had plans for Sulukule.

The first house of the Romani quarter was demolished while the owners were absent. Subsequently, thousands of Roma were evicted to make way for what the city called "urban transformation." Bulldozers came in and the houses were torn down, leaving a flattened plain of rubble and dust. Offices and luxury townhouses were built on the grave of Sulukule.

Evictions and expulsions continue across Europe. Romanichals in England are still being forced from lands they own, deeded lands to which they have title. When the 1968 *Caravans Act*—requiring councils to give plots of land to Romanies—was struck down by the Conservative government in 1994, five thousand people were left homeless. After many Romanies and Travellers were, effectively, railroaded into buying land for housing—and did so, feeling they had no other option—they were then forbidden from using that land to build or install permanent structures. A report from the National Federation of Gypsy Liaison Groups and Anglia Ruskin University says that 90 percent of Romani and Traveller planning applications fail.

A child was crushed to death at a forced eviction in Dudley; three more were burned to death in tents in another eviction in the Brownhills area of Birmingham in 1966. In 1970, when bailiffs were towing caravans off a site, one vehicle overturned and caught fire. A small boy inside was burned to death. Canadian Romani author Ronald Lee recounts that the tragedy inspired Roma activist and leader Zarko Jovanovic to write the words to Djelem Djelem, which was adopted as the Romani anthem at the first World Romani Congress in London in 1971.

Romani children have been traumatized, not only during the evictions but in the course of their daily lives. The National Federation of Gypsy Liaison Groups and Anglia Ruskin University report that nine out of ten Romani children have suffered racist abuse, with two-thirds afraid to go to school, where they have been the targets of bullying and physical violence. This fear goes hand-in-hand with the question that Roma ask every day: *how long will they let us stay here?* (The British government's 2015 definition of Roma and Travellers, for the purpose of planning travellers' sites, states that those who have stopped travelling permanently will no longer be eligible to live in their own caravans on a legal site.)

Back at the end of the nineteenth century and the beginning of the twentieth, when my father's family was travelling in Britain, the situation was similar. Traditionally Roma had been allowed to camp for up to three days on common lands. They had benefited from longstanding agreements with farmers, which stipulated that they could stay on farmlands in exchange for labour. But new rural police forces made it more and more difficult to find places to safely stop.

* * *

After breakfast this morning, looking out over the bergamot, the Solomon's Seal, the Rose of Sharon with its heavy purple flowers, the branches shivering with chickadees and finches, I googled

"Gypsy Evictions U.K." That was after I'd tried "Romani Evictions" and had gotten a number of links, including "evil eye" and "Romania." At the top of the screen I found:

> *We are fully qualified to conduct traveller and gypsy eviction*
> *Immediate help is available for Squatter, Gypsy, or Traveller Eviction*
> *Eviction of Travellers. Nationwide Same Day Service. Fast, effective, low rates*
> *Traveller eviction services. Do you require fast, efficient traveller eviction? Get a quote fast*

Basildon District Council in Essex spent £7.1 million to evict 82 Romanichal and Traveller families, including 100 children, from their own land, which was called Dale Farm. £2.2 million of that money was contracted to a bailiff company. On October 19th, 2011, at seven o'clock in the morning, over 100 police officers arrived at Dale Farm. They were dressed in riot gear. They tasered two people, and sledgehammered a wall behind which elders had sought refuge. The wall surrounded a legal plot of Romani land.

A mother was taken to hospital with spinal injuries after being beaten by police. She couldn't move her legs. Two more women suffered head injuries. Others fled with children in their arms. At seven-thirty, the power was cut off. The breathing machine of an elderly woman stopped working. A man's defibrillator failed and he was taken to hospital.

After midday, two hundred bailiffs came in. Dale Farm was emptied out. In April of the following year, families were camped on the road that had led to the site. There was nowhere else to go.

IDENTITY

Canada must have seemed like a paradise to Daddy. *Did you ever want to go back?* I asked. *To Lancashire?*

No, he said, *I won't go back. Not to that place.*

I didn't understand, until years later, that it was not one place to which he was referring, but many. Not all of them could be seen, touched, heard. All these places, these imaginaries, were layered one over the other: geographical, physical, political, emotional. The allegiances and divisions. The beauty. The night terrors. The place of the senses, of language. *I won't go back. Not there.* He'd raise his arms to wave away something I couldn't see. It was as if he had a paper in his hands and was tearing it in half. And in half again, over and over, so that there was nothing left but tiny fragments that could blow away in the wind. And the words written on it would never be known, so that whatever had been in his life would be gone. Or almost.

He retained the practice of cleanliness. *Do not eat food that has touched the floor. Do not put your plate on the floor. Do not feed an animal from your plate. Do not bring the animal into your bed.* The purity codes, with their beginnings in India, were imperative to the health of a people who, through necessity, moved from place to place. Such codes, deeply and quietly held, could not visibly mark us as different from others. And we were light-skinned, and therefore invisible, in the sense that no hackles rise when we enter a room, walk down the street, talk to a stranger. We melt into the dominant culture.

On the street you would not look at a light-skinned Romanichal and tell yourself *here comes a Gypsy.* You wouldn't think *exotic, wild, dangerous, a crook, a thief.* You would never think to say *I have to watch my wallet around you.* Of the guy who overcharges for fixing your car you might complain *he gypped me,* and not know those words were like a fist in the stomach, that they took the breath from our lungs.

Daddy and his family folded themselves into the climate, the work, the life of southern Ontario. The Lees and Hutchinsons were from England. That was all that anyone needed to be told. The Lees and Hutchinsons were poor but they had a house. One they built themselves. On land they owned.

THE ATTIC

Joey was wrapped in a sheet and kept in a box at the far end of the attic. We never went up there into that dark, although sometimes Daddy did, climbing up through the trap door. I'd hear his footsteps, careful across the joists and stopping at the box. The hinges creaked when he lifted the lid. I'd hear him having puppet conversations in a low voice, as if not wanting to be heard.

Joey was the puppet. At first he was the same size as me. I must have been five or six years old. Daddy would sit Joey on his knee and warble away. I didn't always understand the words. Some of them I knew and some I didn't.

Where did Joey come from, Daddy?
Oh, I made him.
When?
A long time ago.
How old were you?
Just a young chavvie, a few years older than you.

After Daddy died, we were cleaning out the house and I climbed up into the attic and found Joey again. I found another puppet, too, a woman. She had a sharp foxy face and watchful eyes. Somebody said to me, "When you're old, you and that puppet will look like sisters." Mrs. Sopha, that's what my daughters called her. They played with her until her hair came off, and she lost one of her eyes. She was stuffed with straw.

I imagine Daddy carrying Joey and Mrs. Sopha around with him as he moved through his life. As he went from one place to the next. I imagine him building our house, bringing the puppets from the back of the car and up into the attic. Carrying them like children. Like the child he never was.

Daddy would have been twelve when he made Mrs. Sopha. Anthony taught him to build the frame, stretch the leather, carve the wooden eyes and hands, attach the eyes to the mechanism that would make them flutter and wink. You could make them flirt too. You could do all kinds of things with Mrs. Sopha's eyes, perfect round wooden spheres attached with wires and string to the workings inside the back of her head. Her skin was pinkish with little wrinkles worked into the leather, and darker paint rubbed in to deepen them. I thought of the tobacco juices worked into the lines of their hands, Daddy, Ophelia, Lillie, Shadrach, Lizzie, Anthony.

One night after Daddy died, I climbed the ladder and lifted the trap door, opened the boxes to the smell of old straw and painted skin. I looked at their closed eyes, their bodies resting under the sheets. Joey fell apart in my hands. I brought Mrs. Sopha down, and we kept her in the living room.

* * *

Daddy and the family went on travelling, picking tobacco, building houses, tarring flat roofs, putting on shows and more shows for the rich tobacco farmers. They built their house around that time, too, on their little plot of land in Tillsonburg. When he was older, that's when they built the house for Ophelia. I do not know if it is still standing. That was so long ago.

WORK

The collar of Daddy's white shirt was mended and starched. He was growing too fast, for the sleeves no longer reached his wrists. He was thirteen years old. The farmer and his son showed Daddy into a garden filled with roses and vines that climbed up the verandah. They showed him to a chair and he sat with Mrs. Sopha on his knee. Under the elms the tables were piled with food; people ate and talked and laughed while Daddy waited. The bread was white and there was raspberry jam. Beads of water gathered on the pitchers of iced tea and rolled down the sides. Bowls of peaches. Platters of ham. Sliced tomatoes, cold chicken, potato salad. Girls with peach juice running down their chins, staring at Daddy. Pointing at Mrs. Sopha, then laughing and running away. After a time the farmer raised his arm and spoke Daddy's name, and Daddy bent his head and shoulders in a little bow. Everybody clapped.

Mrs. Sopha, new and gleaming, her head turning on its wooden stem, her eyes rolling to the delicate tug of a single string, opened her painted lips to Daddy's young voice in her mouth.

After the show he was taken to the back door, where he argued for the proper amount of money. The farmer's wife called her husband. *Don't you be gypping me.* That was said to Daddy more than once over the years. So many times that he couldn't count. What do you do when someone tells you that? Maybe, so as not to draw attention to yourself, you might pretend it never happened. That those words never came from that mouth. But the words, they get inside you just the same. They enter you like a worm, or a sharp little knife.

At the farmer's door Daddy asked for a drink, and they pointed to the pump. A tin cup dangled from its spout. The farmer told him to leave by the side, not walk out through the gardens or down the long drive. He gathered Mrs. Sopha into his arms and carried her like a child, the tobacco fields simmering under the sun.

EYE

Here's the story of how Daddy lost his eye. Lizzie Lee's *vardo* was slogging back and forth across Lancashire, through the mud, mud all over the wheels. The children gathered firewood, running to sell odds and ends. Daddy played the violin, collected the darts for the dartboard.

I try to imagine Daddy standing by the dartboard. He's been paid, the coin is in his hand, and the man begins to throw. Head raised, body canted, hand pulling back. I try to see the man's friends, shoving and shouting. The dart leaving his hand, the men laughing. Then stopping, horrified, as they see what is about to happen. Daddy, eight-year-old Daddy, looking as the dart flies. It takes only a second to reach him.

* * *

Years before I knew about Dale Farm, I was in the Toronto Reference Library. In front of me was a small exhibit of photographs. "Gypsies in England" it was called. People standing in front of their *vardos*. A basin of washing on a table, a child on the steps, a horse in the field. A boy with eight-year-old eyes looks out at the camera.

Around the corner I stopped. "Gypsies being evicted from a campsite, 1975." Night. Two rivers of people swirling around each other. The Romanies are herded, shoved, a woman pushed, a villager's hand slammed into her chest. Her body angles toward the ground but she's still standing. Into the middle of the swirl leans a man, finger pointed, jaws open, lips pulled back from his teeth. Beside him someone has thrown something, arm high and slanted in the release. In the air, between the villagers and the Romanies, a rock.

A boy hides under his mother's legs, clutching her skirt. He sees her shoelace undone and shredded at the end, sees a leaf stuck to her heel. Sees the mud on her shoes, the flash of her ring as she shields his face. Between her fingers he sees the villagers, the shouting man, the raised arm, the rock, everything. His eyes open the night, parting the dark, seeing what is being done. *Nothing can hide.* I'm caught in the moment of the rock that hangs in the air, in the moment of Daddy, holding myself against the rock, against the dart. Keeping the boy here, keeping Daddy here, holding them with my own breath against the instant that time slices in again and the moment falls apart.

* * *

1975, 2011. The same caravans, the stopping places, villagers, police.

Why do we insist on being who we are? Memory is in our cells, blood, our DNA frilled and spiralling out into our worlds, into our involuntary movements, practices, our acts of living. The human strategies for survival. Poverty, life lived far from the centre, the wheels always moving away, away. The search for food, shelter. What people do to stay alive.

* * *

Mrs. Sopha is inside a wooden cabinet in the corner of a bedroom. One eye is still where it belongs, looking out into the room; the other is in the folds of her skirt. Some visitors who sleep there ask to cover the door, which is glass, so as not to see her or feel her presence at night. The cabinet was found on the street by my friend visiting from Sarajevo. I had told her I'd been looking for something to house Mrs. Sopha, who had been kept on a piece of plywood under a sheet in my attic. When I look at the cabinet now I think of my friend, and the day we carried the cabinet into the house and up the stairs. My friend, in that way, is woven into my family's history.

I take Mrs. Sopha from her cabinet and we look at each other. She has only one eye that works now. I think of Daddy, his single eye. Dark brown it was. The other eye was glass. I think of Mrs. Sopha talking, what she'd say. She is over a hundred years old. There'd be so much to tell. The *didikai*, the *poshrat*, neither of, nor in, one world or another. What could Mrs. Sopha tell me that would possibly help me understand these two divided territories, how to belong in both?

Dust

Tillsonburg
their feet going down the rows
hands at the stem
topping, suckering, priming
the strategy for growing a healthy plant
there are many strategies for living
their feet are walking through the field
their arms are holding the puppets
they are shown into the garden where the audience awaits
there are many strategies for living
they build the frame, the joists, the beams
they hang the doors, nail the shingles, tar the flat roof
they trade: cars, tools, and later cameras, sewing machines, silver
there are many strategies for living

the earth is dry, and dust sometimes blows into their faces

*

Certain things I know. The things I do not know are bigger than they should be. Our lives, our pasts, should not be a mystery to us. We fill in the intervals and dark places with memories and structures, songs, stories passed down, as close as possible to the core, the substance, the event.

MY LIFE AS A ROMANI WOMAN

DELILAH LEE

THE COMMON DEFINITION of "Gypsy" in the dictionary is, "a member of nomadic dark-skinned people of Europe, who move from place to place, traditionally in caravans" or, as my thesaurus adds, "a person living like a Gypsy, traveller, nomad, or wanderer." Further, Romani is listed as, "the language of the Gypsies." If I take these facts as being a true representation of who I am, then how can I honestly be Romani?

I am an educated Canadian-Romani woman who is not dark-skinned; I do not live in Europe or in a caravan; and most of my travelling has been for vacation or for business, and not as a general lifestyle. Am I still Romani (or Gypsy)? My identity and experience, as a Romani woman, has been confusing. When I was a child, my father, Ronald Lee, a Romani writer and scholar, told me that Romani people reject the title "Gypsy" due to the word's negative connotation with the word "gyp"—"to cheat or deceive"—and thus refer to themselves as Romani or Roma. But, when I tell people I am Romani, most assume I am from Romania!

When I was a very young child, my parents were immersed in the Canadian-Romani culture. They played Romani music, danced, sang, and spoke in a language I did not understand. I remember the "*slavas*," big social gatherings with lots of food where women wore long skirts and headscarves and men donned gold earrings and played instruments, revealing gold teeth when they sang. I was also sometimes dressed in long skirts for parties and danced alongside the other women and children. Some were dark-haired and dark-skinned, but there were also those with blond hair, and not so dark skin, like me.

The main reason I did not learn to speak Romani was because my mother was a non-Romani woman and we children spent most of our days with her while my father was at work. When my father was writing his Romani dictionary with the old patriarch Uncle "Wasso" Russell Dimitro, I was old enough to be curious to learn a few words and expressions, but had little opportunity to practice my skills. When I was older, we moved to an apartment, but not in the same neighbourhood as other Romani children, the majority of whom lived in slums because their parents were not educated like my father, and could not secure decent jobs to afford better housing. I learned that most Romani men and women survive by their wits.

When I was school-aged, the messages I received from my parents became confusing. On the one hand, I was told to be proud of my heritage, but, on the other hand, I was advised to conceal my true identity. I was enrolled under my father's adoptive parent's surname, and was told to tell my teachers I was half English and half French-Canadian. At home, I was to refer to myself as half Romani and half "Indian." When I asked why, I was told that *Gadje*, or non-Romani, don't like the Roma (or the North American Indigenous peoples) and that I would be picked on and suspected of theft. It was during this time that I began to feel shame for being Romani. I got the sinking feeling that something about me was not right.

Around my ninth birthday, my father, who was deeply involved in fighting the social injustices inflicted on the Romani people, became a public advocate for his community. He took advantage of every opportunity to raise awareness of the injustices and prejudices, and his passion sparked the enthusiasm of anthropologists eager to help or publish an interesting story. They came to our house with microphones to interview my father and cameras to photograph or film us. Sometimes we remained dressed as we were, but other times we were encouraged to wear our "Gypsy clothes," and I would dance, while my father played music. One anthropologist took us outside for a family portrait. My father walked towards him, and we were told to run past him, which we did, but not to this anthropologist's satisfaction. We were instructed to repeat the action, but this time we were instructed to bump into our dad as we passed him. We were dismayed because in Romani culture, children respect their elders and do not bump into them on purpose! Dad gave us a look to let us know it was okay, and so we did it, with apprehension. The photographer clearly did not understand our culture, and was imposing his onto ours, despite the fact that his intention was ostensibly to reveal the truth.

An article, with a photo of me dancing, ended up in newspapers and magazines, and I was recognized by one of my teachers, who was fascinated. She asked me to dance for the class (without music) and commented on my fluid hand movements. The other kids asked me all kinds of questions. I did not understand what all the fuss was about, and kind of felt like a funny animal at the zoo, although I enjoyed all the attention. When I came home and told my parents, my father was livid. My mother informed me that he wrote a scathing letter to the school asking them to stop singling me out for being Romani. The subject was never brought up again at my school, but I felt as though I should be ashamed about something. I just wasn't sure what.

When I was a teenager, I started bringing friends from school to our home. I was oblivious to the fact that hosting musicians who played Romani music all the time and having tapestries and paintings on the walls of Romani people in caravans was not common in *Gadje* households. When I went to their homes, I began to realize how eccentric we must have seemed to them, and understood why some of them abandoned me. The only friend who seemed unfazed was a Yugoslavian girl whose parents played Slavic music that resembled ours and had similar things hanging on their walls. She felt at home at my home and I at hers. We are still friends to this day.

One fine summer day, as on many other occasions, we donned our Romani skirts and went up to Beaver Lake for a family picnic. My father brought his *bouzouki*, a *tabla*, and some tambourines, and I brought my guitar. After the picnic, we played music and danced and soon drew a crowd. People threw money in my father's *bouzouki* case. Again the "animal in the zoo" feeling returned. I was recognized by kids in my school, who later laughed and called me a hippie. It was the seventies. Some thought I had "cool" parents and others thought I was simply weird. I wasn't sure which attitude to embrace, and shame once again overshadowed my pride. I felt split between my love for Romani music and dance, and wanting to fit in and be like everyone else.

When I was in my teens my father got a job with the Maritime Museum. The demands of that job prevented him from associating as much as he used to with the Romani people, and this alienated him from the community. His newspaper articles and book were seen as a betrayal by the Romani community, who erroneously believed that secrecy was equal to safety. They felt that the more the Gadje knew about them, the more difficult their lives would become. My father believed otherwise and they parted ways. My exposure to Romani people was diminished as a result.

It was around this time that my father launched his book, *Goddam Gypsy*, and I, being the eldest, attended the event. I danced and played my guitar for the press, and was interviewed about what it felt like to be a Gypsy. I don't remember how I responded, but I remember thinking the question was odd, as I had never been anything else and had nothing with which to compare it. My photograph ended up in the newspaper, but I was grateful not to be recognized by anyone in my peer group. I was learning to be proud of my heritage, but I was embarrassed by it at the same time. I began to hide the truth, sometimes even from myself. If I had been born Black, I would not have been able to hide my identity, but the Romani ability to blend in is an insidious attempt at camouflage with grave repercussions for our self-esteem. Revealing our true identities means something negative will follow, namely prejudice and negative assumptions. It becomes an inner secret that we reveal only to those we trust.

By the time I became a young adult, I decided it was better to conceal my Romani identity. The only thing hindering this objective was my love of Romani music, which I played at home whenever I could get my hands on a new album, and my strong desire to dance. I worked as a secretary during the day, keeping my identity a secret, and as a Gypsy belly dancer in Arab and Greek restaurants on the weekends. My dark hair, dark eyes, and Romani dancing style helped me fit right in to this environment. I soon found out that Europeans had a worse attitude towards the Romani people than my Canadian friends, who were mostly curious. Some of my friends did not believe me, while others became all dreamy with cinematic visions of the romantic rebel firing their imaginations.

Dancing introduced me to my first husband, who was Greek. I took to his culture as naturally as a fish to water, and learned to dance to his music. During our honeymoon in Greece, I saw Romani families. We were sitting at a café, and I noticed a couple of children begging with their parents, watching from the sidelines. I was fascinated and asked my husband to take a photograph of me with them. The owner of the establishment, assuming he was protecting his patrons, ran out onto the street and chased the children and their parents away. When I asked my husband why, he said that they were thieves and that they would snatch your wallet if they had the opportunity. I could see in the eyes of the locals that the Roma were viewed as thieves. Later when I looked at the photos, I saw that I resembled them and, had I been wearing a long skirt, no one would have been able to single me out as a Canadian. I dared not reveal my identity to his family when I became aware of their attitude towards my people. Unfortunately, this marriage was doomed to fail.

After my divorce, I went on to earn a degree in fashion design and was eventually offered a job in China. I met my second husband two years later. He worked for the British Embassy and travelled extensively. We ended up posted in Ukraine. In Kiev, I learned Russian and found many words that were similar to the Romani Kalderash dialect I knew. I also discovered that Romani people were treated with the same disrespect as in Greece. I also learned why. The Romani people lived on the fringes of society and had never been integrated into mainstream social life. They were repressed and could not obtain decent work. They were forced to resort to stealing and swindling to survive. The only work available to them was in the entertainment industry: circus performance, music and dancing shows, and animal training. Some were coppersmiths, and the older women told fortunes. They could not stay in one place for any length of time as they were often chased away by the police. And because they were always on the move, their children could never go to school.

In Ukraine, I saw Romani shows attended by local Ukrainians and watched with envy as the girls twirled their colourful skirts. My feet tapped to the music as I sat trapped in my seat. I longed to run away and join them, and to live my life performing. That music reached deep into my soul and reminded me of who I was, in spite of all my efforts to hide it.

My husband was a photographer and managed to obtain backstage passes for a big Gypsy show in Ukraine, featuring Romani artists from around the world. I borrowed one of his cameras, and while he was busy photographing a soccer game, I used his pass and passed myself off as a professional photographer. During their rehearsal, I snapped away. One by one, I watched the troupes arrive by caravan from all around Europe, and set up camp. As a woman, I was allowed to photograph the women and children without censure, to the envy of the male photographers who were only allowed to photograph the rehearsal and the show. I revelled in the music as they played around campfires and practised new dance moves. After the show, I was allowed to join them around the campfire, while the *Gadje* photographers were asked to leave. When I told the performers I was Romani, they were bemused as to why I would want to be like them if I could pass myself off as a *Gadje*. During their after-show party, I danced with them, and we exchanged personal details. One American-Romani man claimed he knew my father. Keeping in touch with Romani families is next to impossible because they are always on the move. We rely on memory and family names to make connections, although the younger generation is starting to make use of modern technology.

I couldn't wait to send the photos to my family. By this time, my father had thrown himself back into the role of activist on behalf of the Romani people, and was working at a university, teaching Romani Studies. I now understood him, as well as the need for his work. Much needs to be done to protect our heritage because the younger generation is embracing Western culture and rejecting their own, as I had tried to do. My photos and experience confirmed to me that the Romani people are a legitimate ethnic group, with members scattered all over the globe. Our family members resembled the people in my photographs; they danced like us and played the music I loved so much. I finally felt like I was part of something, and not just a single animal in a zoo being observed for its oddity.

Until I met the Romani performers, my main reference for Romani people, aside from my dad, was Hollywood movies with *Gadje* actors playing Gypsy roles—stereotyped men riding horses and passionate dark-eyed women with knives in their garters. I could not relate to these images. Pride for my heritage returned when I observed the beauty and richness of my culture. Observing the respect the younger generation had for the old patriarch who stood up and sang, I witnessed something that is lacking in *Gadje* culture, a culture that I feel glorifies youth. When I heard the music, I understood deep in my heart that this music spoke to me more than any other music I had ever heard. I realized that this was a part of me that could not be denied, and I felt proud to claim my identity.

I have met many "wannabe" Gypsies in my life—*Gadje* women who buy into the fantasy Hollywood hype. They live their lives with abandon, use fortune-telling cards to guide their lives, wear long skirts, and sleep around with all kinds of men thinking that they are wild Gypsies at heart. I have also met men whose eyes glazed over when I mention that I am Romani. Visions of a reckless, rebellious, passionate woman fill their loins with desire. If only they knew the truth! Romani women are not free to do as they please. Our society is based on a strict code of conduct. Except within families, women and men do not intermingle. Far from being "dirty Gypsies," an impression assumed by many Europeans, Romani people adhere to strict rules of cleanliness. Modern Romani woman reject some of the strict rules, such as wearing the long skirts and head scarves, but I am sure it has more to do with acceptance in schools and the workplace than a rejection of their way of life.

I am thankful to be a Canadian Romani woman who is not bound by the "stand by your man" philosophy that the European Romani women must endure. I am grateful that I was not sold to a Romani man for marriage at the age of twelve, although many offers were made to my father when I was young. I am glad that my father is an educated Romani man, and I am proud of all the work he has done to raise awareness of and understanding for our people.

With age, I have come to terms with accepting my heritage and I no longer hide behind veils of secrecy. It is time to let go of ignorance and prejudice, and increase awareness. Modern Romani people are struggling hard to battle the stigma, and are educating their children and entering jobs and careers that were previously denied them. However, it is still an uphill battle. Hopefully, my writing contribution will open eyes and hearts to the difficulties faced by Romani men and women.

I hope that, one day, our people will be recognized and accepted as an ethnic group and that laws will be put in place to protect our way of life. I pray that more Romani people will educate their children and become integrated into society so that they will be able to obtain good jobs and not suffer the shame and stigma of being perceived as thieves, living in slums and ghettos. I hope that one day, Gadje people will hear our music and understand the beauty of our culture. I hope that we will learn to not be ashamed to say, *Me sam Rom,* I am Rom. Like Martin Luther King once powerfully said, "I have a dream...."

WHAT IS IN A NAME?

ILDI GULYAS

*I*T DOESN'T *make sense. These things do not match. It makes no sense! Your name says one thing, but the way you look says another. Your face is confusing me. Your name is European, you say? You look Indian, Pakistani, Arab, Latin American, mixed, no, definitely Indian. You are East Asian, I know it. You must be lying to us. You must be hiding something. Why won't you tell us? You are so fascinating, so intriguing. Please tell me, I mean well, my intentions are good, we are Canadians after all. You* ARE *different from us. Tell us what you are.*

*

I moved to Canada when I was ten years old, excited and unaware that it was to become my new home. I loved my home—Eastern Europe, Hungary—the friends, the family, the comfort, the house, all of it. It was 1990, and communism was ending throughout the Eastern Bloc. Borders were opening but the collective mind was slowly narrowing. Nationalism, pride and anti-other sentiments increased. I was not aware of any of it. My parents did an amazing job of keeping me in a bubble that only a child can experience. If I felt, experienced, or saw anything difficult, I do not recall it now. I learned only years later that the demise of communism was the beginning of an ongoing xenophobic Eastern Europe. At the time, it was mostly anti-Jewish and anti-Gypsy rhetoric. The red flags went up figuratively as they came down literally. For my

143

parents, it was time to pick up and get moving before it was more than just words that hurt us.

It was March 1990. I got off the plane in Toronto and shortly after I was enrolled in a day camp. The idea was to throw me into the deep end, to shock me into learning the language. When the school bus arrived, a new experience in itself, our names were called out as we got off the bus. *Ildeeko, Eldeeko, Eldiko?* I quickly realized they were referring to me, so I got up, and followed the kid in front of me. It was going to be the first of many roll calls to come, where teachers pause, attempt, pause again, apologize, and then butcher my name. This was camp. I had arrived. The music of the Beach Boys, soccer matches, plays, and snacks were my daily routine. Not one friend, and not one word of English when I started. But, by September, I spoke almost fluently. I never forgot that first butchering of my name. When everyone in my family was becoming citizens, it was even suggested that I change my name to Hilda. I soon came to hate my name, a name I never gave much thought to before this Canadian moment. A name I did not give myself. I am glad that I stuck it out, though it certainly didn't feel welcoming at the time.

This could be the story of any immigrant child whose non-western name gives them a complex. A story of a colonial system that makes everyone feel their "otherness" when they step ashore. The Jee-Ins who become Janes, the Mohammeds who become Mikes, and the plethora of names we use to strategize with, to change and mould our identities as we try to get jobs, go to school, or go on a date. This is not one of those stories, although it easily could be. I, too, shortened my name and came up with alternatives, and, as a result of the constant mispronunciations, I did not attend any of my graduation ceremonies. No, this is a different story. A story of an unusual name that does not match an equally unusual body. A story in which kind, well-intentioned, curious Canadians bring out the hidden truth. A story in which curiosity leads to revelations, and those just lead to more questions. This is a story of more than just an "odd" name.

I do not recall exactly when the questioning began, but it always went the same way:

Them: Hi.
Me: Hi.
Them: What's your name?
Me: Ildiko.
Them: Oh, that's unusual. Where is that from?
Me: It's Hungarian.
Them: Oh is it? Why do you have a Hungarian name?
Me: Because I was born there.
Them: But surely you are not Hungarian. Are you mixed?
Me: Nope, just Hungarian.
Them: But you don't look Hungarian.
Me: (shrugs). Well I am.
Them: But that makes no sense. You must have something in your background that maybe you don't know about.
Me: (shrugs) Uh-huh.

It happened a few times in my early teens and almost daily when I started smoking, and definitely when I was getting carded at eighteen and nineteen years of age. They asked for ID, and I gave it to them. They looked at me, then looked at the card. Looked at me, looked at the card again. A frown, a sigh, and an inevitable question. "Are you Indian?" And then the line of questioning, doubting, and definitely disbelieving. Each time I would tell them I am not whatever race they thought I was, they would look confused, or upset as they passed me my Benson and Hedges. It was my daily or weekly ritual, depending on my smoking habit at the time.

This was my reality.

One summer in my early twenties, I went to Winnipeg. One of the many events and sights I visited was a food festival in the heart of the city. I was walking through a lovely park on a hot summer day, enjoying the hustle and bustle of the event, when all of a sudden, a Sikh man started speaking to me in another language. I told him that I did not understand what he was saying. He insisted that I did. Next thing I know he was yelling at me in this language. Did he think I was someone else? Did he think I lied to him and I really did understand? To this day I do not know.

I cannot tell you the number of times I experienced similar interactions with complete strangers, customers, bosses, corner store clerks, and liquor store employees. Basically any time my name came up, my ethnicity was also questioned. It was not simple curiosity; it was a debate. It was strangers fighting with me about my identity—questioning it, questioning me. Though many people face the reality of having a non-Anglo Saxon name in a multicultural, western colonial country, I am sure that only a few of us get drilled about our ethnicity as a result.

I would often go home and ask my parents about this. Why are people even asking about my ethnicity? Why do I have to justify myself to strangers? Why am I so dark? Why do I not look Hungarian? And why don't people believe me? Just introducing myself was causing an identity crisis, often daily. At some point, I was told the truth. Oddly, I do not recall having this conversation with my parents, so maybe I blocked it out, but they shared a truth I had not been aware of before 1990. They told me I was half Roma and half Jewish. What? Half Gypsy, half Jew? Oh dear, that is not a good combination, and certainly not good if one lives in Eastern Europe at the fall of communism. The move to Canada, the hiding of my ethnicity from me, it all made sense now. But, as soon as the truth was revealed, a footnote came with it.

As quickly as I learned why I looked the way I did, I was also told that maybe I should not tell people. I was informed that unless I was ready for the potential backlash, consequences like racism, judgments, and accusations, I should just deflect the entire conversation. I strategized what I could say to divert the truth and keep strangers happy. Conversations now went like this:

Them: Hi.
Me: Hi.
Them: What's your name?
Me: Ildiko.
Them: Oh, that's unusual. Where is that from?
Me: It's Hungarian.
Them: Oh, is it? Why do you have a Hungarian name?

Me: Because I was born there.
Them: But surely you are not Hungarian. Are you mixed?
Me: (shrugs) Well I am half Jewish.
Them: Oh okay, that could be it.
Me: (shrugs) Uh-huh.

I quickly became skilled in assessing situations and people in regard to my answers. Sometimes I was half Jewish, sometimes I was just as shocked as the person asking me. "What? I don't look Hungarian?" Sometimes, when I'd had enough, I would be abrupt and just change the subject; these were strangers after all. If my name was going to be said, my ethnicity was going to be debated, and I was not in a place where the truth was an option.

Once in a while I would get a surge of confidence, a surge of pride as I tried to embrace the Roma side of me. Trying to connect through music, through information. I would not tell strangers but, in private, I would explore aspects of Roma identity. I tried connecting with the Toronto Roma community, but I was once told that I was not Roma enough because I did not speak the Romani language. I was crushed. It seemed that I was not Hungarian enough, not Roma enough, not Jewish enough, and also not Canadian enough. At the time, I did not understand colonialism or know that Hungary had outlawed the speaking of Romani. I hadn't understood that my lack of the language was not my fault, nor had I the confidence to challenge the notion that I was not Roma enough. So I retreated to a place of shame and confusion.

Another time, I was at Tim Hortons having coffee with a few of my close friends. We had just returned from a road trip. We had all purchased a piece of Canadiana when one of my friends said that he got "gyped" at the till. My other friend spoke up and informed all of us that using the word "gyp" is racist because it refers to Gypsies and implies that they are people who steal. I had no idea. As soon as the 'g' word had been used though, my heart started racing, my body tensed, and I felt flushed. I was curious to see where the conversation was going to lead. The first friend quickly shot back and said that using the word "gyp" was not racist because being Gypsy was not a race, but a way of life. This friend claimed that Gypsy was a word for being a criminal, lazy, and a conniving thief. They debated for a few more minutes before they both agreed that this was not a worthy conversation to have. I sat there in silence. Tense. Embarrassed. Mortified. Ashamed. Guilty. Guilty for not speaking up. These were good friends, best friends in fact. Was this not a teachable moment? I could not. I would not. I was not strong enough. So I retreated to that place of shame.

There were good times. Times when pride briefly made its way to the surface. One year I took a quick trip to Hungary to visit my Roma family. I learned words in Romani, listened to Romani music, discussed issues, and learned about the culture. I returned to Canada with newfound pride, confidence, and knowledge. Then one day, I was at my dorm room in university when a friend came to visit. We had a nondescript conversation that I cannot even recall, but I just remember him referring to not being a "dirty Gypsy." Like a stab through the chest, tension, flush, embarrassment, shock, shame, guilt. I retreated, yet again, from pride back to shame.

The pattern of going from pride to shame and guilt meant an almost daily rollercoaster of emotions. Since I was in Aboriginal Studies in University, I often looked to First Nations people who, despite the hardships, often sought healing in the pride of their respective tribes and cultures. Why was I not able to harness this? Why not just tell people?

The hiding, the identity crisis, the lies and strategizing all came to a head in 2013. After coming across Roma youth in my line of work, I started hearing comments from co-workers and staff that were teetering on racist. I was sitting at a conference table at lunch at what became a do-or-die moment. A comment was made that I decided I would not tolerate. I braced myself to respond in a way that I knew would be upsetting for some people. My career was on the line. I spoke up and explained who I am. I explained who the youth were. I gave a miniscule historical context, and then sat back. My peers expressed their apologies and quickly backtracked. This moment in time became the hole in the dam through which trust started trickling through. Shortly after, I started telling more and more professional people in my life. It was safe this way. We had human rights and work discrimination policies that would keep me safe. Then, I made a big leap. I left that job to work with Romani youth, a position I held for three years.

Over the years, hiding my identity is still second nature. My friends still do not know my ethnicity; I do not know why. I am not concerned about strangers believing and accepting me; I am most concerned about my own self-acceptance. But just as it was for generations of Roma before me, it is not easy for me. Safety, self-preservation, and survival become a priority. When it is dangerous to be Roma for so long, for centuries, where labelling leads to the gas chambers, to work camps, to slavery, to accusations, to poverty, why would anyone come forward if they do not have to? While some Roma segregate themselves and mistrust outsiders, others try to hide among the masses and assimilate. Whatever the method, whatever the means, it is survival. I am surviving. The fluctuation of pride and shame continues in my life. I cannot help it and I will not apologize for it. It is survival. It is necessary. It is life. The only difference now, in my thirties, is that when I emerge from those moments of pride—such as when I was working with Roma youth for three years, or going to graduate school—that pride is sustained for longer periods of time and is much louder than ever before. I come out with guns blazing. Telling my story, telling my youths' stories, being proud of them, and spreading the word of who and what I am becomes empowering. There are still many times, however, when I retreat, when shame creeps in, when survival takes precedent, but they are becoming less frequent.

For me, being Roma means having internalized the balancing act of having pride and shame, sometimes simultaneously. Being part of an ethnic community and of a people who have internalized an inferior status for centuries is not something one shakes easily. Being the other, being less than, having to hide, having to work twice as hard, and having to survive is something that is not easily left behind. Today, the cycle continues. Circumstances sadly have not made it safe to be anything but cautious. I have the privilege of knowing how and when to hide, a privilege many do not have. I also have the privilege of a strong Jewish community behind me that have instilled in me a sense of pride and a commitment to education. I am slowly but surely allowing my Roma side to also believe it.

WE ARE THE ROADS THAT MEET

ELIZABETH LISA ANN CSANYI

It is not our differences that divide us. It is our inability to recognize, accept, and celebrate those differences.
—Audre Lorde

AS I ARRIVED for my first day of work as a temporary legal assistant at an Indigenous legal clinic, I felt as though I was not going to fit in. I have spent a lot of time in my life not fully fitting in, and I did not think this was going to be any different. As a young Roma woman born and raised in Canada in the eighties, not fitting in was nothing new. I felt like I did not have a group of my own people to belong to. Other than my own immediate family, I didn't know of any other Roma. When people asked me about my ancestry or background, and I told them I was Roma, they either did not know what that meant at all, or they thought it was like I was calling myself a hippie or a fortune teller.

I was born and raised in Toronto, Ontario. I grew up in a Hungarian-Romani family. My grandmother and grandfather immigrated to Canada from Hungary during the revolution in 1956. Together they had four girls and three boys, who my grandmother raised in Hamilton and Toronto. I never had the chance to meet my grandfather, as he passed away before I was born. He played the violin and had a record of his band called the Matyi-Csanyi Gypsy Band. I was fortunate enough to be able to listen to this record, and the love he had for the violin inspired me to learn to play the violin during my childhood. I felt that through the violin, I was able to connect to my grandfather. My grandmother was a strong woman, and I remember she would play Hungarian-Gypsy music and dance around the living room or kitchen while she was cooking some of our favourite Hungarian dishes, like chicken paprika and goulash. I lived with her for a short time and was able to learn some Hungarian, although I found out later that she mixed it with the Romani language. I never thought to ask my grandmother what being a Romani person meant. I simply knew that that was what we were. It was stitched into my very being and I felt it deeply rooted in my soul. One thing I was thankful for was that I had a lot of siblings and cousins, so we never had to look outside of our family for friends. We have always been very close with one another.

For a good part of my childhood, I did not know what being Roma fully meant, so the only thing I could say was, "well, you are Spanish or Italian, etc. and I am Romani." The next question would normally be "where do Roma come from?" At that time, I did not know that, through the written and spoken language of the Romani people, historians discovered that we originated from India around 1000 years ago (Lee). The only thing I knew was that we lived all over the world, especially in Europe where most people did not like us, and that we were, and in many places still are, treated horribly. Someone of European descent once told me that Roma are known as "the niggers of Europe."

My jaw dropped when I heard that. I could not understand why we as a people were hated because of who we are, especially since I had grown up in such a culturally diverse country. It was totally incomprehensible to me that this was allowed to happen then, and still happens now. Whenever I was asked, I always proudly told people: "I am Romani!" My strong and beautiful mother took great pride in being Romani and taught us to also be proud of who we are. For that, I will be forever grateful. Now, when I am asked where I am from or what my background is, I consider this to be a good opportunity to briefly educate those who do not know about the Romani people and culture. The conversation ends up being enlightening for those who ask. I usually learn and grow from these conversations as well.

I wondered how I would address this question when asked by people at my new job, or by the legal clinic's Indigenous clients. I have been told that I look Indigenous, so with my darker skin, I thought I might fit in, and thus not be treated with suspicion, or seen as a threat to the Indigenous clients. I hoped that, because of my skin colour, they would not judge me harshly as an outsider. Roma with lighter skin probably feel the same way in Europe as they can melt into the crowd, seamlessly blending into the sea of the pale-skinned. I felt ashamed that I, too, wanted to blend in. I am very proud to be Romani, so it was weird to want to be a chameleon at that moment in my life. I know now that we should never have to feel ashamed of who we are. I do wonder, however, how many Roma continue to hide who they are so that they can blend in in order to be accepted and to live in society without discrimination and prejudice.

When I walked into the historic building in the heart of Gastown in downtown Vancouver that was to be my place of employment, I was initially surprised at the location and at the appearance of the building. On the outside, the building was made up of large grey concrete blocks and small, dusty windows. The inside was not any better. There was old, smelly carpet and wooden floorboards that were uneven and creaked as you walked on them. Some of the walls consisted of partly exposed red brick and others were painted a combination of dark black, red, and beige that would have been nice if the building had had more windows. I was not surprised when I learned that the office was known as "The Cave" due to the dim lighting and claustrophobic feel that resonated and oozed from every crevice.

It was a far cry from the fancy law office that I had envisioned. There was a thick darkness about this place that raised the hair on the back of my neck. I found out later that the building was once the first jail in Vancouver. They used to load the prisoners in from the back of the office where my desk was located. You could still see the outline of the loading dock at the back of the building, and if you stayed late enough after closing, you would have this burning desire to run full speed out the door. People who worked there often whispered about ghost sightings and

I had my own strange encounter one evening. While sitting at my desk late on evening, I could see down the narrow hallway toward the front of the office. I looked up and caught a glimpse of a man standing by the front where the photocopier was located. At first, I thought it was just another employee who had also stayed late, but when I looked up again, the man was gone. The next day, I found out that I had been the only one in the building that night.

When I started, I was fresh and green, having recently graduated from college as a legal administrative assistant. But soon all the images of luxury and richness I had initially imagined when working in the legal field were quickly erased from my mind. On the *pro bono* side of the legal world, I discovered a system that is fraught with injustice for many Indigenous people who find themselves entwined in the thorny branches of the legal system. This is the reality for many who cannot afford the costs of hiring a private lawyer and must proceed with their legal matters without representation.

I remember entering the office one day and meeting with a locum lawyer who was replacing the managing lawyer on leave. She sat me down and explained that the clinic had up to six law students who worked with the firm each term, and who generally worked only with the legal clinic clientele. These clients, for the most part, did not easily trust or like anything about the Canadian government, as they came from a history of discrimination, persecution, and over-representation in the justice system. At that point, I knew I would find some parallels with issues encountered by the Roma in Europe. And, indeed, I came to see how similar the issues for both Indigenous populations and Romani people really are. This was something I would continually be exposed to while working there.

The clinic was run by the managing lawyer, the locum lawyer, and law students who applied to be a part of the clinic for an academic term. They made a choice to participate in clinical legal education and they had a sincere desire to help out the clients. At the same time, they were able to gain substantive legal experience that allowed them to learn from the clients on different levels. The clinic exposed them to the discrimination and prejudices encountered by the Indigenous population and made them aware of many other issues Indigenous clients faced such as poverty, lack of housing, homelessness, alcohol and drug addiction, and abuse.

It was not all gloom and horror. Love and support were also strongly present in the office. Beautiful moments I remember well were when the Indigenous women's group came once a week to teach and create traditional arts and crafts such as drum-making, beadwork, dream-catchers, basket weaving, and other fabulous works of art. They would drum and sing softly while meeting and I would sit at my desk and close my eyes. The sound of the drum beating and their soft singing voices was like a lullaby to my ears. It was a momentary flight from reality. A sense of calm and love would envelop me for a few moments and I would feel at peace with myself. I was told that the drumming represents a mother's heartbeat (or mother earth) from which we all came. They taught me about the love and respect they had for the Creator, land, animals, and their elders and loved ones who had passed on into the spirit world. I was amazed at how much respect the Indigenous peoples had for the planet, and I loved to listen and learn from them any chance I had.

I never took the time before working at the legal clinic to learn or understand the Indigenous cultures in Canada, and when I look back now, I think that was a big mistake. I listened to the locum lawyer explain that even though my primary role would be to assist the staff, the biggest and most demanding part of my job would be to serve the clientele with respect and with the same standards that anyone paying for a private lawyer would receive. I greatly admired the fact that even though it was a free legal service, the service would not be sub-standard.

I also found out that although it was an Indigenous legal clinic, the students and staff were not always Indigenous. Being of Romani descent, I had dark skin, hair, and eyes, so I could easily pass as Indigenous. It did allow me to feel more comfortable. At the time, I wished that I knew more about Indigenous history so I could better understand the current climate and culture of the community. I now wonder how public perception of Indigenous and Roma would change if people in Canada and Europe would put more interest into learning about the Indigenous and Roma cultures instead of basing their opinions on stereotypes and misrepresentations in the media. I know my perception changed once I learned about Indigenous people from Indigenous people themselves. It was life-changing for me. I realized that what I knew before was a fallacy based on prejudice, discrimination, and stereotypes. I also learned that no matter what culture we are from, there is good and bad in all of them. The problem is that we focus on the bad so much that the good usually becomes forgotten.

The temporary legal assistant who worked there before me stayed on for the day to train me. She told me about the clinic and which items were in progress and which needed urgent attention. I soon learned that everything was urgent. I discovered that this place was not only falling apart on the outside, but also that the administration of services had badly deteriorated. There was no rhyme or reason to the way things were run or organized by the constantly changing temporary assistants. Organization and problem solving are strengths of mine and I was ready to pull my sleeves up and get right to work. And there was a lot of work to be done.

During my first day, the temp said "good luck!" to me in such a sarcastic way that I had to ask her why. She replied, "this place is a dump, the managing lawyer is a monster, and the clients are all messed up!" I looked at her and said, "Well, that sounds like a challenge and I am ready for it!" I like to make my own opinion on all matters based on my own experiences. In the end, it took me two years to re-organize the files, to get my interviewing skills perfected, and to become more comfortable dealing with clients, law students, lawyers, judges, and the legal system. I ended up working there for almost seven years before leaving to go to university full-time and continue my studies in the arts and sciences program. I continue to work in the *pro bono* legal field today.

My first day of work was a blur of information and many moments of great uncertainty. In fact, the position was overwhelming for the first few weeks, until I started to finally understand how things worked there. The locum lawyer was great, and she took the time to explain things to me when I did not understand something.

One day, when the managing lawyer returned to the office from her leave, I was not there. I do not remember if I was at lunch or if it was too early in the morning. When I returned, those first words of warning from the temp on my first day came back to mind. I was full of anxiety and I tried hard to avoid her and what would be our first face-to-face meeting. I sat at my desk after lunch and starting working. A few moments later, I heard the managing lawyer shout from around the corner of her office: "L.A.!" I looked up at the law students who sat at their desks wondering what or who she was yelling about. A few seconds later, the managing lawyer again yelled "L.A.!" I started to feel a great deal of stress because I had no idea who she was calling. A few moments later she came out of her office and screeched, "I am speaking to you!" I had never seen her before and had pictured a big burly man-like woman with wild hair, a crazy angry look in her eyes, and a bat in her hand. (Admittedly, I can be a bit dramatic.)

When she rounded the corner and came into my view, I was dumbstruck. She was all of five feet tall and about 100 pounds. She looked me directly in the eyes and repeated herself, "I was talking to you! Why are you not answering me?"

I replied, "Well, my name is not L.A. It is Elizabeth!"

Then she said, "Well, your name is too long, so I am calling you L.A. for legal assistant!"

I sat and thought for a moment, then responded, "Well my middle name is Lisa Ann so that would work!" She just stared at me and then smiled, seemingly entertained by my response, and asked me to come into her office.

Once I sat down, she asked me a few questions about my schooling and told me a little bit about herself and about the clinic. She mentioned that she and another colleague, who was now a judge, had co-founded it over a decade ago. She gave me the history of the clinic and a little information about herself. She then asked me what my background was. I told her I was Romani. She then smiled again and chuckled before she said "who would have thought ... an Indigenous person and a Roma working together!" I knew at that moment that I was exactly where I needed to be.

I was fascinated by her wisdom, knowledge, and presence. I told my family and friends she was a walking encyclopedia. I admired her ethics, respect, and knowledge of the law, and the fact that she herself was Indigenous. Her father was the hereditary Chief of her clan. She told me that, as a child, she used to spend the mornings with the local medicine woman learning about medicine and traditional healing. Her afternoons were spent reading case law with an Indigenous judge and learning about Indigenous legal traditions. I felt lucky to hear about this. She taught me to listen, to learn, and to be humble.

While working at the legal clinic, I came across many Indigenous people who had experienced some form of abuse and/or trauma in their lives. Through European contact and colonization, many Indigenous people were dealing with several generations of trauma. I thought this was similar to the history of my people. I felt connected to our Indigenous clients, because of the horrible atrocities perpetrated against both our peoples. We were connected by a series of horrific events in history that continue to affect us today in one way or another. It was amazing to me how even though we were continents apart, we were so close in relation to the things our peoples have encountered and endured: murders, beatings, hate, discrimination, persecution, and the list goes on. Indigenous people have a saying: "All my relations." This refers to the connections we all have to one another. I believe that the same goes for all Roma, no matter where they have travelled, settled, or integrated into different cultures. We are all related and connected by our people, our stories, and our histories.

When I was completing an intake one day with a prospective client, I was asked what "Band" I was from since Indigenous people in Canada identify themselves in terms of their Bands, Nations, tribes, treaties, and other categories. Without much thought I said, "Well, I actually come from a Band of Roma." I received a confused look and the question, "Where are they from?" After explaining that I am not Indigenous but of Romani descent, we both had a good laugh since we could relate to each other. I sensed a feeling of comfort from her knowing that I was not against her but with her, that I was aware of what both of our people have been through and that I understood the struggles in life that come from being who we are.

There were a lot of stories that I heard that broke me apart. I listened and I tried my best to let the clients know that I would do whatever I could to assist them, and that I would talk to the lawyer about their legal and, in most cases, non-legal issues.

There were many times when I felt traumatized by the clients' stories of abuse in all of its forms. I would leave work feeling completely deflated and exhausted mentally and emotionally. I felt scarred by the images of those stories; they would roll over in my mind, leaving my heart in pain and my hope for the world and humanity diminished. I am glad I finally learned the truth about the lives of Indigenous peoples and erased the stereotypes that I had grown up with. Knowledge is powerful. The stories I heard about Indigenous people in Canada made me think about the Roma who go through the same things in Europe.

During the time I worked at the clinic, a residential school class action suit was started against the churches and the Canadian government. Residential schools were funded by the Canadian government and administered by various denominations of churches from 1876 to 1996, when the last school closed. Their policy was to assimilate Indigenous children into the dominant Canadian culture (TRCC). This was their answer to the "Indian problem."[1] The schools sought to "civilize" and Anglicize the Indigenous population by taking them away from their families, most times forcibly; putting them in residential schools; and taking away their culture, language, and traditions. Many children were physically and sexually abused by the nuns and priests, and a large number of them died while attending these schools.

Approximately 150,000 Indigenous children attended these schools and at least 3000 of those children died while attending (Canadian Press). Residential schools caused irreparable damage to Indigenous people and their families. The traumas these children and families faced will take many, many generations to overcome (TRC). I have read in some articles and reports that in some parts of Europe, authorities have been thinking about residential schools as a solution to the "Roma problem" (Ward). They should look at Canada as a prime example of the outcomes of these schools: cultural genocide. Let's hope and pray this does not happen.

One day, I was completing an intake interview with a woman in her fifties who wanted to join the class action suit for the residential school attendees. She had not attended residential school, as she was able to hide when the authorities came to round up the children to take them to these schools. Her little sister was not as lucky and was taken away with the other children. This woman wanted to tell her sister's story and for the family to be compensated for the anguish and horror they had to endure.

One day, this woman's mother had received a call from the residential school that her daughter was attending. They said they were bringing the little girl home. The mother and older sister were excited that she was coming home. Her birthday was around that time, so they decorated the house, baked a cake, and got ready for her arrival. A few days later, there was a knock on the door and a tall, skinny white man was standing at the door holding a burlap sack in his hand. He passed the sack with the dead child in it to the mother, muttering something about the child being afflicted by a supposed illness from which she did not recover. She had passed away while attending the residential school. They did not have the decency to inform the family on the phone, or even to bring her home in a casket. This and many similar stories brought me to tears.

I approached the managing lawyer one day and asked her how she dealt with listening to these stories from the clients without losing her composure. She said that if I became too emotionally involved with the client's story, I would no longer be able to help them in the best way. She said that I needed to look at myself as either a shield or sword for them: a shield to protect them with the law and/or a sword to fight for them. Her words brought about an "aha" moment for me. I realized that I was really getting emotionally involved in these stories instead of studying them for what we could possibly do to bring about some legal recourse. That does not mean that I became a robot or a warrior woman on horseback ready to fight to the death. The legal world is sloth-like, moving slowly and taking time to bend and change. Things take time to reach a resolution or closure. A lot of the time, there was no legal recourse. We could not do anything because clients did not have a sufficiently strong legal case. But I always made sure that I gave them some information or referral to other organizations that could help with counselling, meals, wellness, or a listening ear.

I loved what I did so much that I developed a close bond with many of the clients. I see a lot of my own family members in their faces. Racism, discrimination, and prejudice have existed since contact and colonization, and sadly they are still present in both of our worlds today. The anger that the Indigenous and Roma people have towards outsiders is evident and understandable. The sadness and emptiness that fills them and drowns their souls reminds me of the Romani violin crying and taunting its listeners. Then all at once, the rhythm speeds up and the tune becomes light and happy. This suggests to me that we have the resilience to overcome our obstacles, and that even in the face of sorrow we can find love and laughter.

It is time for both the Romani and Indigenous peoples to take control over their own fate and their own lives and to write their own stories and histories. Outsiders have tried to take control of them, with disastrous results. The Roma and Indigenous populations are growing stronger, becoming more educated not only by going to school, but also by learning from one another through oral histories and the sharing of traditions. We are both resilient and full of perseverance. We travel down the challenging pathways of living in a society that has not respected our cultures and traditions and that has treated us with the utmost hostility. We are the roads that meet. And together, we will strive for justice.

[1]In 1920, while tabling a new Government Bill for the Compulsory residential school attendance of all Indian, Metis and Inuit Children, Duncan Scott (a high level Indian Affairs Agent) stated that residential schools was a solution to the "Indian Problem" (see Rheault).

WORKS CITED

Canadian Press, The. "At least 3,000 died in residential schools, research shows." *CBC News Canada* 18 February 2013. Accessed 2 September 2016.

Lee, Ronald. "The Attempted Genocide and Ethnocide of the Roma." *Cultivating Canada: Reconciliation Through the Lens of Cultural Diversity.* Eds. Ashok Mathur, Jonathan Dewar, and Mike DeGagne. Ottawa: Aboriginal Healing Foundation, 2011. 217-232. Web. Accessed 1 September 2016.

Rheault, Darcy. "Solving the 'Indian Problem': Assimilation Laws, Practices & Indian Residential Schools." 2011. Web. Accessed 5 March 2017.

Truth and Reconciliation Commission of Canada (TRCC). 2012: *Interim Report.* Winnipeg: TRCC, 2012. Accessed 6 September 2016.

Truth and Reconciliation Canada (TRC). *Honouring the Truth, Reconciling for the Future: Summary of the Final Report of the Truth and Reconciliation Commission of Canada.* Winnipeg: Truth and Reconciliation Commission of Canada, 2015.

Ward, Claire. "Boarding schools for Roma kids?" *Maclean's Magazine* 12 May 2010. Web. Accessed 6 September 2016.

A ROMANI WOMAN'S
BEAUTIFUL DREAM COMES TRUE

TÍMEA ÁGNES DARÓCZI

M Y NAME IS Tímea Ágnes Daróczi. I was born in Hungary in the spring of 1981. My nationality is Roma and my mother tongue, Hungarian. My culture is Romanian and Hungarian,. The two cultures are not very different from each other, and I consider myself lucky to have both of them in my heart.

GROWING UP WITH SOMEONE

I was named Ágnes because my father's mother and sister both had that name. He told me that I was to be called Ágnes because he loved them both very much. They were important, influential people in his life, and he wished to express his respect and love this way. He also named me Tímea because this was a special name at the time, one with a special meaning. Mór Jókai, the noted Hungarian author, wrote a novel about searching for happiness, entitled *Az Arany Ember (The Golden Man)*. In it, Jókai named one of the characters Tímea, a name that comes from the Greek *Efthymea*, meaning "good" and "respect."

I was a quiet child. I spoke little and always paid attention to those living around me. My parents worked hard and had little time for play. Of course, they took devoted care of me, protected me, and loved me very much. Still, I felt alone. But I was never bored. Fortunately, we had a very large garden and many animals.

I had a special relationship with animals. I could play for

163

hours with a little chick, but I also enjoyed playing with crickets and lizards. I had a dog that had been with me since birth, who accompanied me everywhere and waited for me no matter how long. He was my faithful partner. I needed him because my curiosity never left me in peace.

Each locked door and gate opened for me and, when it opened, I went out, causing my parents no end of headaches. Whenever this happened, they looked for me anxiously, and often they blamed each other for my disappearance. Often, I would visit Aunt Zsuzsika who lived across from us. Aunt Zsuzsika and people like her are angels on this earth. She gave me so much love and, when she was with me, she was happy and laughing. She would have given me everything, but I did not want to accept anything because that is what my parents taught me. But I was very happy when I was able to give her something. Whether it was a pretty stone, a colourful drawing, or a bunch of fresh wildflowers, Aunt Zsuzsika was always pleased. But she was especially glad when I secretly visited her. She said that when I went to see her, she received something that she thought no longer existed.

Aunt Vanya and everyone else on our street felt the same way about me when I was five years old. My dog would always wait patiently at the gate of the house that I was visiting. Slowly, my parents accepted this. It was enough for them to signal to the dog, who would then let them know that all was well, and no one was worried. When my mother bathed me at night, my father would say that he did not like me to be so independent, and that I must ask their permission and tell them when and whom I would like to visit. He said that not everyone is as nice as the people who lived on our street, and that there are those who are evil and who would hurt a little girl wandering alone. But I convinced him that I was not alone.

I told my father about my recurring dreams about a man whose name I did not know. I called him "Someone." I explained to my father that "Someone" loved me very much and watched over me, often playing with me and consoling me when something hurt me. My father asked me to tell him the name of this "Someone," but I did not know his name, only that he was my friend. My father feared that a strange adult was my friend and he put a padlock on the gate. From then on, I could not leave the garden and the house. But "Someone" was still with me, and we continued to play together. He taught me interesting things about nature, plants, animals, and humility.

One day, workers came to repair the well in our garden. Everyone drew my attention to the well, and cautioned me that that part of the garden was dangerous. My father let me peek at the depth of the well while I sat on his lap. I promised that I would not go to the well by myself. I had started my afternoon rest when a voice I had not heard before asked me to go to the well, and I did, even though I knew I should not.

The area of the well that had to be repaired was temporarily covered by a two-by-two-meter concrete slab. I felt compelled to go there for some reason. I discovered a small hole between the concrete and the ground; I put my small foot there, and then couldn't get it out. I did not know what I had wanted to prove or to whom, and I really regretted what I had done. I realized that I broke my promise to my father. The workers' voices rang clearly in my ear and I felt like I was going to die.

Then I closed my eyes and I asked my friend, Someone, to please come and save my foot. And Someone appeared immediately and freed my foot. I went back to my room right away and lay down as if I had never gone to the forbidden area.

My father came home from work and happily embraced me. I embraced him too, but I was crying because I was ashamed of myself. I told him I just wanted to go to bed. My parents wondered why their child, who was always cheerful and on the move, was now crying and insisting that she was sleepy. Of course, I did not sleep a wink. Someone immediately appeared and asked me to tell my parents the truth about what had happened earlier. I did not do it then or the next day either. Then Someone said that truth was the price of his presence with me. Then he disappeared. That was the first time that I felt distant from him, and I was inconsolable.

One day, my mother asked me to accompany her to the train station, to meet a relative she had not seen for a long time. I was glad to go with her. At the train station, there was a semi-circle of benches made of brown wood and stone. The area was decorated with beds of fresh flowers and snow-white gravel. The train platform was a few steps away, and my mother warned me not go there. "Play with the pebbles," she said.

I had gathered two handfuls of shining pebbles when I noticed a large crucifix mounted on finely chiseled stone. It was a little higher than my eyes, but I clearly saw two feet pierced by a nail, bleeding. Looking up higher, I saw my friend Someone on the cross. At first, I stood in front of the crucifix, silent and frozen, then tears streamed down my face. I asked: "Was it my fault?" He saved my foot, and now his feet hurt, and he died for me.

I cried so hard that my mom became alarmed. She picked me up and we returned home without even waiting for the relative we were supposed to meet. No matter how much she tried to calm me down, I could not tell her what happened. My father was at home when we got there. I told my father right away what a bad thing I had done at the well and that I had not obeyed him. And that I accepted any punishment if he would only give me back my friend. I dragged my father to the station and I introduced my friend to him. My father's eyes filled with tears when he heard me say that I thought my friend had died for my sin.

My father asked: "Is this the friend with whom you play?"

"Yes," I answered.

Relieved, he added, "Then I understand everything! Your friend 'Someone' is Jesus, and he is the Son of God. He is the one who, according to the Catholic religion, died for all our sins, but was resurrected on the third day. There are other religions as well. Their followers believe in other deities—Buddha, Krishna, Vishnu, Moses, Mohammed, and so on."

"Dad," I asked, "what is God's religion?"

"His faith in us," my father replied, "that somehow we seek his teachings and yearn to know him personally."

ARRIVING IN TORONTO

I am Roma, but I do not speak the Romani language. I am Hungarian, but I will never really belong in Hungary because of my skin colour. Wherever I am, I am always double, proving that what I am is just human. For me, diligence, love, and empathy are important.

Some people present themselves in good and positive ways, but others in my life have committed errors. Because of their ideological views, they are frustrated and they suffer. This is the reason I had to leave my beloved country. In 2009, I tried to start a new life in Canada as a refugee. However, the lawyer who represented us (and many others) was neglectful and irresponsible. Our application failed and we lost our refugee hearing. We were to be expelled from the country.

We had to find another way.

Mary Jo Leddy and Romero House helped us find sanctuary in a church. This experience is precisely why I am a Roma rights activist. When we first arrived in Canada, we received shelter for my daughter (who was three years old at the time), my husband Jozsef, and myself. We had given up all of our material things; we entrusted our destiny to God. We had many problems with medical care, income, and with providing food for our daughter. But God gave us strength, and excellent people provided us with appropriate help.

We met an Anglican priest with whom we became very close friends, almost as though we were family. I am grateful to him. Then we discovered Windermere United Church where we met the most wonderful people: Minister Alexa Gilmour and Adrian Marchuk. This was when our lives changed. I remember when Mary Jo Leddy asked Alexa to help us:

"Alexa! Tímea, Jozsef, and the baby need shelter."

"I'll show you the way."

Alexa led us to her office.

Many people offered to help, but Alexa and the Windermere United Church community stepped up. The minister's office was not very big, but it gave us shelter. We slowly came to know the church members, and all of them, without exception, were helpful. They are wonderful, blessed people.

We waited three years in sanctuary. Our former lawyer was brought to trial. The Law Society was not ignorant of the 5,000 Canadian deportations of Romanian and Hungarian-Romani families. They had evidence against this corrupt lawyer who had gambled with our children's futures. His actions also hurt Canadian taxpayers when he took money from Legal Aid for work that he did not do. The lawyer neglected his clients' needs and hundreds of their claims failed. In a tribunal in 2015, the Law Society of Upper Canada punished the lawyer because of his professional misconduct.

Negotiations took place. The trial was not held in the church, so we were unable to attend. We asked the immigration authorities for special permission to leave the church while we we waited for the lawyer's trial, but our request was denied. My daughter stopped going to school at this time. All of this led me to fear that we would not be able to remain in sanctuary any longer. I wanted my daughter to be able to meet children of her age, but this would only be possible if we returned to Hungary. My hope of staying in Canada, a place that had become my home, had been strangled. Advocates rallied to our cause, but the federal immigration authorities still would not admit our family as refugees. When we left, I did not say goodbye to anyone. But I did not give up on my dream of returning one day.

We returned to Europe, to Hungary, and remained there for one year, during which time we faced a great deal of Nazi activity. Despite all of the hardships, my daughter was an excellent student at school. While we were there, my husband and I got involved with a social work organization that distributed food and blankets to homeless people. The demand on the organization was high due to the many refugees from the Middle East and elsewhere who were moving through the country at the time. The refugees received donated food and medicine and other services, too. We did not receive too much money for this work, but it was not about that. I felt uplifted and humbled by the work.

With the help of our new lawyer, Andrew Brouwer, we soon received a letter from the Canadian government confirming that our Humanitarian and Compassionate request was approved. Our burden had been lifted; and in June 2016, we returned to Toronto where we have recently settled. The reception we received at the airport was awesome. Dozens of people were waiting there with balloons and a giant sign saying, "Welcome to the Pusuma family!" News reporters were there. We had a little party, and people remarked how much my daughter had grown in the past year. Some people cried.

DREAMING OF SOMEONE

Imagine a situation in which you are so happy and balanced that the air accumulated in your chest almost lifts you and enables you to fly. You are excited and relaxed at the same time, interested, curious, and able to respond to all questions, all as one person.

Have you ever seen, in the beam of your light turned on at night, rising from the pages of a suddenly closed book, the dance of tiny specks of dust, rising with a circular motion, on their indeterminate way? Can you imagine a solid substance consisting of continually moving dust particles and of brightening and dimming light? Can you imagine a door or a plant—or maybe yourself—made of such a substance? If you feel that you are experiencing *déjà vu*, then please forget reality and pay attention, because I am relating a special story to you. My condition is of ignorance; neither time nor space has meaning. I am sitting with crossed legs somewhere. The first breath of air that I inhale lets me know that I am little, about four years old. The room in which I find myself is unimaginably large, still and peaceful, but with enough light. I feel only the slow motion of my blinking eyes, just slow movements. The more I blink, the more information comes into my head, and I find myself increasingly conscious.

I have so many questions, but whom to ask? How did I get here? Why do I feel that this is an important time and that somehow I must measure it? I measure with the number of my blinks, but I do not yet know how to count ... I stop. It probably has no significance. I start to worry so much that I can hardly breathe. I feel like crying but I have no tears. I feel like shouting but I have no voice. Then I stand up, frightened. I am now breathing deeply and stretched. Someone touches the top of my head. I do not know who it is, but I become much more relaxed and able to breathe slowly, rhythmically, and I know that I have to sit down again in my place.

Then I see a dazzling table. Everything on it shines with the same light as I do. My curiosity remains and I know I can walk again. I stand up and head toward it. Standing up, I see clearly that the children are sitting in neat rows. There are many, many children and they sit comfortably in the huge room, almost motionless. From the line of children, I go straight to the table that is ornately carved. There I see grapes the size of peaches and peaches the size of cantaloupes. There is also a golden wicker basket that contains golden loaves of bread. They loaves and the utensils gleam with that wonderful light. I do not take anything; I am just full of wonder at the sight. I am grateful for all the beauty I can see there.

In the area behind the table, there are three steps. At the top of the stairs stands a high, long altar. It is not adorned with anything, yet it is as if the altar holds a special power over me, a power that makes me bow my head. I feel ashamed of my curiosity. Then a man with a marvellous face takes my face in his hands and looks me in the eye. He sits down on the middle stair and places me in his lap. It feels so good that he is here. I embrace his neck with both arms and I tearfully tell him: "I know who you are!"

I love that man, and remember him from somewhere. I know that once he did a lot for me and now that I am here, I want to reciprocate all that he did. But I have nothing. Nothing! I look for something in my pockets. The man just looks at me with his wonderful eyes and laughs, as if he can read my every thought. We communicate without words. As he looks at me, I forget all my questions. He says: "You remembered me, you are dear to me. The present that you will give me will be that you keep me in your memory. If this will be so, I will be with you everywhere, and that itself will be a privilege for you."

Then the man slowly stands up, takes my hand and escorts me back to my place. There he hugs me again, touches his face to mine, and I know he loves me, and I love him. The children, recovering from their awe, approach. Everyone embraces the man who looks each in the eye, caresses their faces, and whispers something in their ears one by one. We children also hug one another. We are very cheerful and happy. Our hugs seem to say goodbye for a time, but no one knows what is in store for him or her. Despite this, we are happy and resolute. Slowly, everyone sits down again.

The giant hall goes quiet again. Now all eyes are on a huge double door. Its size and colour are almost dazzlingly beautiful. When a crystal-clear voice rings out, the huge double doors swing wide open. A child stands up and walks through it. Then the door shuts again. I await excitedly the ringing voice calling me. When it comes, I know I have to stand up and approach the door. And I do. I walk through the door, which is opened by two marvellous, shining angels. They are tall and are made of the same kind of light as myself and the other children. They do not seem as tangible as the man we have come to love. Their task is to take me through a huge garden to another door. Everything to be seen and heard in the garden is so calming that I cannot think of the future. What is important is the here and now. As I advance toward the new gate, I try to memorize everything so as to fulfill the man's request.

The angels reveal that they and two more will be personally responsible for me. When they explain everything to me, it sounds like a big game. They prepare me for dangers but, in my foolishness, I focus on the interesting rustle of the leaves in the garden.

We reach the gate, where the angels embrace me. They do not say goodbye; they just calm me. He raises me up and begins to turn with me in the air, faster and faster, until I shrink into a small dot, so small that I could have gone through the small keyhole of the huge gate. The gate opens and the whole universe opens up before me. Everything is changing, moving, and forming from second to second, just as it does now, in our days.

LIFE IN TORONTO

We have been in Toronto now for a few months. My husband works in a restaurant for twelve to fourteen hours a day, earning minimum wage. I do volunteer work, but I am hoping to find a paid job soon. Jozsef and I plan to one day open a restaurant. I wish to work with people who want to make good things happen. I hope that our daughter will be able to experience kind and pretty things in her life. We would not have been able to achieve this dream here and now without Canada, a country of peace and acceptance.

WOMEN IN ROMARISINGCA

CHAD EVANS WYATT

WHEN WE CONSIDER the "Gypsy" photograph as text, what usual elements are we apt to find? The prevailing ingredient is exoticism, an "otherness" separating this group from its majority context. Such style of photograph, as Chair of the famed Film and TV School of the Academy of Performing Arts (FAMU) in Prague, Professor Miroslav Vojtěchovský, told me, produces a theatre of grotesque characters, irreconcilably different, without redemption. Often, those pictured are presented in garish colour, increasing the isolation. In contrast, *RomaRising* offers quiet, respectful, black and white images of dignity. Launched in 2001, *RomaRising* now has extended to the Czech Republic, Poland, Hungary, Romania, Bulgaria, and Slovakia. The project has but one simple premise: to dispel stereotypes about the Roma making it impossible to deny respect for these now more than 500 people (who represent so many more). Exhibiting an emerging middle class in six European countries, these are people both remarkable and unremarkable, who establish careers and demonstrate the universality of human aspiration.

A Romani Women's Anthology selects from the Canadian folio taken in 2013 and 2014. This greatly cherished experience sits apart from the European work. Instead of including only those who defy flagrant discrimination to accomplish the improbable, in Canada we see the visage of freedom. Whereas in Europe, *RomaRising* concentrated on middle class and professional

173

class individuals, in Canada's broad spread of citizens and new arrivals, we included absolutely everyone who, like any average citizen, works, pays taxes, and cares for their families.

As in Europe, *RomaRisingCA* is in particular a record of women's empowerment. Time and again we encounter women of strength and character stepping onto the stage. Indeed, it is Romani women who brought the work to fruition from the very beginning, and in every country. It was *A Romani Women's Anthology* that stimulated my re-examination of the project through the lens of gender, starting from its inception and initial success on through the years. My contacts have overwhelmingly been women of all callings, education levels, and ages. In the growing series of exhibitions of the work, I find that it is women who have organized my success. My hope is that majorities everywhere will come to recognize that these individuals are talents of vast ability. Regardless of their chosen path, one discovers them to be inspiring embodiments of our common humanity.

Milena Dunkova and family, Toronto

Nazik Deniz, Toronto

Page 176, top: Ivana Cervenakova, Toronto; Page 176, bottom: Romana Petrovic, Toronto; Above: Kristin Molnar, Montreal

Ilona Orsós, Toronto

Lela Savic, Montreal

I STAND AGAINST THE BINARY

Art and Identity

MONICA BODIRSKY

No person is your friend who demands your silence, or denies your right to grow. —Alice Walker

THIS QUOTE from Alice Walker, African American activist and author of *The Colour Purple*, strikes a chord deep within my heart, yet also makes me pause to consider how silence is demanded, and how a denial of our right to grow manifests itself. It invites me to look at pressure—all aspects of it, whether internal or external—in the very specific context of being an artist, a Canadian woman, and a pagan of mixed Romani ancestry. I pause to reflect on the consequences of socio-economic, cultural, and gender biases imposed by a colonizing majority on visible and invisible minorities. I also consider how internalizing a colonizers' paradigm can transform into self-imposed silence. I think about how artists struggle to retain the right to speak freely within the visual arts about cultural identity and about how they may reconcile the internal and external pressures that exist in contemporary Canadian society.

INSIDE VIEW

I have worked consciously for over twenty-five years to integrate all aspects of myself, not only for quality of life, but also as a political statement. I choose to stand firmly in my fluid identity and to disrupt the colonized framework that constantly exerts pressure to choose sides. I stand against the binary and will not pick art instead of design, fine art over commercial art, representation over abstraction, European instead of Canadian, Roma instead of European, ad infinitum. These theoretical oppositions represent nothing more than a need to exert control over and impose order on perceived chaos through over-simplification. In reducing choices this way, colonizers are able to impose pre-conceived notions and beliefs through conformity and assimilation. I resist assimilation and strive for integration. It requires the ability to live comfortably within ambiguity and the strength and persistence to resist imposed identities. So how does discovering Romani roots at the age of forty alter my artistic voice? Born in East York of immigrant parents who also shared mixed cultural identities, this new information did not make me feel terribly different, but did make me want to explore the history of the Roma and to seek community in Toronto where I live.

Ronald Lee, Toronto Romani scholar, author, and activist has done so much to allow for diversity within the community by uniting people of varying education levels, countries of origin, and beliefs. He created the Roma Community Centre in Toronto, and was instrumental in welcoming me into the community. He works as a Romani interpreter and has created a comprehensive Romani-English dictionary and a lesson book on how to learn the Romani language. It was through his generosity that I met many wonderful people and became familiar with a language long lost in our family. His acceptance of those of us with rudimentary Romani traditions encouraged me to delve into my own family history to dig for what remained.

Assimilation has had devastating effects on the identity of our family. Over centuries we changed names, became Christianized, moved frequently throughout Europe, fought in wars, and avoided wars. All were sacrifices made for survival. I found that while much of the information lost can never be recovered, many Romani cultural norms, especially of arranged marriage, arts and crafts professions, and ritual pollution beliefs once assumed lost had continued. They had simply transformed over the years from Romani traditions into family traditions. I also became quickly aware of my own fragility and privilege when confronted with stereotypes about Romani culture. I was never called a dirty gypsy when growing up, simply a dirty immigrant. I grew up in a middle-class home, am pale skinned and was subsequently spared the overt racism that many Romani face. I was shocked and offended when more than one person made attempts at humour while checking their wallet, asked me what was wrong with the word Gypsy, and told me they were Gypsies too by virtue of fashion. I saw the horrid stereotypes of con artists on television and in movies accompanied by energetic klezmer music to heighten the farcical quality of the event. "Gypsy Queen" Halloween costumes, television portrayals of drunken people at weddings with insanely large rhinestone-covered dresses and scamming fortune tellers as representative of Romani culture stirred mixed feelings of anger and shame.

I wrote an article for a Romani website discussing the harmful effects of the fictitious "Gypsy" and was met with a generalized silence except for one very adamant Romani woman who insisted that being negative will get us nowhere and that we should all "play nice." Silence is imposed from without and within.

Some people believe that I represent the entire Romani population. They ask questions I can't answer. Although, this is frustrating, I strive to answer patiently and suggest credible resources that highlight the diversity of the Romani community.

The limitation of language makes it difficult to understand diversity and diaspora; the semantics of multiplicity is a fluid and ever-sensitive process. Though the word "blended" has come into vogue as a "nicer" alternative to the word "mixed" to describe the presence of several heritages or cultures within a family or individual, I use the word "mixed" in the context of my work, and sometimes my feelings.

What is cultural identity? A name, a language, a skin tone, an attitude, or a deep blood memory? I am not sure, but for me it is complex. As an artist, I see art as a means of understanding complexity through exploration. It allows me to speak about personal and communal identity. Art allows me to interpret the world and bring together many disparate physical and psychological elements to make sense of my environment. When

"Justice" 9" x 11", mixed-media collage, ephemera, paint, ink, antique photograph. Uniting the head and heart is the theme for this tarot-card-inspired interpretation of equity.

183

creating, I use the materials that best express my concept, often as simple as watercolour or as complex as combinations of materials such as paper, felt, cheese boxes, broken dolls—detritus to some, treasure to me. The resultant chimera allows me to envision possibilities that embrace the multiplicity of identity, space, and time, and the legacy of commemoration. I can speak about the past, present and future simultaneously and my work is informed by past sorrows as well as victories and looks to future possibilities. My life and art are bricolage.

Bricolage becomes a way of surviving, thriving, seeing, and being, not simply something that is material or theoretical. Wendy Knepper in her essay, "Colonization, Creolization, and Globalization: The Art and Ruses of Bricolage" uses Claude Lévi-Strauss's idea of the bricoleur, and states that his use of bricolage is

> a mode of interpreting and adapting existing materials to new circumstances or needs. While the result may be a new or reformulated myth, tool, a house, a language, or a discourse, it is important to note that Lévi-Strauss does not see it as a deliberate project-oriented view, but rather as an adaptive mode of being in the world. (71)

I was not European or Roma growing up, and as the child of immigrants in a new suburb of Toronto, I was encouraged, like many post-World War II children, to simply say I was Canadian, to blend in and become the embodiment of bricolage.

Many people I know who are of mixed heritage choose a single cultural identity with which to align. Often it is described to me as a political act to reclaim parts of heritage that reside within an oppressed minority. I recognize and respect this act as an important statement for some; however, there are many who do not choose this path because it is challenging to derive support from one's community when one is seeking help to re-define or align oneself with a cultural group that was not part of one's spoken history or childhood. The Romani community is a diaspora, and here in Toronto can form small, seemingly impenetrable pockets. We are a complex group consisting of Muslims, Christians, Pagans, Jews, and atheists. There are Romani speakers of many dialects and many European languages. We are recent refugees, immigrants through the years, and settlers from the 1800s. Finding common ground can be difficult.

Though I was born in East York, I was raised in what was then a new development—Scarborough. It was a place of cultural autonomy and integration, but predominantly assimilatory attitudes. I grew up with children from a wide range of cultural identities who displayed a varied and extremely complex set of reactions to being seen or treated as "other." Some friends were not of mixed ethnicity, yet embraced a mixed identity by virtue of growing up as outsiders to the Canadian Anglo-Caucasian majority. Many friends were visible minorities, but because there was no community of East Asian, African, or Indigenous peoples at the time, community for some did not exist beyond an occasional picnic or religious gathering. We existed as children who had no strong cultural community ties. We were all new or first-generation Canadians.

In a world disrupted by war, migration, and trauma, our collective languages, lifestyles, and identities have been nearly eradicated, or at least so dismantled that many of us have had to repair and re-interpret. Along with this process of external damage to our identities, as a group we internalize colonial disapproval of our culture and may subconsciously and consciously discard the parts of our history that we cannot relate to, do not fully understand, or that seem irrelevant. This reinvention can contribute to splintering within a community who may see it as non-representative of their own experience or cultural identity. Self-identification can be problematic for all of these reasons.

My father was self-conscious about his own "darkness" especially in summer. He used to speak about his own father's skin colour as an issue in the Czech Republic, and said his father avoided the sun because he was so dark that he feared he would get ejected or worse. Followed through the streets and threatened many times, my grandfather kept a large dog with him when he took his wagon with market goods through the village. Rosemary Stehlik, also a Toronto artist of mixed Romani heritage shared her own family memory with me in a personal exchange:

I remember a chant, echoes of a childhood taunt, spoken through the memory of my mother first encountering the Hungarian community in both Europe and Canada as a young girl of mixed Hungarian and Romani heritage: *"Cigany! Csigany! Csig! Csig! Csig! Poros gyár-ba Fiadzik!* (Gypsy! Gypsy! Gyp! Gyp! Gyp! In a dusty factory you bear sons!)"

Colonization encompasses diverse times and locations from the Roman Empire to contemporary Indigenous groups in North America. It has perpetrated a great deal of damage worldwide through constant and aggressive pressure to assimilate. My family assimilated in the 1700s by accepting land to settle in Maria Theresa's Austro-Hungarian empire and, though they left the wagons behind, my family continued to move from village to village for economic reasons carrying their traditional metal-working, musician, and beekeeping skills with them.

THE STORIES WE TELL OURSELVES

I find the process of repetitive brush strokes comforting, the visual mantra of layering and free-flowing movements calming. Painting is an act of healing as it allows me to reflect on my cultural history some of it obscured and other parts exposed, the fragments of language visual and written, the depth, and the way history inhales everything and spits out seeds and indigestible bits for us to sort through. I work through this process to create abstract and representational paintings, which hold my identity and history, inscrutable to some, intriguing to others. This physical manifestation and integration of a complex self within the environment gives me a voice and agency. In varying degrees, all artwork is a self-portrait.

SHADOWS

As artists, how do we examine and integrate our cultural identities and how does this affect our individual and collective artistic voice? Art by its very nature is a process of questioning

"Thinking of You," mixed-media on canvas

and looking inward for answers. Toronto artist Lynn Hutchinson Lee, of mixed Romanichal (British) heritage, expresses some of the questions she encountered:

poshrat
posh: half

rat: blood

half my blood is one thing, half is another
which half is which?

Poshrat in the city. 2016

I didn't think about bringing together my bloodline, my divided identities, and my art practice until 1995, when my sister came back from relatives in England and said *let me tell you about the caravan Dad grew up in.* It was full of mirrors, she said. At that moment I thought of the mirrors and what they'd reflect when you look into them. Not just the eyes, the face, the expression on the face, the willingness (or not) to look through the face and under the skin, but everything behind that. Memory. Memory from my own experience, but not only that; memory that I carried in my cells and blood. Of the ancestors. Of their context, their experience. At that point I began to make art about my dad's people and the troublesome way I fit, or do not fit, into their world.

Lynn Hutchinson Lee's journey strikes a chord with me and reminds me of how I began my own journey through the narrative of shadowboxes. The process of retrieving and examining discards, mirrored my own attempt at making sense of my cultural heritage. The process was one that created a safe space for me to express ambiguity, complexity, and commemorative aspects in a contained and dimensional space.

Once I have created, I spend periods of time reflecting my motivations for creating what I do before moving forward. Perhaps this allows the vital intuitive process to occur: creation without judgment. I am secure that I will say what I need to in the manner I need to. I look back and see a new story created from one that is fragmented and perhaps lost, and it feels hopeful.

I have been asked about my heritage, and some wonder why it is not overt in my work other than a title here and there perhaps, or a family photo hiding among strangers. One person told me at the New Gallery exhibition, *Assimilate/Integrate,* that they did not see cultural pride portrayed in my work. He was quite angry and demanded that I explain why I was not proud. It seems he equated pride with nationalism, an uplifting colour palette, and a clear statement of my heritage. It was a short conversation, but his words haunt me. My own guilt seeped through at not choosing sides, I suppose. Do I need to put a crystal ball and gold hoop earrings into my work to indicate my Romani heritage? That would not only seem trite, but it would also mean trivializing my own culture. What about a painting of recent Romani immigrants to Canada? We are not all immigrants. We cannot be judged as authentic or inauthentic according to Eurocentric points of view. Some of us come from middle-class homes, some do not drink, and some do not get the urge to wander. Some of us share characteristics of non-Roma even if we identify as 100 percent Roma. The need to position oneself as a separate cultural group can be problematic. If Gadje live a certain way, we will do the opposite. The problem of course in reacting against a culture is to allow the culture to still control your behavior. If you spend too much time doing the opposite and your whole life is spent as a political action against the "other," then who are you?

"Mixed" is a description that some feel invites scorn and judgment. I do not have a running dialogue with parts of me, nor do they conveniently separate on the dotted lines that are imposed by colonized thought. I stand in this ambiguity. I live it; I breathe it. I am proud that my ancestors were community advisors, regardless of the medium they chose—whether it was tea leaves, palmistry, coffee grounds, mediumship, common sense, or all of these combined. The skill to listen and advise is part of my familial past, and it is part of me. Is this uniquely Roma? I can't say, but I know who I am and I do believe in blood memory.

Ronald Lee once said, "Monica, you ask some difficult questions." He was referring to my asking about why Romani people do not use tarot cards for actual divination instead of as an economic means of support. That some Roma use coffee grounds and other methods of divination for personal purposes seems to suggest that spirituality is not restricted to economics.

I am happy to ask questions because if there are no easy questions, there are no easy answers. With easy answers, people may slip quietly into a self-imposed cage of stereotypes, or place others there. We get lulled into the illusion of freedom of identity and the sometimes-awkward dialogue of diversity when we engage in picking and choosing which labels to accept and which to impose on ourselves. But with questions, we are able to recognize multiplicity and diversity for what they truly are, and to accept fluidity of identity for what it is.

YOU are the Flower

I speak to myself and then
I speak to a green stem
I say Roma, part Roma, still Roma
Artist and Roma, Roma and Artist
Roma and Spiritual, Spiritual and Roma
Tiny buds appear on the stem – curious
I say tarot, and wear too many rings
Buds now begin to appear in earnest – attentive
I sing, dance with flamenco claps and a twirl of the skirt
leaves spring from the green stem – delighted
I chant immigrant, oppressed, victim,
Petals and blooms like fireworks explode – approval
A tentative word of Romani, one recently learned
Lush, blooms nod in joyous unison they chant – authenticity
I continue my truth – strong,
Sometimes I don't dance – independent,
Intelligent, mixed heritage, articulate, educated
On and on I continue – gene pool now sullied
Austrian, Czech, Middle Eastern name, sober, settled, middle class
A seer who sees too much, is too much. Suddenly the air is thick with a fog of discontent,
The flower betrayed refuses to grow
The flower confused retreats – disappointment mutual.
With power of magic, breath, identity, ancestry

I inhale deeply parts of me
and exhale proudly all of me

—Monica Bodirsky, 2016

"Destin (Destiny)," 2015, shadowbox.

"Destin" (Destiny) is a shadowbox I created in 2015. Donated
to Project 31, an annual fundraising event held at OCAD
University, it was auctioned and went to an anonymous collector.
It is a neatly arranged collection of unwanted goods, a bricolage
of what I had on hand and what others sold in flea markets.
Things that once held narratives now inaccessible, they were
returned to the economy some monetary value and no original

context. Reminders of others' discards is a booming market for those who are fascinated with nostalgia. A teacup may remind you of your grandmother's house and the time you spent with her. I collect things that are both reminiscent of my own story and that also represent the common thread that runs through our collective narrative. The process and components of my art mirror my experience with identity. In Destin, I placed items together, divided, within a drawer. The drawer is a space we usually keep private things, thoughts, and memories. Yet here it is on a wall, in public.

I know what I do and why I do it, but it is refreshing to see yourself through another's eyes. Cynthia Levine-Rasky kindly added her thoughts and impressions about my artwork for this particular exhibition.

> One of life's great pranks is how its apparent everyday seamlessness resists its configuration in memory. Every rendering no more than a cobbling of fragments, the best we can hope for is to hear a persuasive tale or to see a compelling picture. Monica Bodirsky's current mixed media works summon such a picture, conjuring meanings for viewers that are at once familiar yet strange, domestic yet other-worldly, real yet thoroughly imagined.

> Both assemblages and collages at "Intimate Strangers: Mediating History through Narrative," Bodirsky's show at Studio Huddle, beckon viewers to look closely. Shards of remembered lives are presented with rich detail. Antique and vintage photographs, illustration, script, household items, shells, buttons, fabric, paper, glass containers, doll parts, jars, locks, coins, pins take up a shared residence in skillfully wrought boxes the fine contents of which are ours, yet are not ours.

> Whose are they? They are those left behind, the invisible and silent, now made as sepia-toned archives of relatives no one remembers. Bodirsky deftly re-narrates their sensibilities in subdued colours and with a palette of elements each of which is utterly unremarkable on its own. The effect is an invitation to a momentary

relationship with these strangers and with the oddly disturbing minutiae in the small and imagined worlds in which they have been placed.

Both mysterious and delicate, even comforting in the quotidian, Intimate Strangers expresses the uncelebrated arts of women and artisans. There is something in Bodirsky's work that evokes the high holy days of Samhain in the Wiccan tradition. Corresponding to what we have come to call Halloween, these collected moments of the discarded and the lost are re-assembled and re-contextualized. They bring into recognition not only individual narratives, but also the spiritual practice—a women's practice—long interred.

Bodirsky captures the particularity of memory in the moment of its arousal. We are left with everything that matters that turns out to be very little, assembled in a box whose edges are as battered as our capacity to recollect. In Intimate Strangers we may abandon the effort in this, a small place of refuge.

OLD ROOTS

I did not grow up with any spirituality. There was silence, and a lack of church attendance. There were discussions along the lines of: "find out for yourself," and "the woods are our church; we do not need someone to help us talk to spirits or a higher power." I took my father's words to heart. Both my parents were traumatized by the war as young children and teenagers. They often told me they lost their childhood and, because of this, encouraged me to play. My brother and I enjoyed our time at a cottage north of Toronto near Algonquin Park, and were always silent and grouchy on the return trip to the city. We felt free and unfettered in nature, allowed to find our own voices. I now follow an earth-based spirituality.

We never discussed our ethnic heritage to any great extent, and it was always a mishmash of borders shifting, family moving, migrating, and several languages that used to be spoken. German was spoken by both my parents, but my father always seemed frustrated and said, "But we are not German, we are not Czech, we are not ... any of those." "So who were/are we?" I would ask. "Canadian," he would say. My mother held on to a few Russian and Polish words and spoke of *kishke* (stuffed derma) as fondly as *rotkohl* (red cabbage). She mentioned Prussia (a region whose language was almost completely extinguished) in northern Germany, Sweden, Denmark, and Silesia—a place that no longer exists. My father spoke of Hungary, Austria, and Moravia, and knew very little about his own family—his uncles and grandparents were always moving and carried their skills with them from village to village. They were caught in the Napoleonic War, World War I, and then World War II. All that is known is that the name "Bodir" apparently originated in the Middle East, and "sky" is a Slavic ending meaning "from." Each subsequent generation splintered from previous ones. The disconnect that my father frequently discussed was with his maternal and paternal grandparents whom he does not recall having met. I never met any of mine.

We have a history of being cast to the four winds, in many cases never to be reconnected. Records in churches, if they existed at all, are gone, families changed their names, religions, and languages to survive, and each generation began anew. The constant reinvention left a wake of fragmented stories, but it also created in us a strong sense of self in the absence of community and a good sense of humour. The fragments retained in information were few, but treasured because of their preciousness. I listened attentively to memories of herbal healing, living off the land and a special relationship to nature, family members who were advisors and artists, basket makers and musicians, tailors, entertainers, and metal smiths. Bricolage continued with the need to make art. I have always been driven to create something tangible in the midst of unseen, unmanifested essence.

DIVINATION

Spirituality came early in the 1970s and appeared in my artwork. It took on an air of mystery, darkness, and shadows—an invitation to peer into unknown or unexplored spaces. At the age of eleven, a friend gifted me a deck of tarot cards that she did not want. I have been reading them ever since. The seventies were open to psychic phenomena, Ouija boards, séances, witches and my own intuition. I lived happily in the shadows.

From early childhood, I always wanted to create mystical art, specifically a deck of oracle cards. But suddenly it occurred to me that with Romani heritage, perhaps I should shut this down to avoid contributing to the stereotype of Gypsy fortune-teller? It was my understanding that my ancestors used divination as a way of life within their own group, both as a form of income and for purposes of healing. Despite some misgivings, I created a deck anyway, knowing my contribution may not be viewed since:

Romani readers do this for a living.

Most often they are "cold readers" who check for their non-Romani clients' reactions while advising .

For most Romani people, it seems to have nothing to do with the artwork of the cards or psychic ability, cards are just an available tool. We are a diverse community and this is not always the case.

Spirituality is one way to access pre-colonial connections and knowledge. It is a way for me to reach back into what I consider to be a free time and space before languages and traditions were oppressed and women were subjugated. For some, spirituality is viewed as a stupefying opiate to critical thought. For others it goes beyond communing with nature and becomes academic and activist.

The word *"aquellare"* in Spanish is used to describe a gathering of witches, women who were understood to be evil. Julie Shayne, in her book *They Used To Call Us Witches: Chilean Exiles, Culture and Feminism*, uses the word "witch" as a political reclamation of the feminist self embodied by the Chilean refugees accused of plotting against dictator Augusto Pinochet's regime of terror from 1973-1990. She eloquently connects artmaking, politics, resistance, feminism, and survival.

I can relate to Shayne's book through my own artmaking, political and spiritual beliefs. In a space where little culture remains, I am free to return to the womb of universal and shared feminine history and strength. I have agency in this ritual silence and I can piece together what is remembered, known, and yet

*Using graphic design and fine art skills and my experience as a reader,
The Lucky Lenormand Oracle Deck was created. I view it as both a tool and artwork. I am
grateful for the freedom to express myself and feel lucky indeed.*

to come in a new context. Rosemary Stehlik has made a similar journey and describes her relationship between art, feminism and spirituality:

Living with my Great Grandparents in Nagykovácsi comes to mind with my mother relating the feelings of being an outcast in many spheres of Life due to Societal concepts of Segregation, Prejudice, and Xenophobia. Somewhere in my DNA, this cellular-level of trauma has informed my Subconscious Self whose Visual Paradigm is often informed by and focused upon the subjects of Shadow Work, the Outcast/Solitude, Alienation, Female Occult Strength, Nomadic Spirit, Collective and Individual Fears, Occult Power, Oneiromancy, Shamanic Themes of Transformation, Cosmic Connection, and the Personal and Transpersonal Collective Unconscious Realms of Human Identity and relation. The Folk traditions living in childhood memory ~ Dream recall for Divination, Tarot, Herbalism and moving with the Cosmic Seasonal tides have assuaged any level of Alienation enforced upon my life by Society. My Heritage has cultivated my awareness of self as Female Artist in Patriarchal Society dancing with the Mysteries; my unique circumstance cultivating what it means to be Born into what I deem:

"Existing between the Worlds."

Not "white" enough to be Hungarian

Not "brown" enough to be visibly Romany.

Removed from the Romany tongue by Great Grandparents bent on protecting future generations from persecution.

Scapegoat.

Outcast.

Feared Feminist.

Non-Conformist.

Witch.

Oneiromancer.

Seer.

Visionary...

...Despite the antagonisms of time, obstacles have cultivated a Timeless, Cosmic Relationship with myself as a Creatrix Vis-a-Vis the Cosmos housing my Being in Realms of Timelessness which assists transcendence of the barriers of Separation forged by Society.

SKIRTS

Forced to wear skirts to public school as a young girl, I saw them as a way to hinder movement. The so-called free movement of

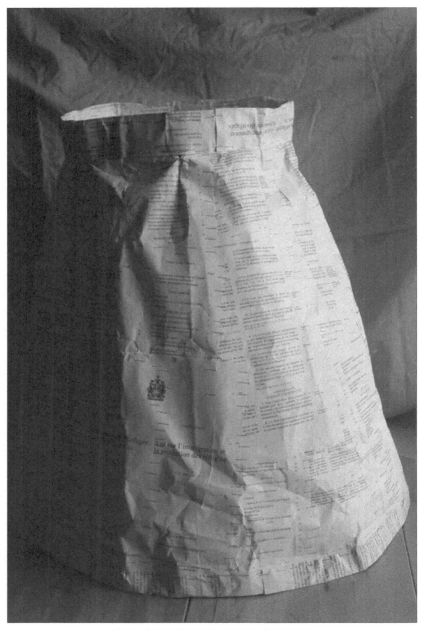

"Policy Skirt", Printed Immigration Act, staples.

a skirt was illusory. In a skirt, I felt hobbled, unable to run and explore as I could in pants; in skirts we were expected to keep our legs crossed and act like "young ladies," not children. More silence imposed.

So the skirt project began, and the Chirikli Collective—Lynn Hutchinson Lee and Hedina Tahirović-Sijerčić—generously invited my participation and with it a very old and long-forgotten dialogue resurfaced. Having recently graduated from the fibre department at OCAD University, I had already explored my tentative relationship to fabric and fibre as a gendered and restrictive space. I understood, however, that Romani women's skirts can also symbolize places of power. A Romani woman's skirt hem is considered contaminated, and a simple toss of her skirt in the direction of someone could curse them or render them ritually polluted. A skirt therefore can be a Romani woman's power, but only when restricted to acceptable use. The parallel between the physical and social restrictions of the skirt and the Canadian government's attitudes towards Romani refugees is apparent.

I constructed a skirt by printing "Protecting Canada's Immigration Act" on 8 x 10 pieces of bond paper and stapling them together. This represents the dichotomy of resistance and submission, and questions the notion of imposed identities.

A second skirt was created by digitally repeating a pattern containing two photographs of bulldozers tearing down Romani settlements in Europe. The mesmerizing beauty of a bright pattern combined with horrible images of destruction creates a contrast. Its purpose is to draw people to the pattern which, when examined closely, serves as a wake up call from complacency. I am questioning ways of seeing the Romani reality in Europe and our awareness, or more accurately, our lack of awareness.

NEW ROOTS

Encouraged to assimilate and not to identify as any one nationality in particular was a very real part of my childhood. Perhaps this was out of fear of rejection, perhaps out of understanding that complexity of language, geography, and beliefs will be

"Pagan Roots,"
12 x 24 inches,
mixed-media water-
colour, ink, antique
photograph.

misunderstood. My cultural identity, gender identity, art and spirituality are now integrated. I am an artist, spiritual, and of mixed heritage. My ancestors fell in love with one another despite the pressures to remain divided. They mixed, mingled, loved one another, had children, survived, and thrived despite language loss and surrender, changes in geographical locations, political differences, religions adopted and discarded, oppressors marrying oppressed. They are all ancestors. My art is my voice realized and is a celebration of community. My late parents saw many horrific things that no children should have witnessed, yet the worst thing about the war according to both was "having to choose sides. Brother killing brother. Sister speaking against sister." In honour of all of our relatives past, present, and future, I stand against the binary.

WORK CITED

Hutchinson Lee, Lynn. Personal communication, August 2016.

Knepper, Wendy. "Colonization, Creolization, and Globalization: The Art and Ruses of *Bricolage*." *Small Axe, Number 21* (10.3) (October 2006): 70-86. Print.

Stehlik, Rosemary. Personal communication, August 2016.

Shayne, Julie. *They Used To Call Us Witches: Chilean Exiles, Culture and Feminism*. Lanham, Maryland: Lexington Books, 2009. Print.

ROMANI ADVOCACY, IDENTITY, AND INTEGRATION

Music and Myths in Montreal

MELAENA ALLEN-TROTTIER

A S A HISTORY BUFF, I have been fascinated for decades by the "there-but-not-there" representation of the Roma. They are present in so many places, but only seen in the shadows of history, in the margins of the books, so to speak. From a Canadian perspective, looking through the eyes of a new and not-very-populous country, it seems unfathomable that such an enormous group of people existing for centuries could be so overlooked in the annals of history. Yet we know it is happening in many countries in Europe in the present day: Roma are forgotten, ignored, undocumented, and deported. In Canada, the Roma are more visible, yet still not fully in control of their own narrative. My research explores the ways in which two different groups of Romani advocates in Canada—one less likely than the other— have engaged and seized control of their own public identities and narratives.

My decision to study Romani music in Canada for a doctoral dissertation in ethnomusicology was risky, given the low numbers of Roma in Canada and the voluntary nature of their identity. Was "Romani music in Canada" a viable topic with so few Roma, and, if so, how many Roma would be required to make it viable? I would need to argue this successfully to my academic committee and supervisor, and then I would need to stake my own money on finding out if I was right. To complicate the idea, well-meaning colleagues and contacts from European

202

countries told me, kindly, that the Canadian Roma were not "real Roma." In order to study "real Gypsy music," they said, I would need to go to abroad. As I had already met several "real" Canadian Roma who played "real" Romani music, there was no way to understand the advice of my colleagues except in terms of a schism between Canadian and European understandings of the Roma.

What did it mean, then, to be a "real Roma" in Canada, and why were they not seen that way by Europeans? What about Canadian Romani music? Did it exist as a concept with its own identity, or was it only redacted, derivative of European genres? I had to cross Canada to find the answers, which were far more ambiguous than I expected. In retrospect, I should have known better than to seek homogeneity across such a diverse culture.

At the beginning of my research, I had assumed that Romani musicians would produce "Romani music." While this is semantically correct, I found that the musical tradition in Canada is most commonly referred to as "Gypsy," which is used in the sense of a wide genre label like "jazz" or "classical," with no ethnic restrictions on the musicians. It was clear that I would need to study "Canadian Roma" and "Canadian Gypsy music" as two separate but inextricably linked concepts, set in a uniquely Canadian context that disinherited the rigid hierarchies of European countries from which many of the Roma originated.

The basis of my doctoral dissertation, then, was to explore the processes of identity construction vis-à-vis building the diasporic "Romani nation" of the two most visible groups of Roma in Canada: the Romani advocates and refugees of Toronto, and the Montreal-based Romani and non-Romani "Gypsy musicians."[1]

While the Roma advocates are frequently tied to emergent Romani nationalism, which focuses on political and historical narratives of injustice and loss, the majority of the Montreal "Gypsy musicians" are apolitical by choice, focusing on myths of freedom and power. They maintain a degree of control over personal and professional cultural identity that remains elusive for the general Roma population of Canada, and which is virtually unknown in European countries.

CANADA: THE CONTEXT

The two most common "Gypsy" myths in Canada are binary in nature. Canadians of non-European origin tend to self-consciously believe in "Gypsies" as semi-magical nomads, fortune-tellers, and free spirits, based on a well-established literary tradition that portrays them as exotically-dressed and at peace with nature. It is common to hear Canadians use phrases such as "I have a Gypsy soul" to imply traits like wisdom, freedom, and intuition. By contrast, Canadians of European origin are more likely to use the word "Gypsy" in a thinly-veiled xenophobic manner, sometimes prefaced with the words "dirty" or "thieving." Both myths are inaccurate, but only one is pejorative.

Due to Canada's distance from Europe, and the fact that Canada is peopled with immigrants from many places other than Europe, the mythical and largely benign literary trope of freedom and magic is, in my experience, much more common in Canada. Because of the low numbers of Roma in Canada, neither the name nor the culture are well known, and, in defiance of current advocacy efforts to replace the often-pejorative "Gypsy" with "Roma," "Gypsy" has acquired significant momentum as the genre label in the music industry and is unlikely to change any time soon.

Several of my research contacts told me that they viewed Canada as a country in its infancy, with deep commitment to social equality but few traditions. Canada offers newcomers the opportunity to escape from fixed social hierarchies and corresponding exclusion, allowing a degree of social mobility and control over one's identity that is rarely available in European countries with strong Romani minorities. For Romani musicians, Canada offers an opportunity to learn from and create music with people of diverse cultures as equals, and to market the product to an audience that is virtually free of preconceived expectations about "Gypsy music."

A TALE OF TWO CITIES: THE BEGINNING

Central to this ethnography was the fieldwork component. Although it was intended to be multi-sited among several cities, from my home in Alberta, I could not find enough Roma in the other cities to make a leap of faith. The research became focused on two communities: Montreal, with the most "Gypsy musicians," and Toronto, with the most Roma. I had hoped to create a meta-analysis or definitive work on Canadian Romani music, but the project soon took on a life of its own, and formed itself into an inquiry about the different ways that the two population bases created and maintained public "Romani" or "Gypsy" identities.

Not only did Toronto and Montreal have entirely different cultural personalities, but considering they were only six hours apart by car or rail, there was curiously little interaction between them. In Montreal, where there were no dedicated Romani resources or social networks, I met comfortably middle-class Romani musicians and educators, distanced from the immediate need for advocacy. While they recognized the desperation of Roma abroad, there was a sense of ease and integration in daily life that seemed to preclude worry.

The apolitical nature of the "Gypsy musicians" is similar to that of the Romanian *lautari*, an elite group of Romani musicians as studied by Margaret Beissinger. She speculates that they form a third socio-economic class that is neither Roma nor *Gadze* (non-Roma). The *lautari*, for the most part, have been neither raised nor educated among the Roma, and they do not identify themselves as being truly Roma, although neither are they fully accepted by the Romanians, who, at the same time, are utterly dependent on them for live music. The *lautari* are generally not interested in Romani politics, and some stated that music and politics were mutually exclusive (Beissinger 48). It is also worth mentioning that two of the most prominent musicians in Montreal, Carmen Piculeata and Sergiu Popa, would fall directly into this *lautari* classification.

Toronto, by contrast, is a refugee magnet. It offers dedicated provincial services for incoming Canadian Roma plus a well-established social network of hundreds of families, many of whom live in close proximity in many neighbourhoods through the city. There, Romani culture is public and visible the way that "Gypsy music" is public and visible in Montreal. Toronto Roma are well connected to their families abroad, and, at least until the refugee process is complete, committed to "being Roma" in a political and advocacy role. The need for advocacy, for funding, and for validation is so strong that it is impossible to mistake: Roma abroad are in peril, and the Toronto advocates whom I met were working tirelessly to ameliorate the situation.

MONTREAL AND TORONTO: THE NUMBERS

While there are thousands of Roma in Toronto, many of whom can be easily found at the Roma Community Centre, I found very few Roma in Montreal in seven months of living there over two years. Ethnographic fieldwork is supposed to "snowball," with each contact leading to three more contacts and so on, but my connections were circular; after a month or so, all of my Romani contacts led back to each other. Despite this, the "Gypsy music" scene in Montreal was a genuine community in and of itself, with complex connections, traditions, and its own musical identity. It was also inextricably connected to "Roma identity." I decided to stay.

"Gypsy music" in Montreal was a big business, and anything to do with "Gypsies" was highly sought after. At the time of my fieldwork in Montreal in 2009 and 2010, there were eleven active "Gypsy music" groups or individual artists, and there was even a dedicated music school, "École Jazz Manouche" (School of Gypsy Jazz). The groups and individual artists were: Les Gitans de Sarajevo, Carmen Piculeata and the Montreal Gypsy Orchestra, Kristen Molnar and Te Merav, Jorge Martinez, The Sergiu Popa Ensemble, Briga, Kaba Horo, Djoumboush, Soleil Tzigane, Sarah Barbieux and Caravane, and Gaji Gajo. Some musicians told me that the highest compliment they could give (or receive) was that they had played something "like a Gypsy."

The only "Gypsy music" group who regularly performed for the members of the Roma community was Les Gitans de Sarajevo. Some members of this group were non-Roma, which is interesting in itself as a situation that would rarely, if ever, occur in European countries. Les Gitans played sporadically at Café Sarajevo, a small bar run by a non-Roma, the closest thing Montreal had to a Roma community centre. I had been a few times prior to 2009 before Café Sarajevo closed permanently and, at the time of my fieldwork, no other venue had replaced it. Other than private house parties, live "Gypsy music" in Montreal, as far as I could see, was generally aimed at a mainstream audience. The two "Gypsy musicians" who were interested in advocacy work, Sarah Barbieux and, to a lesser degree, Sergiu Popa, mostly engaged with a non-Roma crowd.

In Toronto, among the thousands of Roma there, all my inquiries turned up only three active Roma or "Gypsy" music ensembles: Micheal Butch and the Gypsy Rebels, Ungro Rom, and Robi Botos. While Robi Botos plays primarily for mainstream audiences, the other two groups are less well known publically. At the time of my fieldwork, Ungro Rom was still an emergent group, while Micheal Butch was playing regularly both for mainstream audiences and within the Roma community.

What Toronto had instead was a great deal of informal and unpaid music, live and recorded; it had the anthem at protests, children's performances at school assemblies, and Romani dance classes at the community centre. Music in Toronto was used to raise awareness, to raise funds for refugees, and to keep an extended and diverse community together. There was a great deal of live and recorded music focused inwards at its own Romani community, whereas Montreal had a great deal of music directed outwards, at mainstream Montrealers.

TORONTO AND MONTREAL: THE PEOPLE

At the Roma Community Centre in Toronto, I heard story after story of European Roma being taunted, abused, hated, and denied basic human rights like voting, education, and health care. Indelibly stamped as "Gypsy," they lived as second-class citizens inside national administrations that viewed this as an acceptable norm. As a new parent, one of the saddest stories I heard was about a Romani toddler being denied food in daycare while the other children ate.

The level of hatred towards Roma in many European countries is unlike anything Canadians have ever experienced. Our closest and most shameful parallel is the long history of First Nations abuses. While reform has been a long time coming, the First Nations community is now guaranteed full rights under the law, in theory if not always in practice. However, institutionalized abuses are still very much in evidence in many countries in which the Roma live. The Toronto Roma tell some of the saddest stories ever told. The affective experience for both speaker and audience alike is one of sorrow, loss, and grief.

In Canada, however, that chain of hatred is broken. As a relatively new country in which little is known about the Roma, Canada offers a safe place in which new immigrants can choose an ethnic identity that is not predicated on human rights abuses or strictures. Those who wish to identify as Roma are free to do so without stigma or denial of services. Likewise, many of my Roma contacts told me that some Roma simply walk away from their "Roma" identities, which is especially easy in ethnically diverse cities.

My Montreal Romani contacts were drawn from a very different demographic. Most were well educated and had arrived in the city with marketable skills; some had chosen Montreal specifically due to its international reputation for live music. Many had married outside the culture and had little interest in maintaining Romani traditions or culture on a personal level. Given the same open-ended interview format as in Toronto, my Montreal interviewees wanted to talk about how to play a proper 11/8 rhythm, the complexities of getting grants and gigs in the Montreal music industry, and where to get the best bagels.

Ethnic or national identity as "Roma" (or, more commonly, "Gypsy") was self-conscious and usually only came up in the context of marketing the music. There was a keen awareness that Montreal audiences were in love with the mythological "Gypsy" ideal, and a strong interest in keeping it that way. Colloquially, being a "Gypsy" in Montreal was "cool." Rather than walking away from the culture, the "Gypsy musicians" went to some lengths to embrace it.

Much of my research, then, focused on the ways in which the successful Gypsy musicians (Roma and non-Roma), who were business-oriented strategists and self-promoters, negotiated and marketed a very positive "Gypsy" identity predicated on myth and "feel-good" affective qualities that was greatly at odds with anything I had seen in Toronto or read about in European countries. This identity, while based on the underlying Romani culture and drawing heavily on its musical traditions, also bypassed the difficult and contentious history. Musicians who did not wish to overtly engage in "Gypsy" dialogue were likewise not constrained to do so except in ways that suited them personally. Carmen Piculeata, who had blue eyes and played classical music in cargo shorts, defined himself publically as a "Gypsy" through his violin virtuosity. Many of my Montreal contacts agreed that virtuosity in the "Gypsy" style was a uniquely Roma trait that, due to the immersion quality of the musical transmission, could not be replicated by an outsider (and as a music educator, I am inclined to agree). Therefore, within my "Gypsy musician" contacts, virtuosity in the "Gypsy music" style was its own proof of Romani identity; no further visual displays (such as dress) or musical choices (such as repertoire) were necessary.

This omission of Romani history was of course convenient to the musicians from a business perspective, but over months in Montreal it became clear that it was also not personally relevant to the musicians, who, while keeping a public identity of Roma or "Gypsy," had purposefully chosen to break with European traditions in order to create new ones. Although some Montreal-area musicians, such as Sarah Barbieux, were actively engaged in advocacy work—while also channelling images of myth and spectacle—it was not the norm at that time.

LOSS OF IDENTITY IN TORONTO

In the nature of diaspora populations, relatives bring more relatives, and the population concentrates in a central area. During the years of my research (2009-2013), the overseas awareness of Canada as a "safe haven" for Roma had spiked, and there was a sharp increase in the number of refugee claimants, concentrated almost exclusively in the Greater Toronto Area (GTA).[2]

The federal Conservative government under Stephen Harper, in power from 2006-2015, was uninterested in paying even lip service to the Mulroney and Chretien ideals of "diversity" and "multiculturalism." The Harper administration viewed the rise in refugee applications first with alarm and then with purposeful strategies of exclusion. During these years, it was a matter not only of national policy but of pride that most of the Roma claimants at that time were denied entry and subsequently repatriated (Swan).

To justify the refusals, the Conservative government utilized mainstream media to publicize the refugees as "bogus," describing them as intent on defrauding the public purse, making heavy use of the "thieving Gypsy" trope that is, or was until that time, little known in Canada (Toth 18-19; Conway 11). While many of the media reports and editorials about the incoming Roma were sympathetic to their situation, media outlets also published interviews and press releases that were supportive of the federal administration (Ayed and Ou). By publicizing and mainstreaming the "Gypsy thief" narrative, the Conservative government planted the seeds of discrimination that re-created the atmosphere of the countries from which the Roma were fleeing.

The word "bogus" is a particularly powerful word to enter the media as it casts doubt on the relevance of any further identity that the Roma themselves might wish to disseminate such as "teacher," "parent," "artist," and so on. Simply put, if the individual's right to claim refuge is not valid, then further definitions are irrelevant to the public discourse. At one point, the impact on the community itself was so severe that the moderator of the Toronto RCC Facebook group requested that people stop sharing those media releases, because it was damaging the morale of the incoming Roma to the point that some were considering abandoning their refugee claims (Csanyi-Robah). It is impossible to imagine that the Harper media releases about the Roma did not have a significant effect on public opinion as well as on the Roma community itself, and indeed, several years later when Harper ran for re-election on ethnic issues like the niqab, there was an upward spike in reports of hate crimes towards Muslims (Fine). In both instances, Harper showed his resourcefulness in dominating public discourse around vulnerable groups (Roma refugees and Muslim women) to situate himself as the benevolent protector of the Canadian nation from hostile outsiders who would threaten social unity. Ultimately this bid failed, and now, while the Roma refugees have respite from hostility in mainstream media, they must seize the chance to disseminate public identities on their own terms.

AMBIGUOUS IDENTITIES IN MONTREAL

In the ethnomusicological world, it is noteworthy to find an ethnic genre in the diaspora that transcends ethnic boundaries. But like jazz music and the emergent Bollywood craze, Gypsy music in Canada is now so popular with a mainstream audience that it forms a genre in its own right with subdivisions such as "Gypsy Jazz," "Balkan Gypsy," "Gypsy Funk," and so on. Thus the "Gypsy" genre in Montreal is assumed to be transmissible past ethnic barriers, up to but not including the level of virtuoso (a very rare degree of musical proficiency surpassing mastery), for which, all the musicians agreed, one really did need to grow up immersed in the Roma culture; virtuosity could not be taught to outsiders. There is, however, limited scope for virtuosity in Montreal, as the culturally-specific sound is not understandable to most Montrealers—its rapidity and tonality are overwhelming for those who have not grown up in the idiom. As a result, competent but less exciting non-Romani "Gypsy musicians," drawn from ordinary middle-class Montrealers, perform widely around the Montreal environs.

In this context, ethnic heritage was worn very lightly among the Montreal "Gypsy musicians," and even as a researcher I sometimes had difficulties working out who was Roma. The musicians were not quick to volunteer the information, and while at first this seemed stagey or deliberate, it happened so many times that I realized that it was not as important to other people as it was to me, the ethnomusicologist. This disinterest represented a contradiction to the majority of the ethnomusicological literature focusing on cultural identity, in which the contacts are generally quick to identify their ethnic and cultural backgrounds. As an added level of ambiguity, many of the people I interviewed had only one Roma parent, so their decision to identity as "Roma" or not was wholly situational.

For the "Gypsy musicians," the main criterion for deciding who was a "real" "Gypsy musician" was a high degree of proficiency in the idiom. Dialogues of authenticity within the musical community, then, were almost exclusively limited to the technical expertise and performance practice of the musician rather than his or her ethnic birthright. This phenomenon was also explored by Chong, in her discussion of cultural transmission in a Balkan women's singing group, in which she asks: "… is passion … combined with extensive research of that culture enough to constitute a credible cultural bearer?" (Chong 36) There can never be a single answer, but general consensus among the Montreal "Gypsy musicians" seems to be that it is.

Despite the common use of "Gypsy" as a broad genre within the industry, and used consistently in this manner by the "Gypsy musicians," there was, in my opinion, still a very real audience expectation that most, if not all, of the musicians, would be Roma (or "real Gypsies" as they would have probably been called). If a Japanese ensemble promoted itself with images of Japan, Japanese people, and Japanese cultural themes, then showed up at a local community centre with blonde Swedish musicians, most audience members would be surprised and/or disappointed in their underlying expectations of "the real thing." While treating the "Gypsy" label as a broad genre within the music industry, it was nevertheless marketed primarily as an ethnic genre by foregrounding cultural aspects, and it is reasonable to assume that the audience was pre-disposed to think that the musicians were "real Roma."

The musicians, while not making false statements that they were Roma, nevertheless did not try very hard to disillusion audiences either. So if a non-Romani musician wanted to play "Gypsy music" in a long skirt on stage, then that was definitely within her purview, but it was done with awareness that the audience would surely assume that she was Roma even though she was not. In short, while the musicians treated "Gypsy" as a non-proprietary genre label, they were aware that audience assumptions about their ethnicity would work to their professional advantage.

What is fascinating about this phenomenon, though, is that

the non-Romani and Romani "Gypsy musicians," a telegenic, highly skilled middle class who are well integrated into Montreal culture, became *de facto* ambassadors for Romani culture. For many Montrealers, the "Gypsy musicians" are the only Roma they will ever meet. The fact that none or only a few of them were born Roma is not relevant to the lived experience of a mainstream audience that cannot tell the difference.

At Montreal's 2007 Romani Yag, a three-day advocacy festival showcasing Romani and non-Romani "Gypsy musicians," I met Carmen Piculeata, one of the main performers, who is one of the best ambassadors for Romani culture that I have ever met. During his concert, there was some consternation among the organizers (who were not Roma) that his evening performance featured Romantic classical composers, such as Lizst and Chopin, rather than traditional "Gypsy music." The inestimable Ronald Lee, a locally famous Canadian Roma advocate and author, who was sitting beside me, was shocked by this sentiment and exclaimed, "You can't tell a musician what to play!"

Lee and Piculeata were in perfect accord: when I interviewed Piculeata about that decision in 2008, he shrugged and said simply that he was promoting his upcoming album. He added that, as an upper-tier musician, it was his privilege to choose his own repertoire rather than pandering to audience expectations, which made him feel like a "street bitch" (Piculeata). While Carmen is not interested in advocacy in any sense, he was nevertheless the strongest advocate for the Roma that evening, refusing to accommodate audience expectations of "traditional music," and forcing many people, including the organizers, to question the role of "Roma" public identity. As Ursula Hemetek states so adroitly: "Ethnomusicologists' mediation of cultures has paved the way and given a platform to minority musicians who are now free to choose to deny the 'ethnic' stereotypes expected by the majority" (53). Piculeata's simple message that "Roma musicians are brilliant, and we play any kind of music that we want to," was, in its simplicity and independence, a very strong and clear statement about what it meant to "be Roma," an impression that persists despite the jumble of numbers and statistics of human rights abuses.

"GYPSY" MUSIC IN CANADA:
TRANSFORMATION AND IDENTITY

Musically, the "Gypsy music" offerings (such as live music and recorded music for sale) in Montreal are often a collaboration of the European "Gypsy" style with mainstream North American contributions or substitutions. Some of the well-known Romani musical traditions, particularly the penchant for 'extreme ornamentation and long virtuosic interludes—processes that are very similar to jazz music—have become simplified and changed to be accessible to: (a) the other musicians in the band, who may not be able to play at such a technically advanced level; and (b) a broad audience base who cannot understand the advanced sound. In this, again, there is a parallel to jazz music, which lost much of its audience when it became too aurally inaccessible. Recreating the traditions was not the goal, anyway, as most musicians stated explicitly that they wanted to create a new "Gypsy" sound rather than slavish adherence to European styles. The only group I met in Montreal whose style was wholly derivative of the European Roma tradition, untouched by Canadian influences, was Soleil Tzigane ("Gypsy Sun"), composed of Bulgarian non-Roma brothers. Without exception, every musician that I interviewed in Montreal referred me to this group as having "the best Gypsy music in Montreal." In this sense they meant the "most traditional" Gypsy music, again referencing the European custom of what is meant by "real Gypsy music."

Soleil Tzigane's live music was indeed incredible, musically brilliant and perfectly suited to its expatriate audience. They were virtually impossible to find, though, as they had no media presence and no marketing processes. In that sense, and in the sense of the music being redactive, Soleil Tzigane was markedly different from the other "Gypsy music" groups in Montreal.

Cultural transformations occur when musicians with different ethnic backgrounds make their own contributions to the music. This mélange happens naturally in groups with, for example, a Serbian bass player, a Turkish dancer, a Moldovan--Romani accordionist, and a Haitian drummer, all performing under the umbrella of North American rock music. Within the group, the musical *lingua franca* of "Gypsy" might be more theoretical than practical, and the product becomes a perfect light snack for a Montreal global audience which is itself Serbian, Turkish, Haitian, and so on. In Toronto, similar processes were happening for the same reasons. In Montreal, the practice of borrowing musicians between groups led to a somewhat homogenous and localized "Gypsy music" sound.

I would argue that the new repertoire and the new multicultural styles constitute a uniquely "Canadian Gypsy" sub-genre of music. However, opinion on this among my contacts was divided; while some musicians felt that "Canadian Gypsy music" was well-established enough to be a sub-genre in its own right, other musicians argued that it would have to stand the test of time like other traditional music; as a genre, it would perhaps be viable in fifty or a hundred years. Whatever the consensus among our small group, it is worth noting that the phrase "Canadian Gypsy music," although understandable in meaning and sporadically in use, has not yet gained momentum among a broader audience.[3]

THE MONTREAL "GYPSY MUSICIANS":
BEST-CASE IDENTITY CREATION

The contrast between the identity-creation processes of Montreal and Toronto was enormous. At a time when the Toronto Roma were being slandered in public media by the federal government, the "Gypsy musicians" of Montreal had, through manipulation of media resources, purposefully strategized positive elements of the same culture to create a strong local market for "Gypsy" cultural products. How had they achieved this?

First, they were in the perfect environment to negotiate ethnic identity. Montreal is a unique city in Canada, with its bilingualism and European heritage, coupled with an aggressively egalitarian approach to Canadian multiculturalism. "Ethnic" is a way of life there, where ethnic products surpass their local communities to reach a wider, globally savvy market that is hungry for differentiation on the world stage. Also, the popularity of live music in Montreal cannot be underestimated; not only is there a great deal of provincial funding for the arts, but paid venues are packed in a way that is not seen in other large Canadian cities. Montreal audiences are avid consumers of ethnic products and live venues, a niche that the "Gypsy musicians" exploit skillfully.

While Montreal is well connected to the European global marketplace with strong ties to European countries, especially France, the city is at the same time curiously local. Many of the Montreal musicians that I interviewed were completely unaware of Canadian politics outside the Quebec border. The province of Quebec is like a small country to many of its residents, marooned in a sea of English, and in that analogy Montreal is an insular community, wholly self-reliant and a little bit smug, extraordinarily in love with itself. Further, the "Gypsy musicians," by virtue of their public careers, were demonstrably neither refugees nor welfare cheats, and if Harper's negative press had somehow managed to penetrate the Francophone buffer, it is unlikely that anyone would have taken it seriously.

The small Romani population in Montreal has also worked to the advantage of Romani musicians, in that they have been forced to integrate quickly with locals. With no real Romani community to speak of, the immigrant musicians established strong personal and business relationships with native Montrealers who knew the languages and the culture, where to perform, and how to get grants like those offered by the Canada Council for the Arts. The Romani newcomers acted as music teachers to the Canadians, sharing their imported repertoire and performance practices while validating the "Roma" component of the "Gypsy music" groups. For their part, the locals helped them integrate more thoroughly than any government agency or program would have been able to do. Music in Montreal is highly competitive and standardized, though—even busking in the Métro (underground train station) requires a permit—and I heard stories about brilliant Romani musicians who left Montreal after failing to come to terms quickly enough with their administrative and financial responsibilities. With a dual-language requirement, fierce competition, and few social safety nets, Montreal is difficult for musicians who cannot integrate. This led to a sort of Darwinian effect in which the remaining groups were those who were highly integrated, but which, as some musicians pointed out, were also biased in favour of local Montrealers, most of whom are already bilingual. In theory a French-only speaker could establish a successful music career within the Montreal environs, but anyone hoping to gig or sell albums in other provinces, or the United States, would also need to speak English fluently. Thus new immigrants hoping to succeed in the music industry struggled to learn not just one language, as in Toronto, but two languages quickly.

As business people, the musicians not only create their product, but must also brand and sell it amidst a great deal of competition. In almost every situation, the most successful musicians are strong self-promoters, technologically savvy, and fluent at media relations. Established musicians who are (or who hire) skilled publicists are far less vulnerable to the sort of public manipulation of identity that happened to the Toronto refugees.

But musicians are equally capable of branding the less desirable myths of "Gypsy" culture too: Kaba Horo labelled their "Gypsy Groove" music as "100 percent contrabanda," possibly referencing the "Gypsy-as-thief" myth. While this is seemingly a pejorative or, at best, backwards strategy for the Roma, it must be mentioned that "bad boy" imagery has a long history of positive associations in the world of popular music, which links it with freedom, original thought, and rebellion; colloquially, it can be "good to be bad." The counter-culture reference of "contrabanda" in this case serves to highlight and reinforce the intended demographic.

If Harper had personally shown up in Montreal to lambaste the Roma, the efficient musicians would have doubtless found some way to brand and sell that too. It would be easy to follow Kaba Horo's very successful Juno award-winning strategy by staking a claim in the counter-culture. One might imagine how they could express a justifiable anger against the state, and situate the Roma refugees who seek justice and freedom as rebels against "the Establishment." Many popular genres such as punk, jazz, and rap started as counter-culture genres, or at best, "underdog" genres that represented little-known cultures until popular music pulled them into the mainstream.[4] The final and perhaps most important point about Roma and non-Roma collaborations in Montreal is that, because the most economically viable "Gypsy musicians" (Roma or not) originate primarily from the educated middle class, their dissemination of "Gypsy" or "Roma" culture is congruent with one that situates it within the range of the middle class. It distinguishes it from one that assumes its place at the bottom of society, like the image that might be advanced by those who entered Canada as refugees fleeing persecution abroad.

SELLING AFFECT: FREEDOM AND LOSS

Montreal Roma actively market the feel-good "Gypsy" tropes such as the party spirit, musical virtuosity, and a strong sense of the exotic, with ties to the wondrous and the semi-magical. The music is usually upbeat and intended for celebrations; to share the "Gypsy" culture in this sense is to have a welcome escape from routine. The experience is affective and fun. At the same time, the great cultural distance between the two cities, seemingly much further apart than six hours, meant that Montreal audiences were not expected to stretch their credibility by believing in the "feel-good free Gypsy" myth while also watching new Roma refugees line up for food banks like they do in Toronto.

The impact of the disconnect between "local" and "mythological" is discussed by Mackey with regards to the First Nations people in Canada:

> Although Native people are highlighted in Canada's heritage, they are at the same time frozen in the glorious past of teepees and headdresses. Many live in poverty in small, unromantic homes on reserves.... Would homes such as these, if placed in the middle of the Canadian Museum of Civilisation's courtyard, have the same effect? (78)

The Toronto Romani advocates and refugees, in their turn, are equally as affective in nature as the "Gypsy musicians," but the affect—based on literal truth—is one of loss and grief rather than freedom and fantasy. Many times I was hard-pressed not to cry during interviews. While no one can deny the validity and magnitude of the injustices, and the tremendous losses on both cultural and personal levels, the mood created is uncomfortable and sad. Further, the sense of loss is neither a positive identity in terms of what a Romani person *is*, nor does it engender a new heroic myth.

It is easy to say that the Toronto advocates are in the business of marketing knowledge and rationality, not mythology or affect, but there is a definite place for myth and heroism in any new national endeavor. These myths do not have to be the ones already circulating in Montreal, that work to fulfill non-Roma audience expectations based on the literary ideal. They could be myths and heroic attributes of any type that the Roma decide are meaningful, such as those of unsurpassed craftsmen, legendary equine specialists, or fabled coppersmiths. Carmen Piculeata and Sergiu Popa in Montreal are advancing the myth of Roma as virtuosic musicians. While this is literal truth in their case, the generalized promotion of their "Gypsy virtuosity" paints all Romani musicians with the same brush, particularly since the general Canadian public cannot tell the difference between a virtuoso and a highly skilled studio musician. Whatever the myths, it is important that they are seen to be genuine, and also that they are instigated by the Roma themselves. Injustices are a valid platform on which to form a nation-state, but not enough to build a complete national identity (Guibernau 26).

Canada's own anthem references the "true North strong and free," and later "glorious and free"—but factually, is Canada really "strong," "glorious," and "free," or were the words chosen primarily for their emotive appeal? By contrast, the Roma anthem speaks of loss: "Once I too had a big family / but the Nazis murdered them." Strength is mentioned only as a potential: "We will succeed where we try." Again, the references to injustice and loss provoke an affect which is profound but not substantive; after the abuses stop, what is the identity of the Roma? What would the words be to that anthem if it were to be recontextualized here and now?

The reluctance of the Montreal "Gypsy musicians" to engage more fully in advocacy efforts, such as fundraising, could easily be seen as contrary to the goals of advocates who are constantly seeking more funding and volunteers. At the same time, the musicians are forging a new public Romani identity through manipulation of imagery that promotes idealized and mythological elements of Romani culture such as magic and the exotic, freedom from social mores, and a "feel-good" affect. Donald Trump, a current political contender in the United States who is widely known for his mendacity, is campaigning successfully on his highly-emotive "Make America Great Again" slogan, both creating and disseminating a mythological past that many voters want to believe. No one expects a national myth of any country to be literally true; there is room in the public imagination for concurrent discourses of heroic myth and ethnic injustice.

From national anthems to advertising jingles to Wagner's heroic Germans, music has a long history of changing the world based on its emotive, affectual, and occasionally mythical qualities. Certainly there are many places in which rationality—the judicial righting of wrongs —is needed, but in terms of public relations and building a cultural identity within a country that is essentially a blank canvas, emotiveness and myth are powerful tools. The Montreal "Gypsy musicians" have an enormous potential for advocacy based on their current popularity.

CONCLUSION

The Roma "Gypsy musicians" of Montreal constitute a *de facto* privileged class of Roma in Canada. Since there are virtually no societal or in-group restrictions on the ways in which these individuals enact their Roma identities, they do so in ways that are the most advantageous and meaningful to them personally. No longer predicating their identity on the role of "undesirable other," Canada's most inadvertent, and perhaps most progressive, Romani advocates are composed of Roma and non-Roma alike— the "Gypsy musicians" who are opening middle-class doors for Roma culture in Canada. While the advocates' emphasis on the global and historical is sometimes in conflict with the musicians' focus on the mythological and the feel-good affective nature of the music, both perspectives are necessary in the creation of the diasporic Romani nation. It would be to the great benefit of both groups to work collaboratively to a larger degree.

[1]This chapter represents an overview of my research and fieldwork. Further details are available in the full dissertation: *Canada's Roma and the "Gypsy Musicians": Identity as Dialogue and Musical Practice* (University of Alberta, 2013).

[2]The acceptance rate—reflective of rapidly changing policies and great legal controversy—plummeted at the same time as the claims increased radically. In 2006, 52 percent of the refugees were accepted, compared with a 2 percent acceptance rate in 2010 (Warnica), and 3 percent in 2011. The rate of applicants from Hungary rose from 34 in 2007 to 2,297 in 2010 (Warnica) and in 2011 this number rose to almost 5000 (Swan).

[3]The concept of "Canadian" music in general is not well established, since Canada is seen by many as having no real culture of its own, and as solely derivative of the dominant European cultures. R. Murray Schafer, the famous Canadian composer, provides an excellent discussion of this phenomenon in *Canadian Music: Issues of Hegemony and Identity*.

[4]One of the best and most creative "Canadian hybrid" Romani performances that I ever heard was in Vancouver in 2004, listening to Mario Ines-Torres, a brilliant Romani flamenco singer, improvise "Romani rap" with a local Vancouver rap band, A and P. Likewise there are many First Nations rap artists in Canada who use the genre to tell their stories, and it has always seemed to me to be an undeveloped opportunity for the Roma to combine popular music with the narrative of injustice.

WORKS CITED

Abu-Laban, Yasmeen, and Christina Gabriel. *Selling Diversity: Immigration, Multiculturalism, Employment Equity, and Globalization*. Peterborough, ON: Broadview Press, 2015. Print.

Allen-Trottier, Melaena. *Canada's Roma and the "Gypsy Musicians": Identity as Dialogue and Musical Practice*. Doctoral dissertation in Ethnomusicology. Edmonton: University of Alberta, 2015. Print.

Anderson, Benedict. *Imagined Communities: Reflections on the Origin and Spread of Nationalism.* London: Verso, 1983. Print.

Ayed, Nahlah, and Ed Ou. *CBC News: World.* "Hungarian Roma hope for sanctuary in Canada." 12 December 2012. Print.

Beissinger, Margaret. "Occupation and Identity: Constructing Identity among Professional Romani (Gypsy) Musicians in Romania." *Slavic Review* 60, 1 (2001): 24-49. Print.

Benhabib, Seyla. "What Lies Beyond the Nation-State?" *The Claims of Culture: Equality and Diversity in the Modern Era.* Ed. Seyla Benhabib. Princeton, NJ: Princeton University Press, 2002. Print.

Bow, Erin. *Plain Kate.* New York: Arthur A. Levine Books, 2010. Print.

"Call us Roma not Gypsies!" Vancouver, BC. Independent publication by the Western Canadian Romani Alliance. Includes "Fact Sheets # 1 – 8" by Ronald Lee, Toronto, Ont.: Romani Community & Advocacy Centre, No date. Print.

Chapman, Malcolm, ed. Martin Stokes. *Ethnicity, Identity and Music: The Musical Construction of Place.* Oxford and London: Berg Publishers, 1994. Print.

Chong, Carolyn. "Constructing Identities in a Women's Balkan Folklore Ensemble." *Canadian Journal for Traditional Music* 33 (2006): 32-47. Print.

Cohen, Robin. *Global Diasporas: An Introduction.* London: UCL Press, 1997. Print.

Conway, Alana. *Examining the "Illegitimate" Refugee Label: A Case Study of Roma Refugee Claimants in Canada, 2008-2009.* Master's thesis in Anthropology. Ottawa: Carleton University, 2011. Print.

Csanyi-Robah, Gina. Facebook communiqué from the Toronto Roma Community Centre. Used with permission, 2012.

Daughtry, J. Martin. "Russia's New Anthem and the Negotiation of National Identity." *Ethnomusicology* 47 (2003): 42-67. Print.

Fine, Sean. "Muslim Convert Attacked While Wearing Niqab in Toronto." *The Globe and Mail* 4 October 2015. Print.

Gellner, Ernest. *Nations and Nationalism.* 1983. Malden, MA: Blackwell Publishing, 2006. Print.

Gilman, Phoebe. *The Gypsy Princess.* Richmond Hill, ON: Scholastic Canada Ltd, 1995. Print.

Gheorghe, Nicolae. "The Social Construction of Romani Identity." *Gypsy Politics and Traveller Identity.* Ed. Thomas Acton. Hatfield, Great Britain: University of Hertfordshire Press, 1997. 153-171. Print.

Gheorghe, Nicolae, and Andrzej Mirga. "The Roma in the Twenty-First Century: A Policy Paper." *Eurozine* (2001). Web. Accessed September 2012.

Guibernau, Montserrat. *Nations Without States: Political Communities in a Global Age.* Cambridge, UK: Polity Press, 1999. Print.

Hemetek, Ursula. "Applied Ethnomusicology in the Process of the Political Recognition of a Minority: A Case Study of the Austrian Roma." *Yearbook for Traditional Music* 38 (2006): 35-57. Print.

Lee, Ronald. *Goddam Gypsy.* Montreal: Tundra Books, 1971. Print.

Lee, Ronald. Exhibition notes from JoEllen Brydon's visual art exhibit. Peterborough Art Gallery, Peterborough, Ontario, 2006. Print.

Levine-Rasky, Cynthia. "Who Are You Calling Bogus? Saying No to Roma Refugees." *Canadian Dimension* 46.5 (2012). Web. Accessed August 2016.

Mackey, Eva. *The House of Difference: Cultural Politics and National Identity in Canada.* London: Routledge, 1999. Print.

Piculeata, Carmen. Interview by Melaena Allen-Trottier. Montreal, QC, 2008.

Ringold, Dena, Mitchell A. Orenstein, and Erika Wilkens. *Roma in an Expanding Europe: Breaking the Poverty Cycle.* Washington, DC: World Bank, 2005. Web. Accessed March 2011.

Schafer, R. Murray. "Canadian Culture: Colonial Culture." *Canadian Music: Issues of Hegemony and Identity.* Eds. Beverly Diamond and Robert Witmer. Toronto: Canadian Scholars' Press Incorporated, 1994. Print.

Stokes, Martin. *Ethnicity, Identity and Music: The Musical Construction of Place.* Oxford: Berg Publishers, 1994.

Swan, Michael. "Canadian Refugee Reform Makes It Us vs Them." *The Catholic Register* 8 March 2012.

Tahirović-Sijerčić, Hedina. *Dukh—Pain.* Toronto: Magoria Books, 2007. Print.

Tax, Sol. "The Fox Project." *The Applied Anthropology Reader.* 1958. Ed. James H. McDonald. Boston: Allyn and Bacon, 2002. 250-254. Print.

Tóth, Judit. "The Incomprehensible Flow of Roma Asylum-Seekers from the Czech Republic and Hungary to Canada." Centre for European Policy Studies. November 2010. Web. Accessed September 2013.

"Veiled Attack: Muslim-Bashing is an Effective Campaign Tactic." *The Economist.* 10 October 2015. Print.

Vermeersch, Peter. "Marginality, Advocacy, and the Ambiguities of Multiculturalism: Notes on Romani Activism in Central Europe." *Identities: Global Studies in Culture and Power* 12 (2005): 451-478. Print.

Warnica, Richard. "Canada: The Roma's Next Stop?" *Maclean's Magazine* 16 December 2011. Print.

IT IS IN THE BLOOD

SASKIA TOMKINS

I WOULD LIKE to begin with a note on terminology. You may be familiar with the terms "Gypsy," "Roma," "Traveller," "Romani," and "Tinker," all of which I use in this essay. My family commonly used the word "Gypsy" to describe anyone who was not settled in a house and spent their life on the road following seasonal work. It is odd that the term "Gypsy" conjures up two diametrically opposing images: the first is promoted by Hollywood (the wild, carefree, exciting Gypsy Rose type); the second is promoted by fear and ignorance (the dirty, thieving, negative stereotype of someone who is always trying to outdo the "honest folk" in society).

I was born in England, and, for as long as I can remember, I was fascinated by the cover of an album that my parents owned. The cover featured a dark woman in a long red dress dancing with wild abandon by a campfire, hair and flames flying, with a horse-drawn caravan in the background. It was called, appropriately "Gypsy Campfire Songs." I would put it on and dance around the living room, imagining myself to be that woman. Driving home from my great-grandmother's funeral around the same time, after seeing my entire maternal family gathered together in one place, my mum observed: "My family look like horse-traders; they wouldn't look out of place at a horse fair." A strange thing to say, but a truth. One branch of English "Travellers"[1] was known to include many horse-traders, as well as tinkers. Over

My grandmother.

the years, stories emerged from the family vaults. My great-grandmother would frequently entertain Granny Smith, an elderly Gypsy woman, on Sunday afternoons in the kitchen. In the UK, a Gypsy would rarely come into a house full of cats to drink tea and chat unless he or she was related to the occupants of the house. There were rumours that my family had circus people on my great-grandmother's side, but nobody would ever say, "Yes, we have Gypsy blood." The term "circus people" is slightly more acceptable than "Gypsies" in racist England, although they were often one and the same.

I started learning to play the violin at age seven and took to it quickly, even playing Bach with a freedom that teachers could not easily explain. I soon took an interest in music from all corners of the world, and from many different cultures. At the age of fourteen, I met an amazing elderly gentleman by the name of Donald Kendrick in London, who spoke fourteen languages fluently and countless others "not quite so well" (his words). We would go to folk dances together—Cajun, Bulgarian, English, and so on. We had lots of fun. I found out that he was the secretary for the International Romani Guild (IRG) and was often appointed to act on behalf of illiterate and semi-literate Roma in the courts, giving them a chance of fair representation. It was a volunteer position that he took to try and correct some of the injustices imposed on the Romani community.

Donald recognized something in me, and joined me up with the IRG, so when I visited the Czech Republic at age seventeen,

Clan Hannigan, 2013

the local Roma would accept me and share their music with me. When he took me to Bulgaria a year later to demonstrate Cajun dance in factories (another story for another time), on my free time, I could go off and learn from the Roma people who lived in the mountains. On the mountainous border, we experienced an extraordinary historic meeting between Turkish and Macedonian Roma, Bulgarian village people, and us English eccentrics— sharing music, dancing, and food. Donald even translated while a young Turkish Zurna player declared his undying love for me and threatened to throw himself off the cliff if I did not marry him (I did not; I hope he is still alive). Instead, I married a musician from Northern Ireland who is very proud of his cultural roots, and plays music that is strongly identified with the Irish Traveller culture. He, too, has heard rumours of Traveller blood in his ancestry, and has worked extensively with Travellers from all over the British Isles including the Stewarts of Blair. The musician Traveller families preserved the storytelling, music, and songs of

Clan Hannigan, 2015

the countries they lived in, which would have died out if left to the rest of society.

The touring musician's life is very much based on the road. These musical travellers feel displaced except when on a stage, and are situated slightly outside of society, relying on their family groups for support. My husband and I are fortunate to work with our family: all three of our children are performers, too. We moved with our family to Canada in 2007 and our first few years were spent busking and hitchhiking to gigs in the snow with twelve instruments, two small children, and a toddler in a stroller. Thankfully we have patient children, and I have to say the generosity and trust of the people we met in Canada is beautiful.

In order to make a living and to fulfill my interests, my music-making is varied: at the moment I play mostly Celtic and French music with my family as *Clan Hannigan*; classical music with a local orchestra and with trios and quartets for weddings; and I self-penned pieces with my duo, *2ish,* that nod towards jazz and roots music with much improvisation, in which I find freedom and joy. Recently I have been fortunate enough to work with Romani musicians in Canada—namely Robert Horvath and Jozsef Botos, both incredible musicians on classical and jazz piano and guitar respectively. We recorded Bach's "F Minor Piano Concerto" (BWV 1056) and Vivaldi's "A minor Guitar Concerto" (RV 356) together as part of a septet. While the general population may have an image of the Roma musician playing "Gypsy music"—a romanticized version of Hungarian folk music made popular by the West—in reality, the Roma musicians I know play jazz, classical, tango, rock, blues, and whatever else takes their fancy, just like any other musician from any other culture. My musicianship does not fit into a box, and we should not presume to squish other musicians into boxes, whatever their cultural heritage, unless they ask you to do so.

Back to my own family: there is a distinctive look around the eyes that some lines of English Travellers have, that I see in myself and in family photos. It's easy, with an ambiguous ancestry, to revert back to the romantic images fired up in my childhood imagination by the record cover belonging to my parents, and by movies, but a reality check is always good, and with the knowledge of world history that I now possess as an adult, that would be foolish. Instead, every so often, I trawl the Roma and Traveller section of the UK genealogical archives online, looking for clues—photos, family names, anything really—that would give me something more concrete than stories. I am proud of my family's possible heritage and of the blood that may run in our veins. Up to now, I have had no luck with my search for the truth and have to content myself with a saying from a good friend of mine: "Never let the truth get in the way of a good story".

[1] I should note that, in England, the phrase "Traveller" was used to refer to people of Romani origin, though in the 1980s it became attached to the new age movement and was often used as a derogatory term to describe young people living on the road. These people were often stereotyped as being grubby Caucasians, usually sporting dreadlocks and with a dog attached to a lead made from string, who may drink alcohol in the streets and are often seen to be begging.

DJANGO ON THE GUITAR

ARIELLE DYLAN

With Django on the guitar
I can almost forget
The journey:
A Diaspora marked by
Benjamin's barbarism,
Complete with slavery, persecution,
And the Devouring.
Where masturbating guards,
Aroused by sadistic acts,
Commit banalities of evil
Among a chorus of bones
And the stench of burning flesh
Seared dirge-like in my imagination

With Django on the guitar
It is almost possible to consider
That which never changes:
A level of freedom
To which one might aim
If anger and resistance
Were less sensible.

THE OLD WEDDING DRESS

SARAH BARBIEUX

Long wedding dresses are hanging one beside the other in the wardrobe at the back of the old Jewish dry cleaner's shop. They stay there; they hang and they wait, like medieval ladies waiting for their suitors to return after their useless warlike conquests. They dangle and they age like women who were not able to live their own lives, who had only been daughters or sisters, wives and mothers, without ever having had the experience of also being genuine friends, intellectual companions, respected teachers or healers, initiators or creators. They get dusty and bored, one thread after another. Since they are no longer in fashion, they worry that their chances of coming alive again are very slim.

But the old dry cleaner had managed to recognize their value, perhaps through nostalgia for his mother Rebecca, whom he had loved and respected when he was a small affectionate boy, growing up close to her in this shop. Even after she had rejoined her ancestors, he continued to cherish and honour her. She took great care of her wardrobe full of old things, and spent a lot of time there. Often, she seemed to be talking to herself.

At least, that's what he believed.... But it was quite different! Because, for several decades, his mother was secretly conversing with the old dresses in the wardrobe.

She wasn't crazy—quite the contrary! She simply knew how to listen with profound attention. The dresses spoke amongst themselves. They told each other everything, without embarrassment, but with dignity. They never interrupted each other and they waited their turn to make comments. It must be admitted that they had the time—all of their time—that is necessary to make memory vibrate in tune with the truth.

In front of the wardrobe, there were dresses that had been cleaned. When one departed, the others shed a pearl-like tear. Before realizing the origin of these mysterious droplets, the dry cleaner's mother exclaimed: "We will have to figure out where this leak is coming from one day or another!"

These sentimental drops did not cause a big mess, of course, but nothing escaped Rebecca's sharp eyes. In vain, she had called all the plumbers in the Marais neighbourhood. No one had been able to trace the source of the tiny leaks.

"Pff! They don't make plumbers like they used to!"

But she immediately let the subject drop, knowing full well that there were so many more important things to deal with, understand, and meditate on....

Sometimes, she fasted before noon. On those mornings, she didn't go downstairs to the shop. It was not about religion, but because she knew from experience that when she would go to work in her back storeroom, she would be able to hear better what the dresses had to say.

That day, it was the oldest who spoke: "I am a very old wedding dress and I was entirely handcrafted in early 1936, in a small village in Burgundy near Nevers, by a young seamstress who was shy but gifted and not from the region. She delicately stitched onto me all these little round buttons covered with pearly cloth that was the same as the material I was gracefully constructed from. The buttons cover half the sleeves and fit perfectly with my princess style. There was a lot of love in her work and, sometimes, I felt that she was praying when she passed her needle over my silky fabric. Each piece that she completed carried the seal of her tangled vows, which were as many as the orders she was asked to fill for many seasons and occasions." (The dresses liked to give details; they thought that small details revealed big realities.)

"So I was created for a young countess whose parents were about to disown her because she fell in love with a young man from Sicily who wrote poems and songs and also played music with his mandolin. The young countess had refused the advances and arrangements of a fiancé from a supposedly good family: a legitimate son, courteous and well-intentioned for sure, but imposed on her by her parents who were too respectful of the proprieties of the time and not enough of the feelings and desires of their own daughter. However, the young woman had stood up for herself; she had been sheltered by her maternal aunt and, unlike many of her contemporaries, she could marry the man of her choice!

"Oh, please excuse my stream of words, but this story deeply touched me at the time. It is also the story of my birth.... So I will continue.

"When the young ex-countess greeted her older sister, who had come to see us both, her sister exclaimed: 'How beautiful! It makes me want to find a suitor quickly.' I was delighted with the comment, but I tried not to imagine having to wrap around so many breasts and buttocks at once! I was already seeing my precious seams rip one after the other, my little round buttons explode, and my velvety fabric sag—the best way to age prematurely!"

And all the other dresses, with their threads and their ribboned borders, started laughing in unison. With a smile on her lips, Rebecca walked to the counter to serve a client who had pressed insistently on the small pewter bell button that sat at the right of the cash box.

Rebecca, who suffered from being slightly overweight, was neither inhibited nor humiliated by the comments of the Burgundian dress of 1936. She knew only too well that we were as we were, and that's all! She felt proud to have given birth to several children and to be about to become a grandmother. Even when she was young, she already thought that a rounder woman was more beautiful by nature.

It was the mid-seventies and she had heard through her cousin, a teacher who lived in Boston, about a new book called *Our Bodies Our Selves*, which was translated into French by a group of women, one of whom was an occasional customer. Rebecca thought the world was small and that was infinitely reassuring.

Her client was called Sophie and she already had spoken at length about the struggles of women here and elsewhere which were increasing in the changing society. There were so many new ideas to discover. Rebecca felt this wave of optimism reaching the depths of her being, she who had been overwhelmed by melancholy, sadness, and fear for so long that she knew them only too well.

Part of what terrorized her most was the torture and sexual abuse inflicted on women, and worst of all, on little girls. Her trauma was so great that her whole body collapsed into itself and all her physical processes seemed to lock down at the slightest hint or information about these events. That's just how it was. There was nothing to add, nothing to understand, or even to discuss. Going to the sea was what did her the most good. She adored the seashore and especially preferred the Mediterranean. But it also gave her great pleasure to stand, facing the Channel, on the cliffs of Étretat in Normandy, where one of her sons could take her more regularly since it was not so far from Paris. The waves of the Côte d'Albâtre (Alabaster Coast) cleansed her overflowing emotions, purified her dark thoughts, enlivened her vital energy, and calmed her disordered mind.

Afterwards, at low tide, she delighted in going down to the beach to bathe her feet, ankles, and calves while walking along the shore. At each visit, she gathered all kinds of shells and, with translucent glue, used them to create small dolls with ruffle dresses for the daughters of her favourite clients. She also left the most rolled up and compact shells in large bowls of transparent glass on the round table next to the counter, low enough so that children, especially boys, could plunge their fingers and hands into them, discovering through touch these petals from the sea, living witnesses to the power of life.

It was almost night-time, and Rebecca stayed later in the back storeroom, mending a jacket and sitting in the most comfortable chair in her shop. Between sighs of concentration and the purring of the steam engines that were still running, the voice of the old dress reached her sharp ears.

"I thought that my life as a dress would pass for decades in the same family, in the same region, and that I would take it easy in large fragrant cedar cabinets. To be well packed in warmth, safe, away from work, transfers and complications, in a world where everything runs like clockwork. But three years after the wedding of the young ex-countess, everything was chaos around me."

Rebecca suddenly wanted to return to the sea....

Then the dress told how she had passed from hand to hand and remained shelved for years at a different dry cleaner's, listening to the stories of others. And one day in early spring, she was bought and sent by boat across the Mediterranean to Algiers. Rebecca paid attention, as she would have liked to hear tales and stories about her favourite sea. But there was nothing, since the dress crossed the ocean in the hold of a cargo ship.

"I had been sent to the sister of an old camel driver who had made his marriage proposal to the father of a very young girl of eleven who was also arriving from France. He thought to please his youthful promised one with the idea that I was from France too. It was 1969. I felt so uneasy in that situation and wondered what exactly the meaning of my existence was. I was torn. But I learned from the old man's sister that the union had been cancelled because the girl had run away with her wolfhound and provisions to the mountains of the Saharan Atlas in order to escape this horrible fate. The villagers said that they had heard the dog howling for several nights and that his baying mingled with the angry and shrill cries of the runaway girl."

("It's crazy how Mom often wants to leave for the sea at this time!" Rebecca's children thought....)

"As for me, they folded me, wrapped me in blue ribbons and sent me back where I came from. An antique dealer bought me a few years later. I was suffocating in his attic; there was no light and the dust weighed me down. But as luck would have it, one fine summer afternoon the antique dealer freed me, aired me, and placed me on a large vintage armchair near a green and tender lawn. He set me up that way on many consecutive Sundays for a few years and, in my solitude, I had a strange and unhappy dream: I dreamt that a man who had been tortured by life and wars went to ask his own daughter to marry him on her eighteenth birthday. He had brought his suitcase with him and asked her to follow him to Switzerland to get married. The rest was vague because the girl's tears drowned this macabre dream."

This time, on that Monday afternoon, Rebecca was content to go along the border of the Seine, to loiter on the quays and stop in front of the booksellers to look for the children's stories that she so loved to offer to her neighbours (after having read them herself, obviously, and sometimes even after copying whole passages or transcribing the synopsis). Rain or shine, she would go again, never tiring of passing through the *Parvis de Notre-Dame de Paris*, and feeling her heart lift with the many mystical vibrations she could perceive without any contradiction to her own ancient spiritual traditions.

The most exciting days in the back storeroom were when one of the dresses that had been cleaned or sold, left. Thursday morning, it was the turn of a simple, lightweight, inexpensive dress, with no rustle or veil, to get insistent glances, a rubbing of the chin and a pouting lower lip from a sympathetic friend. But the celebrations were too short-lived to have an impact on that dress that had been pleased too quickly by the thought of being worn. It was a marriage on paper only, and the bride, rather guilty and with a touch of cynicism, chose a gown of a completely different colour. The dress did not leave her spot that morning, but got the gossip from a beige suit that came to the dry cleaner's a few days after the dreary ceremony. (Even dresses have souls. What about those who believed for so long that women did not?)

Sometimes Rebecca thought about marriage in general. She had heard stories about forced marriages in history; they made her shudder in disgust. She also thought about the nuns from her childhood who had passed by in the Parisian streets and declared that they were married to Jesus. This idea was confusing but, at the same time, it amused her. She had a particular admiration for the teachers, those who gave themselves to their vocation, and she speculated that they were married to education. Occasionally, she had questions about the matchmakers who initiated meetings and brought couples together. She also questioned conventional marriages, entered into in order to be part of the mainstream, or as required by families, societies, cultures, and conditioning. Through it all, she had a weakness for the celebrants around the world, even if it impressed her that someone could unite people through this "sacred" link. Too often, she was of the opinion that not very much was really sacred, but she kept this to herself. Although she was realistic and practical, banality did not interest her.

Time passed with its share of events, realizations, surprises, and deceptions. The "36" had already left the dry cleaner's shop many years ago. Then, one day in December, Rebecca got a phone call from her old cousin in Boston whose daughter had been living in Montreal for a long time.

"My granddaughter attended a show recently and she took photos. When she showed them to me, I recognized one of the old dresses that had been displayed in your shop. It looked the same in every way. I'm sending you the pictures in the mail and you will tell me if it really is the dress; I'm curious to find out. I will also ask my daughter if she filmed that day, because I know that she does that for events that please the little one. I'll let you know."

In her heart, Rebecca hoped that in those photographs she would recognize "The 36," as she liked to call the Burgundian wedding dress. In numerology, 36 becomes the number 9. This number of cycles, oneness, and altruism was appealing to the deeply generous nature of this woman who had given everything throughout her existence. She had lavished advice, hopes, listening, care, and other kinds of attention on those around her. She knew that "The 36" was like her, woven from the same thread of life, and she missed her.

It was Rebecca's son who received the photos and showed them to his mother, who was touched by them. He did not understand everything, but he intuitively welcomed his mother's feelings, thoughts, and reflections as part of a great mystery, and as characteristic of all mystics worthy of the name.

Rebecca took the pictures and brought them close to the last wardrobe. Then she tried something a little crazy. Holding the package of photos in one hand and lighting her *Papier d'Arménie* —as she was used to doing because she didn't appreciate certain smells that came from the dry-cleaning that some people called "pressing"—she sat down among the hanging dresses and took the small number of photos out of the envelope, exposing them one by one in front of the masses of white, pearly, embroidered, and silky fabrics. The most yellowed one ground her hanger and asked her neighbour: "What is she saying? What is she saying? I knew her well, she was beside me for a long time; she thought that she had a special destiny."

Not suspecting that Rebecca could hear her, she was surprised when the photos came into contact with her lacework. "I can feel her; I can hear her!" And as if in a trance, the ancient gown discovered her psychic gifts of channelling and storytelling, and, rolling up her ornamental trimming, began to speak in the voice of "The 36."

"Hello, my friends. I am well. Listen to my story! In the summer of 1978, a fine young man from Martinique bought me for ten francs. My colour contrasted with his bare arms when he offered me as a gift to the young woman with thick hair who tried me on right away. I fit her like a glove! She wanted to know where I was from and when I had been made, so the seller, smiling at the sight of the young woman, gave her the date and place. The young man complimented her on her outer beauty, which for him was a reflection of her soul. It didn't matter if he tried to sleep with her; the compliment was gentle, non-intrusive, and full of healthy sensuality. They were not a couple, not even really lovers; there was no demand from him, just a gift.

"The young woman was half Gypsy. She had been told not to talk about this since her childhood. She should forget about it, and besides, being only half Roma, what did it matter? But she fiercely missed her father's family, her blood, her original language, her memory, her legacy, and her roots. She could not bring herself to forget or deny it, and it was there, in the sun that made her eyes squint and her forehead wrinkle, that the young woman told her West Indian friend about how, in August 1427, the first Roma arrived in Paris on the *Parvis de Notre Dame*. When they were asked where they came from, the chief of that tribe answered that they were from Little Egypt. She added that this was the reason why the tribe received the name 'Little Egyptians,' which was transformed over the years into 'Gypsies.'"

(Rebecca had a better understanding of why she was attracted to the *Parvis* of the cathedral, and then she remembered the frequent intermarriages between Jews and Roma. She even began to wonder about her own origins. Who knows?)

"What luck! I've been playing my best role for twenty-five years. Indeed, the young woman who had brought me to Paris with her in her luggage, and temporarily stored me in the damp basement of a building she left, found me again through a friend who had gone to visit her in Canada, in the Greek neighbourhood in Montreal where she lived in the early eighties. I crossed the Atlantic by plane. When he held me out to her, I realized that she was very happy to see me, because she had missed me. I became the costume of a white fairy "from the distant steppes of a world without name that has no borders and who will tell you the well-known Russian legend of the old Babushka!," which she repeated at every performance. Every year, in makeshift theatres, when the Northern snow begins to fall on the cities and villages of this chilly country, I have the best job in the world. This girl, half *Tzigane* but completely engaged in her profession, gave me a new life that I would never have suspected. I sparkle, I parade backstage and in front of the mountain scenery, I twirl to the rhythm of drums, I fly and I dance to make the little girls dream. I embody a purity of the imagination; I shine, enthusiastic, under the coloured floodlights. At the end of the show and in front of the curtain, I bow with gratitude. The music of the applause makes the strings of my artistic senses keep vibrating throughout the rest of the year. In my sweet repose, I inspire the depths of children's peaceful sleep with wishes and wonderful dreams."

Until now, Rebecca had never heard the other dresses speak, but from this time on, she knew that they all had the potential to tell a story. She felt so happy for "The 36," who was now living everything she had always wished for. Although she herself was already old, she had a feeling that she too could now share the fruits of her own creative sensitivity. She imagined the costume cupboard of this artist, full of outfits and other accoutrements, and she began to invent other stories that she attempted to write when her time and energy allowed her to.

In the fragrance of the *Papier d'Arménie*, sitting on the solid wooden bench by the closet at the back or in her comfortable mending chair, Rebecca transcribed the stories she heard in her head and in her heart. Imagination had taken over from listening. Like a whirlwind, the stories would spring up, clear, from memories that were interspersed with her visions. After each inspiration became writing, she conscientiously arranged and typed the swarm of words on the computer that she now knew how to use (a twenty-first-century "must"). She re-read, annotated, simplified, and completed her manuscripts, and she did not stop as long as she felt a shiver, an emotion, an inner healing.

When she finally thought that they were ready, she had each story printed on small hardback rounded formats to which she added simple illuminations in vibrant colours. Letting out her breath, she carefully deposited a drop of essential rose oil on each of them, and, with a smile, she gently placed her booklets on the little round table near the bowls of pearly shells.

MISERY LOVES LOVE, MISERY LOVES ME

ELIZABETH LISA ANN CSANYI

Love and I
Have never been friends.
Only enemies.
It has cheated on me and I am defeated,
Left me without a chance.
From the very beginning
I have lost the fight.
I should have given up,
But still, it wanted to dance
And play around,
Laughing hysterically behind my back.
With its cold hard knife
It pierces my heart.
I drown in my sorrow.
The air fills the holes
In my soul.
I cannot breathe.
There is a crushing heaviness,
A burden to carry,
In addition to Misery.
Its company is Love,
And it starts all over again.
My love, love my dear.
Death and rebirth but never

Satisfying.
Addicted to the pain that love brings,
I fear I will die
Alone, without love.
True love, eternal love, a child's love
Without my Roma legacy to remain alive
I will die and
All of me will go to my grave.
My tears will fill my body and
pour into the ocean.
Maybe that is what the ocean is:
Salty tears from all those
Before me who have gone
Through heartache and pain.
My tears belong to it and so should my
Heart.

"THERE IS ONLY ONE GYONGYI"

GYONGYI HAMORI AND BLUMA TERAM

THE EARLY YEARS
"We always had love."

MY LIFE BEGAN in Communist Hungary in the autumn of 1951, in Kek, a small village northeast of Budapest where Roma and non-Roma lived. My mother, Maria Bodi, was born in the village of Kemecse in 1921, and my father, Jozsef Horvath, was born in the village of Patroha in 1927. They met at a celebration event in Kek, married, and had my brother, sister, and me. As the eldest son in his family, my father was responsible for both his widowed mother and our own family. My mother, who was six years older than my father, initially stayed home to care for us children, but due to my father's meagre income as a musician, my mother had to work outside the village cleaning and doing laundry in rich people's homes. My parents were not destined to remain married; they separated when I was three or four years old. My father remarried, but he never deserted us, and continued to support us along with his second wife and four children.

All the men on my father's side of the family were musicians. He was a wonderful musician who played several instruments and made certain that he passed this rich tradition down to my brother, and, to a certain degree, to me as well. I was lucky because he taught both my brother and me to play the violin and the cimbalom, the hammered dulcimer played by striking two beaters against the strings. My enormously talented brother played the dulcimer, guitar, violin, and bass. My mother's younger brother also played the violin. I loved the dulcimer as a child, but now I also play a little guitar. A few months ago I started to learn to play the piano without the benefit of a teacher. My motto has always been that it is never too late to learn.

During my school years, we were destitute, and the family had to find ways to survive. When my father could not find work as a musician, he worked in construction and made bricks and mortar. It was hard labour as the brick ingredients were mixed manually, by foot. At the age of ten, I too worked and, like the other women, my job was to take the building material out of the vat and shape it into bricks. To augment our income, both my parents hired themselves out as farm labourers. There was a time when I worked on a farm side-by-side with my mother, but, for the most part, I lived with my grandmother while my parents left the village to search for employment. It did not matter how hard we worked; money was always scarce.

We were four family members living in one small room. It was always so noisy that when I wanted to read, I had to read out loud just to hear myself. Our home was adjacent to my grandmother's house and to my father's house, where he lived with his second family. We all shared a garden where we grew some vegetables. We slept on straw, on the floor, until we eventually acquired an uncomfortable bed with a straw-filled mattress. I slept with my mother and later with my married sister. There was no bathroom, hot water, beds, electricity, or stove, and it was difficult to keep things clean. No matter how difficult it was, my mother had a reputation for maintaining an exceptionally clean home. When I was about ten years old, we suddenly acquired "great wealth" and were able to buy two beds. At about this time my mother started to teach me how to cook. We ate very simply: potatoes and some bread. We made bread with flour, a little salt and water, and baked it on a wood-fed fire. We rarely ate fruit, meat, or fish. I cannot remember how many times I went to school hungry, and when I returned home from school there was still nothing to eat. Most times, however, I was able to eat once a day; usually *vackaro*, a crusty Hungarian bread, and some beans. I never had a winter coat or boots, and throughout my elementary school years I remember always being cold.

Luckily our elementary school was a mixed school, which meant that the standards were higher. Some teachers liked me, but at the time I could not understand why others did not. I knew that I did not have nice clothes or shoes and that they believed the Roma were "stupid," but I was a good student. Their disdain for the Roma was displayed in a variety of ways. One small example was that, despite being a fine student who was never late, I was not allowed to sit at the front of the classroom. There was always a fear inside me, and I felt that I had to prove myself to be good all the time. This is one of the reasons I also participated in all the extra-curricular activities at school—I wanted to try, and excel in, everything. Although I could only study at night by means of a lamp, and our living conditions were impoverished, I would not be deterred from proving that I could be as smart as anyone else. This was an exceedingly sensitive issue for me. The one time that I received a poor grade—because my non-Roma classmate was not able to lend me her book as she normally did—I cried for hours.

Hungarians used to warn that everyone should "be careful" because Gypsies are *stupid, selfish, will steal from anyone, and will return nothing. They are poison; they do not want to be, or are incapable of being, educated; and they are no better than beggars.* The teachers' racism and discrimination made me feel small, as small as a louse, but I was determined to prove to them that the Roma are not stupid. Despite all the negative images that branded the Roma, I worked unrelentingly to become the top student. I came first in drama, poetry, reading, and Hungarian grammar, and in grade four I received a certificate for my poetry reading. I remember one small example of the strength of my resolve. It was a warm day in May or June. My mother had done the laundry and my one and only dress had not dried yet. Although my mother told me to stay home that day, I escaped and ran to school wearing only my undergarments. Similarly, despite not having bus money to attend drama performances or owning a uniform or costume, I somehow managed to participate in the drama program.

In grade five, a schoolmate gave me a lined notebook that he had not used. I had never owned a book or notebook before. I had one pen, some graph paper, and nothing else. The library was a sanctuary; I read everything I could, and I loved poetry, prose, and drama. My brother and sister did not have books either, but they too were not bad students. While my parents were not educated and could not help me with schoolwork, they did encourage me to learn so that one day I could have a profession and an easier life. My hardships at home—no money, lack of space, too much noise, not enough clothes, lack of school supplies, and being always cold and hungry—were met with defiance. Because I knew I could not cry forever, I would not cry. I was curious about everything, and I was going to satisfy my curiosity. I loved learning and would continue to do so, and I never shied away from a challenge. I was such a good student that I tutored other students right through grades five, six, seven, and eight. I particularly loved the classics and I could also speak a little Russian. I especially loved Russian songs, some of which I can still sing today. As mathematics was not my favourite subject, it remains a puzzle how I actually enjoyed studying high school statistics and eventually became an accountant.

How did I get through all these tough times? God and my parents were by my side. My parents would say, "Don't worry, my daughter, if you can, the best way is to learn and maybe your life will be easier than ours. You do not have to suffer like we do." Strength came from my memories of the closeness of my many extended family members and the Roma community, who were constantly coming together to sing, dance, and play music, and who used any reason to have a party. Strength came from sharing the good times, bad times, and love. We were particularly happy when my father and others returned home from working in neighbouring cities, and everyone got together. I reaped enormous strength and pride from the fact that, as a top student, I was successful and could be a role model in our community. This demonstrates that Roma also celebrated victories. Most importantly, despite our abject poverty, we always had love.

My nature has always been to be curious. As a child, I wanted to know if I could do as well as any of the Hungarian children in school. On the one hand, I used to think that they were simply born smart; that a Hungarian child already knew everything from his or her mother's womb. On the other hand, I suspected that this was not quite true, and I was going to prove that I could be as smart as any of them. When I completed grade six, I was the recipient of an award for being the best student. Credit for my success also goes to my Hungarian language teacher and my grade six Russian teacher, who took good care of me, and of course, to my parents who always encouraged me.

Affirmation of my success came on a Mother's Day when, as the best student, I was chosen to open the ceremony. I borrowed clothes from another girl and stole flowers from a nearby cemetery. The scented rose and lilac flowers gently wafted over me as I spoke about the meaning of Mother's Day. Many, in an audience of hundreds, cried as I recited my rehearsed words. Surely God forgave me for stealing flowers from a grave considering that it was for such a good cause. Further confirmation of my status came with being chosen by the school principal to receive financial support to attend high school. Hallelujah!

Discrimination against the Roma continued throughout my high school years. Despite doing as well as ever on my exams, my work was always rewarded with lower marks. My teachers openly declared hatred of the Roma, and I had to repeatedly endure malicious anti-Roma sentiments: Roma are stupid, dirty, beggars, corrupt, thieves, untrustworthy, etc. Skinheads would confront the Roma, challenging our existence in Hungary. They spewed hatred, were violent and dangerous, and would tell us to "go back to India." My reaction, as always, was to double up on my studies.

Between the ages of eighteen and twenty-one, I was fortunate enough to attend the four-year program at the Hunfalvi Economic College in Budapest. This was a school with a great reputation for training students in economics and trade. Graduates came out with a double designation as an accountant and a statistical/strategic planner, and the hope of moving into the middle class.

During those years, I lived in a student residence and had several part-time jobs.

When I was a child, we were governed by a communist regime. It was a time when people could find employment; not just the Roma, but everyone. Despite the fact that companies constantly held meetings that were inefficient and wasted a lot of time, members of the communist party received benefits—such as a higher salary, or not having to wait ten years to receive a telephone—and could acquire authorization for trips that were heavily subsidized. The Roma, who did not join the communist party, were in double jeopardy: first because we were Roma, and second because we were not members of the communist party.

Job interviews usually worked well for me, as I could be assertive and use positive body language. While I was sometimes nervous and well aware of discrimination against the Roma, I nevertheless had a good attitude, I listened and observed well, and I was educated. I worked in the construction industry, factories, and hospitals, and as a teacher in a children's institution. In one hospital, my duties included custodial, maintenance, electrical, and plumbing work. I did it all. I was a reliable hard worker and received an hourly wage, although I always received a lower salary than a non-Roma. In one hospital where I was hired as an accountant and administrator, and performed some secretarial work, I was paid fifty percent of what non-Roma earned, despite having better skills and experience. That time my heart was broken, but what could I do? I had worked for about ten years in a factory where I had become one of the 30 percent of women who could successfully operate and fix a crane. Although I was somewhat fearful, because the work was difficult and a mistake could be fatal, it was time for me to explore a new direction. By this time, I was thirty-eight years old and married with two children. My son Charlie was fourteen or fifteen years old, and my daughter Hajnalka was ten years old.

With the fall of the communist government in 1989, companies went bankrupt and thousands of workers were laid off from their jobs, but the Roma suffered even greater losses. Our situation deteriorated as anti-Roma sentiments grew and employment opportunities became increasingly paltry. My brother, for example, lost many job opportunities and had to resort to driving a truck; my salaries of course were always lower.

Towards the end of the communist regime, I heard that a new time was coming and I was keenly aware that I had to prepare for it. It was common knowledge that the new Hungary needed workers who were knowledgeable in economics, computers, and languages. So to prepare myself for the new Hungary, I took computer classes and did fairly well. At that time, I also thought about becoming a social worker because I understood that the Roma would become even more impoverished and would not stand a chance in the increasingly discriminatory labour force, particularly as many Roma lacked education. My thoughts turned to how I could serve our people, and I ignored advice to avoid working with Roma. How could I abandon my people in such dreadful times? While working in a construction company as a cost accountant, I went to night school: Tuesday and Thursday evenings I studied accounting, and on Sundays I studied social work at the John Wesley College in Budapest.

Eventually I graduated from the social work program and landed my first job at the Dzsumbuj Help Community Development Center. The Dzsumbuj was part of the inner city (9th district) of Budapest and a classic slum established in 1937. People lived near abandoned factories and derelict lots. They were overcrowded and poor, but the houses were clean, and had running water and toilets. Most of the Roma were unemployed and lacked primary school education. Crime rates, alcoholism, and drug use were high. Children tended not to complete elementary school and young people engaged in risky sexual behaviour. These problems further exacerbated prejudices and discriminatory policies against the Roma.

I was one of three Roma workers who were hired at Dzsumbuj, and I was assigned a large number of clients, all of whom lived within three buildings with a total population of 1,400. My job was to connect with families and schools, provide information, facilitate children's return to school, develop recreation programs, and in general to deal with the multiple issues confronting the Roma. I was very proud of our work, and we functioned as an efficient team that allocated the various responsibilities fairly.

To my delight, I had the opportunity to introduce the needs of the program and the Roma to the British Ambassador. He came to Dzsumbuj and learned first-hand about the issues we were facing. He not only understood the issues, but he also subsequently supported the daycare program to the tune of $150 per month. He ensured that the children had fresh fruit daily, a carpet, and toys, and he addressed other needs. The Ambassador also provided fifty tickets to attend *The White Bird of Poston*, a fifty-minute children's opera by Eli Villanueva. It was my first opera and I loved it.

Unfortunately, I left my full-time employment at Dzsumbuj due to my strong disagreement with an intervention that I felt was unethical. However, I continued to work at Dzsumbuj on a part-time basis. I co-ordinated the recreation and the breakfast programs, recruited food for the children participating in the breakfast program, and organized and taught in the children's recreation program, in addition to tutoring history.

In 1997, I was privileged enough to host a few radio talk shows that gave me the opportunity to debunk myths about the Roma. As callers made rude and ill-informed stereotypical statements about the Roma, I was able to manage the conversations in a way that demonstrated their ignorance without being discourteous. Instead, I used an educational approach to try and correct their wrongful impressions and prejudices.

"GYPSY WOMAN"
"What should have been a happy day for me was just the opposite."

My parents were so kind; they never pushed me to marry or to have children, which at the time was unusual. There are different Roma groups who require a girl to marry by the time she turns fifteen, but my Roma group, Rumongro, is different in that sense.

At the age of twenty-one, I met my husband at a tea party in a restaurant. I refused to dance with him since he was a bit drunk and aggressive and I felt uncomfortable with him. I was just on my way out, but he insisted I dance with him, so I danced with him without removing my coat. He was never my idea of the kind of man I wanted to marry, although I did continue to go out with him. He was also not Roma and intermarriage was frowned upon. Yet he asked me to marry him. My mother told me to think about my life: that he would be the father of my children and that "what you choose, you have to live with." By then, I had come to think of him as a nice man who was a good worker but sometimes drank. My mother agreed to the marriage, as did his mother, but his father did not like Gypsies and had never had a Romani person in the family. His four sisters cautioned him that he would lose friends and no one would want to have a relationship with him because of me. I could only wonder to myself "what did I do that was so wrong?" His father advised him that he could "use me" but not be serious about me. I heard him say many sickening things about Gypsies. On the other hand, neighbours told my husband that I was beautiful, educated, and a hard worker. He had only completed grade eight and had no profession, although he was a friendly person. We were so different: I was the poor quiet Roma girl who studied and worked hard; he partied and drank. We got engaged with only our two mothers in attendance. After a year-and-a-half engagement we were married at City Hall with only my brother as a witness. Not a single one of my relatives came to my wedding, but after the ceremony at City Hall many of his relatives did show up. We continued the celebration at a restaurant. Neither my mother nor my brother attended, and I was all alone at my wedding. What should have been a happy day for me was very much the opposite. I went around the back of the restaurant and cried.

Within a year and a half we had a child, a son, but just after he was born my husband became a very angry person. He called me "Gypsy woman" and many offensive and belittling names. Although I cried a lot, I still had hope. No matter how many times I tried to speak with him, nothing helped. He continued to go to parties, drink, disappear for days at a time, lie, and be aggressive in every way.

We were married for twenty-seven years, and we had a son and a daughter. During all those years, I struggled to hold down two jobs. My health was affected; I was hospitalized, nervous and very unhappy. I had no friends because I felt so ashamed, and I had no support, love, or kindness throughout those harsh years. My days and years were weighed down with work outside our home and inside our home: I had the sole responsibility for our children and household without the benefit of financial or emotional support. I did all the washing, even of shoelaces, and the ironing of all our clothes, including the bedclothes. There was never a moment to rest or relax. Still, I did not tell my mother what I was going through as she had reminded me that I could not come back home once I married him: "That is the Roma way." I did, however, maintain contact with my mother and brother; my mother-in-law and sisters-in-law loved my children, but not me.

My life was filled with an abusive and loveless marriage; filled with certificates, skills, and talents that I gave away for fifty percent of what my work was worth, never getting paid for overtime; filled with wearisome housework, full-time and part-time jobs; filled with the demoralization and suffering resulting from discrimination and unfairness of every kind. Still, somehow deep inside of me, I never truly understood why, because my résumé was excellent. I was experienced and professional; I had seven certificates; I was trained in so many areas; and I was knowledgeable, honest, and hard working. Yet I was Roma, and I was rejected time and time again. At this point I was very tired.

My brother knew a couple who had been to Canada and, after hunting down their contact information, I spoke with them about their Canadian experience. While I was initially somewhat wary, I did verify their information. There were many reasons for me, at the age of forty-eight, to begin to imagine a new life in Canada. My profound unhappiness in my current life and marriage, the fact that my children were grown, and ultimately my ever-present sense of curiosity generated strong thoughts of leaving my husband and Hungary. Eventually, the idea of immigrating to Canada solidified into a firm decision. With the emotional and financial support of my brother, the stage was set for my departure. For various reasons, my twenty-year-old daughter and I sought refuge in a shelter.

After all the arrangements for our flight were completed, I returned home one last time to say a tearful goodbye to my son and three grandchildren. The following day, I boarded an Air Canada flight that steered me towards my new life. I was filled with hope for a kinder life, a new language, good jobs, and the hope that the rest of my family would soon join me in Canada.

ACROSS THE BORDER: JUNE 11, 2000

"As soon as I arrived in Canada I loved it. Everyone asked me, 'How can I help you?' Everyone—people in the streets, neighbours, shelter staff, lawyers, bus drivers, everyone— was so friendly and nice."

When I arrived at Pearson Airport in June 2000 as a refugee, immigration authorities interviewed me. Or, to be more precise, they attempted to interview me. We could not finish the interview because I felt sick to my stomach and was constantly running back and forth to the washroom. I was weak and had a lot of stomach pain. At a later stage in my immigration process my legal aid lawyer asked why I had written only one sentence to justify my request for refugee status while other immigrants generally provide at least one full page of explanation. I laughed because the only response I was able to provide was that the immigration officers most probably got tired of me as I vomited non-stop and was not able to say or write more than one sentence. When asked the reason for coming to Canada, all I said was that "life is very difficult in Hungary." That was it; that was my sentence, nothing else—I was in so much pain, I simply was not able to speak. Of course, there did come a time when I was finally able to advocate for myself in much more detail.

Once the immigration officers released us at about 1:30 in the morning, I walked out to meet a couple who I knew from Hungary. They took me to a building somewhere on Weston Road. After a four-hour sleep they drove me to a women's shelter at Bathurst and Dundas. I loved it! I loved my roommates, neighbours, and everyone in the streets who were so nice and helpful. The Hungarian-speaking social worker at the shelter supported me in every possible way, and we later became friends. My life was overflowing with newness, excitement, surprises, anticipation, and appointments.

Within two weeks of arriving in Toronto I was taking an English language class at the library. My dictionary went everywhere with me and was invaluable during my meetings with the immigration doctor, social assistance workers, lawyers, and others. My only translator was my dictionary, and whatever few words I managed to absorb within a few short days. I vividly remember when, on my way to the legal aid clinic, I got lost by getting on the wrong streetcar and the trip thus taking me over four hours. The driver was very patient with my broken English. He actually stopped another streetcar and told the driver to take me to where I needed to go. This is something I will never forget. I was so happy I almost cried. Everyone seemed to have a nice heart and accepted me. My whole reason for coming to Canada was that, as I had written in my claim, life was very difficult in Hungary. And here I could not figure out if I was on earth or in heaven.

My social worker suggested that I start doing volunteer work, but at that time I did not even know the meaning of the word "volunteer." She explained that volunteering would give me a chance to keep busy, acquire new skills, meet people, and learn about the Canadian culture. While still living at the shelter and studying English, I volunteered for Toronto Dollars, a Canadian charity that was a project of St. Lawrence Works. The charity raised and donated funds to local charities that offered help to people who were unemployed, homeless, or living on low incomes. The work was fun and the atmosphere lively. I met and chatted with all kinds of people and, while I did not understand everything that was said, I used my dictionary to communicate as best I could. I distributed flyers, sold cold drinks, managed the exchange of dollars, and performed a variety of other tasks. My time with Toronto Dollars introduced me to friends with whom I am sociable to this day. I loved being involved in the organization, I loved the work, and I was happy to be busy. When the organizers realized that I was an accountant, they asked me to sort out two large bags filled with months of receipts and to reconcile the daily expenditures. I was only too happy to use my skills and to be given the responsibility. To complete the task, I worked two weeks full-time at home and was told that I did an excellent job. During this same period, a friend who worked as a dishwasher in a Hungarian restaurant suggested that I work with her. I was given the job as dishwasher and worked for free, although in short order the restaurant owner changed her mind and paid me. I worked seven days a week, two to three hours each evening and made $20 a week.

When my daughter arrived in Toronto a month later, we stayed together at the shelter for one more month. She knew a little English from elementary school, so when she arrived it made things a bit easier for me. We applied for social assistance and began searching for an apartment. People in the streets helped us find our way to different addresses. On two separate occasions when we got lost, strangers offered us rides in their cars and brought us to our destinations. I could not believe it. I wrote home telling everyone that we were not living on this earth, we were in heaven now, or at the very least we were living in a fairy tale book. They wrote back asking, how come? I responded by saying each time we go to a store or bank we were given a smile, and everyone was polite and helpful. They always asked, "How can I help you?"

In August 2000, my daughter and I signed a lease for our first apartment at 1430 King Street, Apt. 309, just in front of the No Frills supermarket, and we moved out of the shelter in September or October. I fell in love with the streetcars and would watch them from my window. I loved the noisy hubbub of the city: the traffic, the city noises, and the bustle of Canadians as they went about their daily affairs. I do not like the quiet. In Edmonton (where we lived from February 2002-May 2004), it was dead and there were no streetcars. One day, I stood at my window and counted all of seven cars drive by.

The immigration process was a very long one as both our refugee applications were rejected. After living in Toronto for one and a half years, Hungarian Roma refugees were still not being accepted. Our lawyer recommended that we try in a different province as the IRB in Toronto was not accepting Roma cases form Hungary. My daughter and I opted for Edmonton, and we left in February 2002. We ended up living there for two years. In Edmonton, I completed the PRA and the Humanitarian and Compassionate (H&C) application requesting permission to remain in Canada.

LABOUR OF LOVE – SOURCES OF PRIDE
"It is so important to teach our culture, its language and customs, to future generations, otherwise they will be in danger of losing their identity, culture, and pride in being Roma."

One day, I was walking in the streets and I saw a sign that said CultureLink. I thought to myself, what is this? My curiosity led me into the building where a friendly and smiling security officer asked, "How can I help you?" He showed me how to get to the second floor where the CultureLink offices were located, and the first person I saw was Paul St. Clair, the settlement worker. He could not speak Hungarian, so sought help from someone who did. To my astonishment and absolute delight, out walked three young women whom I knew from the Dzsumbuj Help Community Development Center. I had been their social worker! We were very happy to see each other again, and they immediately asked if I would continue the recreation work that I developed in Dzsumbuj—teaching traditional Roma song and dance. I did not have to think twice and instantly volunteered. With Paul St. Clair's support, I recruited children, youth, musicians, and whoever and whatever else was needed. We organized practise sessions at CultureLink and, before we knew it, we were set for our first performance at Harbourfront.

Six months later, my Canadian work permit arrived. I took on a three- or four-month project doing outreach with the Roma community acting as a translator with the welfare, education, health, and justice systems. Two evenings a week, I volunteered at CultureLink to run a women's group and program for children ages four to sixteen. During the day I worked at various jobs such as babysitting, and cleaning homes and offices. The children's program needed funding, and when I found out that funding was available through the city, I wrote the grant application in Hungarian and found an English translator who I paid $100 per page. The grant was completed, submitted, and approved. At the moment of victory, when we received the funding for the children and youth program, I found out that I had to leave Toronto for a short time due to my immigration status. This was a bittersweet outcome for me, and I felt a profound sadness at my inability to implement the program. When I called Paul St. Clair from Edmonton to ask about how the program was coming along, his response was "there is only one Gyongyi." They could not find another volunteer to take on the program.

My daughter and I returned to Toronto without knowing what the outcome of our H&C application would be. I continued my work with Roma youth at CultureLink; organized picnics, winter parties, and monthly activities; facilitated a women's group; volunteered as a translator accompanying Hungarian Roma to various medical, legal, and welfare appointments; continued to study English; and improved my computer skills. All this activity and busyness kept away the symptoms of depression that I had been experiencing at the time. Staying in touch with all my new friends also helped.

On March 13, 2006, I was invited for an interview with the Federal Ministry of Immigration. When I arrived, I was given a letter telling me that my H&C application had been approved. Hallelujah! Within a week or two I was already registered with the Skills For Change program, a program that provides skills training for immigrants and refugees so that they can find jobs, create new lives for themselves, and make contributions to Canadian society. Despite the fact that I wanted to take accounting, it was recommended that I start a retail service course until I could pass the accounting exam. Unfortunately I did not enjoy retail work and I was not able to pass the accounting exam because, even though I was well versed in the content, I could not type. I returned to CultureLink and continued to volunteer with children and youth. I studied English at Parkdale School and continued to clean condominiums, offices, and homes—a job that I did not particularly enjoy—and carried on with translating services.

In 2004, I was one of the first women to serve as a Board Director for the Roma Community Centre (RCC). While at the

RCC, I received a grant to develop a drama program. Roma women were invited to dramatize the history of the Roma. As the women did not feel comfortable speaking in English, I improvised and used music instead of words. This was a particularly important dramatization of the Romani story because even our own children are unaware of our history, and many of them do not know the Romani language. To help educate our children and the general public, we developed a brochure that provided an historical outline.

We felt that it was so important to teach our culture, its language and customs, to future generations, because otherwise they would be in danger of losing their identity and pride in being Roma. Public education must confront negative stereotypes and replace them with positive understandings of Romani history and culture. Romani women need education—particularly that which teaches skills for personal development, such as literacy— to provide them with every possible opportunity to participate in Canadian life and to embrace both their Roma identities and new identities as newcomers to Canada. Violence against women, for example, is a very sensitive issue that makes a woman feel very small and like a lesser human being. In Canada, however, the laws are different. Here a woman can call 911 and she can always find a helping hand. If someone asks her, "how can I help you," she can tell them. I felt women needed to have information to benefit from all that Canada has to offer.

My involvement with the Roma Community Centre (RCC) was two-fold. I was a paid staff member as the outreach worker and office manager in 2009, and the remainder of the time I volunteered my services in a variety of capacities. At CultureLink, the Roma Community Centre, and the Toronto District School Board, I organized various social and recreational programs for children and youth, as well as learned, taught, and translated for the school board. I also taught Roma children Hungarian and personal development in the International Language program and was contracted for one year by the Parkdale Intercultural Association, a non-profit, community-based organization that provides free settlement programs and services to refugees and new immigrants.

Another source of great pride and fond memories was my participation in the Red Tree Collective, in which I worked with artist Lynn Hutchinson Lee on two different projects— *Song of Sorrow,* and *Shukara Lulugi (Beautiful Gypsy Girl).* The Collective was a cross-cultural interdisciplinary partnership with diverse artists and activists. Here I am posing in front of the mural that four other women and I painted, a mural that shows the rich traditional Romani culture and our hopes for the future.

The Roma Community Centre jointly hosted an exhibition of our work with CultureLink, which was held at Sojourn House, a non-profit that provides shelter and essential services to refugees and assists them in integrating into Canadian life. At the end of the project and to celebrate our achievements, I cooked a huge pot of delicious cabbage rolls that we gobbled up at a concluding celebration.

Volunteer work helps me in a multitude of ways, including preventing me from falling into a depression. For fifteen years up until today, I have contributed, and continue to contribute to the Roma community. I happily took up the challenge of volunteer work only two weeks after arriving on Canadian soil (by working with the non-profit organization Toronto Dollars), and I continue to volunteer as a translator and facilitator for many Romani newcomers to Canada to this day.

LOOKING BACK
"...Step by step, slowly, slowly, we began to rebuild our lives."

Since my daughter's arrival, and stumbling through all the steps of registering her for school, applying for welfare, finding a place to live, learning English, volunteering, and finding paid employment, step by step, slowly, slowly we began to rebuild our lives. I am incredibly proud to say that I have always been a hard worker and I never failed to challenge myself to do better, to be better. This is something that I continually strive to do. I am pleased with my seven certificates, my versatility, and my resilience and energy to try new things. I never want to cry again, and I will never be ashamed of being Roma.

As I noted earlier, my parents gave me the gift of encouragement and strength, as did my brother, and a couple of special teachers, and other role models. When we were in Edmonton and even after we returned to Toronto, I suffered many disappointments, and my daughter was very ill with heart problems, but I always hung on to the words of one of my heroes: Scarlett O'Hara. After having read *Gone with the Wind* and seeing the movie, I can honestly say that Scarlett O'Hara is the reason that my spirit and body have not been broken. She has been my role model. One of her famous quotes has seen me through some very dark days when I thought I could no longer go on: "As God is my witness they're not going to lick me. I'm going to live through this and when it's all over I'll never be hungry again nor any of my folk."

A powerful and everlasting source of strength for me is God's love. When I was feeling depressed, a neighbour suggested that I attend her congregation. I balked and was not interested. However, with nothing to lose, I finally attended her Pentecostal Church. Eventually I came to feel the power of God. On September 5, 2005, I was baptized. Since then I see miracles and

Gyongi, Toronto, 2016

love everywhere. Helping others is the work of God and this is something that I will always do, no matter what my situation.

Through God, I moved away from hate, discrimination, and persecution, to support and love. I have moved from hurt to healing, and with God's help I have learned never to give up. Between God, Scarlett O'Hara, Canada, volunteer work, and the support of non-profit organizations, new paths have opened up for me. I have friends, meaningful work, and love. Hungary is not

261

my country. I feel as though I was born in Canada, and I am a one hundred percent proud Canadian citizen.

My one concern is for the youth. They too must be taught to never give up. They will be blessed with the key to success and happiness by continually learning, by standing upright, never lying, always doing their best, respecting everyone, and just loving the people who surround them.

If I am to be remembered, I want to be remembered as a selfless person, and as someone who always gave her best.

WHEN ROMA CAN DISAGREE

The Need for Diverse Representation

JULIANNA BEAUDOIN AND JENNIFER DANCH

THIS CHAPTER is a reflective essay that explores some of the challenges and contradictions that exist in the arena of Romani scholarship and representation. By drawing on our respective experiences as a Romani advocate (Jennifer) and non-Romani ally (Julianna), we intend to shed light on some of the hidden obstacles that arise when working on Romani issues. Specifically, we believe that there are patterns that silence the very people and voices that deserve attention, a tendency that then feeds into the larger issues surrounding the representation of a persecuted ethnic group.

After centuries of facing retribution for speaking out for their rights, Roma have made significant inroads on the long and difficult path to self-representation in public arenas. When Julianna began her research on Romani persecution in 2002, she struggled to find any North American Romani authors and voices in popular or academic spheres; today, Romani narratives are more accessible in books (such as this one), journals, popular blogs, in their own organizations, and many other areas. Jennifer recalls her first few years of living in Toronto in the early 2000s when she did not know any other Roma in the city, never mind an entire network of activists or academics focused on Romani issues. Slowly, through the ongoing work of grassroots groups like the Roma Community Centre, as well as the advent of online networking tools such as email and Facebook, Canadian Roma have strategized collectively on how to have their voices heard by the Canadian mainstream.

By no means, however, are we suggesting thsat the battle is won; rather, the struggle to eradicate "Gypsy" stereotypes and negative associations is unfortunately as necessary as ever. Romani ethnicity has been historically misunderstood, and Roma have sometimes been denied the right to claim ethnic origins or identities at all. There exists a strong belief by many Europeans that Roma are sub-human and animal-like, and thus not deserving of human respect, rights, or services.[1] Furthermore, in the present mainstream vacuum of accurate information on Roma realities— compounded by historical and mythical Gypsy stereotypes— popular media fills a factual void. For many people, the "reality" show *My Big Fat Gypsy Wedding* constitutes the whole of the body of knowledge regarding Roma. Despite condemnations by and petitions from many Romani communities and advocates, the show remains a major, if not sole source of information for the public. Indeed, this particular show and its various offshoots present an excellent Roma-specific example of An Kuppens and Jelle Mast's description of exoticized Others in intercultural reality television:

> Exoticism is based on a dichotomization between the Self and the Other, in which the other is valued as primitive, savage, underdeveloped, simple, authentic, close to nature, dirty, animalistic, and the like, while the Self is regarded as the absolute opposite (modern, civilized, developed, complex, inauthentic, alienated from nature, clean, human, etc.) (804)

Thus we begin to understand the extent to which Roma must constantly challenge the romanticized or stereotypical depictions of themselves.

Romani self-representation efforts thus intensively engage with the ramifications of such depictions, in effect responding to what others have "told" them about themselves both as individuals and as an ethnic group. And while self-representation efforts have indeed grown and become more accessible through technology such as the internet, such efforts are hard-won and almost entirely consumed by what we see as a reactive pattern. What we mean by this is the tendency whereby already vulnerable communities or groups (who often lack financial resources and social capital) are tasked with educating the public and combating negative stereotypes or beliefs about them.

In such cases, this cycle for the Canadian Romani community often begins with an anti-Gypsy piece that encourages readers or viewers to feel hateful towards or even encourage acts of violence against Roma. For example, in 2012, conservative pundit Ezra Levant included on his television show a segment called "The Jew vs. The Gypsies," in which he spewed hate speech and deplorable accusations, all the while homogenizing Roma as inherent criminals. Such a message is not necessarily the cause of the problem, but a symptom: anti-Roma sentiments and attitudes prevail in general society. However, such a pointed and public incident virtually demands a response from the Romani community lest silence be mistaken for encouragement or proliferation of such beliefs. Compounding this particular scenario was the fact that, at that time, Romani refugee claimants were awaiting their decisions and hearings from the Immigration and Refugee Board. By the end of 2012, a new refugee category (Designated Country of Origin) that would affect most Romani claimants was in progress to become law. The call to reform the refugee system with such measures was in no small part affected by public belief that "certain" (i.e., Romani) claimants were abusing the system. The DCO category meant fewer legal rights, which, in turn, increased Romani refugee claimants' precarity in Canada. Consequently, this made it more difficult for them to speak out on their own behalf against an unfair system. The DCO designation was eventually found to be a violation of the Canadian Charter of Rights and Freedoms in 2015,[2] but the damage had been done for those who were forced to navigate an unfair system. Thus, even a small media segment can have wide-reaching consequences.

The Romani community, then, must devote their time and energy towards deconstructing such messages, a process that could include such time-consuming things as press releases, television and radio interviews, and community meetings and protests. Even for well-funded organizations, this is challenging, as the nature of media life cycles means that press releases are usually needed within 48 hours of breaking news, lest they become un-newsworthy. Such responses to stories and policy changes need to be well reasoned and articulated—not an easy task when our relatively newfound Romani-focused organizations in Canada simultaneously juggle other responsibilities towards the community, including settlement/refugee system assistance and cultural programming. The pressure to respond to media stories is further reinforced by the needs of the NGO organizations: in order to compete for funding (a very scarce resource), an organization must convince granting agencies that their projects and peoples are deserving of funding. This is difficult, to say the least, when a disproportionate majority of news stories about Roma are negative, stereotypical, and/or homogenizing (Beaudoin). Therefore, it is evident that the Romani community is tasked *not* with efforts that would directly benefit their members in a concrete manner, but instead with the burden of having to provide the counterpoint to an opinion that should never have been given such attention in the first place. In an online communication in 2012, Gina Csanyi-Robah, the former Executive Director of the Roma Community Centre, writes:

> Instead of focusing on the hardships of refugees or the positive things we are working hard at with Canadians who care—I have been mobbed today by media to answer questions about Romanian Roma being smuggled into Canada who are likely to commit criminal acts. Is anyone else getting damn tired of hearing about Gypsy criminal propaganda?! I sure am. It has shaped my entire life.

Caught in this reactive cycle, Roma are *de facto* made responsible for educating the general White Canadian society about their own discrimination, while simultaneously expected to present a swift and unified response to such incidents.

Within such a vacuum of self-representation, every Romani voice that does receive a mainstream platform of some kind is thus overly weighted. Upon reflection for this work, we quickly realized that this was precisely another symptom of the larger problem we grappled with in trying to write a chapter that captured *all* the important issues we see as relevant in this discussion. How to write a short piece on the pressing needs of Romani communities and people and collaborative work when there is so much to say? How can two people discuss all of the intersecting factors and processes that contribute to Romani problems? This would necessarily entail tracing histories, outlining policies, and so on, which leads us back into the pattern in which the authors are responsible for educating their audience on all such topics with a unified and clear vision. The risk is a presentation of sound bites easily digested by both the general public and the broad Romani community.

Unified messages can indeed be powerful tools for a group like the Roma, which can signal to the world, "We will not tolerate persecution any longer; we will speak out." However, unified narratives end up contributing to another, related problem, one in which certain voices and messages are privileged and reinforced. Often, these voices are Romani leaders or non-Romani allies, people with an education and/or the ability to utilize various public resources. Although both are beneficial at times, we cannot help but see the problems that arise when they are the *only* narratives that are reliably reproduced. We are cognizant of the seeming contradiction we present in naming this issue; after all, Jennifer is a Romani community organizer and Julianna is a non-Romani ally and scholar. We are certainly not disparaging the work of community organizers and allies; rather, we seek to question the inadvertent consequences that arise when these two categories of voices are believed to be representative of the greater Romani whole.

During one of our conversations for this project, when we were stuck on how to proceed with discussing such a complex topic, Julianna asked Jennifer what she would like to see in academia with regards to Romani issues. Jennifer paused before answering that she believed it would simply matter to have more Romani people *in* academia. Not necessarily writing or researching Romani issues, but simply being present and active, and thus normalizing

Romani perspectives. Indeed, the sad truth is that there are no Canadian Romani scholars in the legal arena (where Jennifer is currently studying), and while numbers of Romani academic are on the rise, they still comprise a disproportionately small population. This is an issue with which Julianna has struggled as well; she is frustrated by the tendency in academia to speak *for* people, without simultaneously advocating for better systems wherein people can speak for themselves or simply participate in such systems.

This conversation brought us to the insight that our current system of representation is also a force that is limiting Romani participation and dialogue. We realized that there is such a tremendous amount of pressure on those community members who *are* the voices that it leads to stagnation, burnout, and disenfranchisement. Romani individuals have more opportunities than ever to make their voices heard, but recall, these "opportunities" are often steps in the reactionary cycle described above. Moreover, we, as the general public, often do not recognize the sheer amount of effort such participation takes. Consider the everyday pressure that individuals face, such as working full-time or multiple jobs to pay bills, taking care of families, and more, and compound this with the understanding that community mobilization is, ultimately, driven by volunteers. Then consider the challenges that newcomers additionally face, such as precarious status and language/culture barriers, and we begin to better understand that being a representative for one's community is a labour of love, born from recognizing the need for long-term change. It is not a role in which one sees many short-term benefits for oneself. It is also important to recognize the pressures that exist when one is seen as a "representative" for the community, both from within and outside the community. Not only must they somehow reflect all of the community's diverse needs but, given the paucity of public voices, it is seen as all the more critical that spokespeople are virtual paragons of excellence. Of course, having exceptional spokespeople is a good strategy for any campaign or movement, especially those that the Roma engage in to fight vehement anti-Gypsy attitudes. A spokesperson with flaws could allow detractors to seize on vulnerabilities to "prove" so-called Gypsy stereotypes. However, it is unfair—and ultimately limiting to all involved—to demand that only *certain* Romani individuals should be allowed the opportunity to speak on their group's behalf.

This speaks to the very nature of the concept of authenticity as applied to those voices that are allowed to represent others. When Jennifer was in Europe, she heard numerous non-Romani academics and activists encouraging Romani youth to stay in their home communities and organize there, rather than leave for university or join an NGO. She saw that, while these non-Romani allies were attempting to do their own "good deed" by encouraging Romani youth to become involved in their local communities, youths' perceived usefulness to social change was judged solely by their proximity to their home village and family. A Romani spokesperson who is disconnected from their place of origin is seen as inauthentic, and thus ineffective. This type of thinking affects women in particular who have already had to break gender stereotypes in their quest for representation, whether it was through the simple fact of receiving education, their willingness to be outspoken and raise their voice, or perhaps because of estrangement from their families due to gender-based violence.

This type of "benevolent" but presumptive thinking regarding authenticity is not limited to Europe, however. In Toronto, numerous community agencies that serve Romani clients, or that work in communities where newcomer Roma live, have noticed an ever-present (even rising) anti-Gypsy intolerance and rhetoric. In the neighborhood where Jennifer works, this manifests in the form of non-Romani homeowners complaining to their local politicians about their Romani neighbours. She also knows of landlords who charge more rent to Romani families. Progressive politicians and agency staff may recognize this intolerance for what it is, but are nonetheless unsure how to address it. Here is the dilemma: agencies are often looking for an "authentic" Romani leader to tell them what to do about such issues. If not a specific leader, they at least seek a united mobilization of Roma in these communities that they can then support as allies. When an agency calls asking to talk with a Romani representative because they want nominal input in helping "solve" certain problems, they not only assume that every member of the thousands-strong community knows each other but, more importantly, by reinforcing a demand for a singular Romani opinion, they ignore the systematic exclusion that Roma have faced for decades. We must remember that these situations are arising in the total absence of Romani politicians, Romani employees of community agencies, and public funding for Romani organizations.[3]

At the same time, within Romani organizations there are also constant challenges to the concept of authenticity. We think this comes, in part, from the ongoing struggle to defend against an internalized "Gypsy romanticism," wherein some members use this basis to challenge others' histories, cultures, and identities. But it also comes from the justifiable reality in which Romani communities, used to receiving only a small part of the pie—whether in the form of media attention, funding, or the ears of decision-makers—are conscious of the benefits of choosing a spokesperson or spokespeople who have the potential to get the most traction in those realms. This in turn leads to strategy dissension, as the community is forced to choose between working on advocacy and awareness-building in a broader Canadian context, or working on more local, specific projects within the Romani community to benefit its members directly.

By self-limiting the voices of the Romani community to certain people, a disservice occurs for the Romani movement overall. The global Romani community is as diverse a group as one can have, and we feel that should be its strength—not its weakness. This means encouraging a diversity of experiences and personalities to speak out even if these individual members do not agree with one another. Implicitly demanding a unified voice when it comes to the kinds of political change Roma want, despite the admirable goals such a strategy strives to achieve, ensures that only *certain* narratives are enshrined. A prerequisite to genuine representation is the recognition that more Romani people are needed in *all* spheres, even those whose opinions we may disagree with. Having been part of community mobilization for many years, we have both encountered dissenting opinions many times. In fact, our collaborative work[4] has grown stronger since allowing for such difference of opinion, even with each other; after hearing Jennifer's objections to a community project Julianna had been a part of, Julianna better realized some of the project's inherent problematic aspects and worked on attending to these aspects.

Imagine the difference we would see in the world if more Romani perspectives were enmeshed in all aspects of life—from media, to law, to immigration, to art, and more. Moreover, imagine the benefit that could arise when some of these perspectives are inevitably different from one another and, rather than being seen as community conflict or weakness, they are viewed as a matter of course. We should not expect a unified vision from Roma; rather, when Roma can disagree in public and such disagreements are not used as an indictment against their ethnicity or identity, this will be cause for celebration. This will signal a self-representation that has grown beyond mere tokenism, and instead reflects genuine participation and representation.

As for considerations on *how* a more diverse representation can be achieved across fields and public arenas, we should all continue working on varied and multiple solutions that reject a one-size-fits-all strategy. Increasing Romani participation through education is often cited as a goal; yet, while access to education is certainly an important component, it is not a panacea. Such a sole focus on education simultaneously pushes more responsibility onto Roma themselves while ignoring the reality they face in the form of reprisals and political backlash. As we have stated, speaking out is a difficult task made even more daunting by the reality in which speaking up for oneself as a Romani individual makes one a target. While conducting her PhD research, "Lily," one informant of Julianna's, described fear as one of the most limiting factors for Romani representation in mainstream media:

> When people don't have a voice—when they're terrified to have a voice—because they [have been] told: "if you speak [out], you're dead." And that goes on for generations and generations. To develop that voice, it takes generations to start changing things. For example, right now, we're

getting a more powerful voice, but it's not nearly enough. (qtd. in Beaudoin 23)

Persecution against Roma is still widespread and largely unacknowledged; many Roma remain fearful that speaking up will incur further violence. Thus, in order to challenge the status quo, Romani voices are needed not only to work against centuries of stereotypes, but also to ensure that there are spaces where Roma can *safely* voice their experiences.[5] When newcomers and the most marginalized members of Romani communities can freely share their thoughts and perspectives and be truly heard, rather than fear recrimination, this will be an indication that true change has occurred.

In the same vein, when we see continued, varied and, yes, dissenting Romani perspectives as part of the norm, there will be the potential for a meaningful transformation for what it means to be Roma, both by external and internal community members. Currently, funding agencies, politicians, policy-makers, and others tend to criticize Roma collectively when there are differing opinions and beliefs, or if they dare to present a narrative that is unpolished or not quite media savvy. It is perceived as a lack of legitimacy or authenticity when Roma do not present a unified front, and using the wrong language or tone reinforces the erroneous, but ever-present, racist mentality that Gypsies cause their own problems or that they do not know how to help themselves. By setting these invisible barriers to participation, a higher expectation is placed on Roma than others. Every Romani individual is treated like an ambassador for the Romani people. When an individual's behaviour is projected onto the entire ethnic group, her every (perceived) misstep or error is ready to be used to perpetuate ongoing stereotypes. How is this fair? Anyone who has worked in a community organization knows that people *can* and *do* disagree about almost everything! It will be only when Roma feel their voices are included and valued (regardless of any pre-conceived idea of what being "Romani" means) that true self-representation will have occurred. And this will only happen when there are Romani agents across all sectors and social movements. Provided this opportunity, we emphasize that *your voice matters*.

[1]For example, Pérez, Moscovici, and Chulvi explore this animal ontologization specifically in relation to real life treatment of Romani groups.

[2]See the decision of the Honourable Mr. Justice Boswell for the Federal Court of Canada in YZ *v Canada* (Citizenship and Immigration), 2015 FC 892 (CanLII).

[3]For further context on this point, consider Jennifer's lament on this subject in one of our dialogues: "And no one will fund Romani groups because of the widespread belief that Roma can't effectively organize themselves, they can't be accountable with money, they don't have the capacity to complete a project without oversight, they don't have the infrastructure.... How can Romani groups prove these things and have the ability to grow without ever having the opportunity?" Julianna adds that this is a further detrimental example of applying a single narrative onto diverse groups: "Even if one Romani organization fails, for example, why should other Romani groups be denied their own opportunities? Simply put, they are being held to an essentialist expectation wherein all Roma are lumped together."

[4]For example, see Rehaag, Beaudoin, and Danch.

[5]As noted in an article discussing Romani advocacy efforts in a European context, "it is very telling and indicative of the political climate in Macedonia that all the activists quoted wished to preserve their anonymity for fear of further recrimination" (Rorke).

WORKS CITED

Beaudoin, Julianna. *Challenging Essentialized Representations of Romani Identities in Canada*. PhD Dissertation, University of Western Ontario, 2014. *Electronic Thesis and Dissertation Repository*. Web.

Csanyi-Robah, G. Online communication, 2012.

Kuppens, A., and J. Mast. "Ticket to the Tribes: Culture Shock and the 'Exotic' in Intercultural Reality Television." *Media,*

Culture & Society 34.7 (2012): 799-814. Print.

Levant, Ezra. "The Jew vs. The Gypsies." Sun News Network, 5 September 2012

Pérez, J. A, S. Moscovici, and B. Chulvi. "The Taboo against Group Contact: Hypothesis of Gypsy Ontologization." *The British Journal of Social Psychology* 46.2 (2007): 249-72. Print.

Rehaag, S., J. Beaudoin, and J. Danch. "No Refuge: Hungarian Romani Refugee Claimants in Canada." Osgoode Legal Studies Research Paper No. 12/2015. *Osgoode Hall Law School Journal* 52.3 (2015): 705-774. Print.

Rorke, B.. "Young Macedonian Roma Demand the Right to Equal Representation." *Open Society Foundation* 27 September 2012. Web. Accessed 5 September 2016.

ROMA SISTERS

JULIA LOVELL

Sisters:
How special is this word.
My heart sings a song for you
I hope your hearts have heard...
Your beautiful faces shining
Remind me of the moon,
And those familiar smiles
Are like the sun in afternoons.
Sisters, sweet Roma sisters
Shine on...
This day I blow my love your way,
For this and every other day.
Thoughts of you, thoughts so sweet
Drift through the winds of my mind.
This to let you know I am always here
for my Roma sisters, gentle and kind.

Sati Sara bless you and may love
fall upon your footsteps and on
those paths yet unknown.

CONTRIBUTOR NOTES

Melaena Allen-Trottier is a classical musician and third-generation Canadian from Calgary, Alberta, with a strong interest in the Roma and "Gypsy music" in a Canadian context. Both her Master's degree in Music Education and PhD in Ethnomusicology were on this topic, and she is a passionate Romani advocate. Within the field of ethnomusicology, her areas of interest are nationalism, multiculturalism, immigration, advocacy and social justice, Canadian studies, and globalization. She speaks English, French, and Romani (Kalderash dialect). Melaena has lived in many places in Canada including Vancouver, Montreal, Edmonton, Calgary, Ottawa, and Prince George, as well as remote farming areas in British Columbia and Alberta, and she has travelled extensively in Toronto, Kingston, Regina and Red Deer. She currently teaches music in Calgary and ponders the topic of flexible and negotiable identities as they relate to her two young children on the autism spectrum.

Sarah Barbieux was born near Paris in 1958. Of Romani and Mediterranean background, she has worked in performance arts since 1977 as a multi-disciplinary artist (music, dance, theater). In 1980, soon after arriving in Canada, she founded the troupe *Caravane*, in Montreal, for which she has won stage arts awards from *Culture Mauricie*. Since 1995, she has continued to compose, adapt, perform, and dance Romani and rumba-flamenco musical styles, as well as participate in conferences on the theme, "Who are the Roma." In 2001, Sarah created and organized the *Rendez-Vous Romanichel*, the first festival in Québec dedicated to the Romani culture. In 2006, with her daughter Thaïs Barbieux, she created the Romani song-and-legend show *Les fleurs de fougère*. Sarah's writing has been published in the poetry collections, *Sar o Paj (Like Water)* and *L'Exil heureux*, and in the literary journal, *Drunken Boat*. She is the author of *Gitanes... de mère en fille (Éditions Belle Feuille)*. Future works include a solo album, a collection of poetry and short stories, and more.

Monica Bodirsky is a Canadian artist of mixed European and Romani heritage who holds a Bachelors degree in design. She recently published an oracle deck, the Lucky Lenormand. Her 2D and 3D artwork is informed by a broad range of experiences as graphic designer, First Nations history program coordinator, writer, and spiritual mentor. As a community activist, she was a member of many boards, including serving as President of the Native Women's Resource Centre in Toronto (2002-2006), and of the Romani Community Centre of Toronto in (2010-2011). When not exhibiting her own art, she holds international thematic residencies and creates commissioned work for clients. Monica is a sessional instructor at OCAD University where she was nominated for the Borden Ladner Gervais Equity Award for Faculty in 2015. She resides in Toronto with her husband Allan.

Julianna Beaudoin is originally from the United States, where she received her BA in International Studies and Anthropology. She moved to Canada for graduate school, where she continued to pursue research on discrimination against Roma. She received her MA and PhD in the Anthropology Department, in conjunction with the Migration and Ethnic Relations Program, at Western University. Julianna volunteered for many years with the Roma Community Centre in Toronto as well as other organizations, and served as a witness on a Supreme Court case relating to Romani refugee claimants. She is passionate about public advocacy and has presented her work in a variety of venues. She lives in London, Ontario with her spouse and daughter.

Elizabeth Lisa Ann Csanyi was born and raised in Toronto, Ontario. A Canadian citizen by birth, she is of Hungarian Romani descent. She moved to Vancouver, British Columbia in 2001 where she has worked as a legal administrative assistant for over ten years. Having a passion for books and writing since a very young age, Elizabeth has written poems, short fiction and non-fiction stories. She continues to work in the legal field and looks forward to continuing to develop her writing style. She has strong family ties, and building harmony, understanding and a common acceptance is a life-long assignment for her. *Opre Roma!*

Gina Csanyi-Robah's family came to Canada in 1956 as Geneva Convention refugees escaping the Hungarian Revolution. She was born in Toronto in 1974 to a Hungarian Romani mother and a Hungarian father. Gina began her work as a Romani rights activist in 2004 at the European Roma Rights Centre and has been at the forefront of the Roma civil rights movement in Canada since she joined the Roma Community Centre (RCC) in 2007. After serving as the Executive Director of the RCC, she founded the Canadian Romani Alliance in 2014, an organization that promotes human rights, community development, and public education. In 2012, she addressed a Canadian Parliamentary Committee and the Canadian Senate about the prejudicial reforms to national immigration policy. The recipient of many awards, Gina was invited by the Office of the Human Rights Commissioner to speak at the United Nations in Geneva, Switzerland on April 8, 2014. Gina is a certified teacher who has taught in both the Toronto and the Vancouver District School Board. She currently works for the Mosaic Institute as the Program Manager of the Canadian Race Relations Award winning project, "Next Generation: Canadian Global Citizenship." Her greatest joy in life are her two young children, Yasin and Eva.

Jennifer Danch grew up on a dairy farm in Ontario and now lives in Toronto where she is studying law at Osgoode Hall Law School. She previously worked as a social worker and community organizer for many years in the areas of food security, housing rights, and gender-based violence. Of Romani, Hungarian, and Irish descent, Jennifer served as a board member with the Roma Community Centre between 2011 and 2015 and as a Chair of its Advocacy Committee. She is currently an advisory member of the Canadian Romani Alliance. She has worked extensively with Romani Hungarian refugee claimants both in Toronto and Hungary, and in 2015 co-authored a report with Sean Rehaag and Julianna Beaudoin entitled "*No Refuge: Hungarian Romani Refugee Claimants in Canada.*"

Tímea Ágnes Daróczi is a Romani woman born in Hungary. She, her husband, and her daughter claimed refugee status in Canada in 2009 but, like thousands of other applicants, were rejected. The family sought sanctuary first for eighteen months at Holy Cross Priory near Toronto's High Park, and then for almost three years at a United Church in Toronto's west end. Advocates rallied to their cause but were unsuccessful in persuading the federal immigration authorities to admit the family as refugees. Due to their rapidly diminishing hopes of remaining in the country, the family returned to Hungary in December of 2014. When their new lawyer, Andrew Brouwer, was successful in winning their Humanitarian and Compassionate case, they returned to Toronto in June of 2016 where they have recently settled.

Arielle Dylan is a professor of social work at St. Thomas University in Fredericton, New Brunswick, where she teaches in the Mi'kmaq Maliseet Bachelor of Social Work program and the on-campus Bachelor of Social Work program. She is Macedonian with some Romani ancestry. She has conducted research with Indigenous peoples and their perspectives on negotiated agreements, land use, and related issues. She has served on the Board of Directors for the Canadian Romani Alliance. She lives in Fredericton with her family.

Born of musician parents, **Chad Evans Wyatt** spent his formative years first in New York, then in Paris. This cross-cultural experience laid the groundwork for two projects in the Czech Republic: *101 Artists*, and then *RomaRisingCA*. Bringing to light the Romani middle and professional class, commonly thought not to exist, was a natural for him. *RomaRising* has been exhibited in nearly forty sites and published in three books. New folios are nearing completion for Bulgaria and Romania. Chad lives in Washington, DC.

Ildi Gulyas was born in Budapest, Hungary and has been living in Canada for twenty-six years. She has an Honours BA in Aboriginal Studies from Trent University and academic credit toward a post-grad diploma in Child and Youth Work. She worked for the Ontario Ministry of Children and Youth Justice Services as a youth probation officer for ten years before moving on to a position closer to her heart, as a Roma Youth Outreach Worker with Yorktown Family Services. After three years of youth work, Ildi decided to return to school and is currently enrolled as an MA candidate in the Social Justice Education program at the University of Toronto/Ontario Institute for Studies in Education (OISE). Upon the completion of her MA she hopes to contribute in a meaningful way to the success and achievements of Romani youth within education. She resides in Toronto with her special-needs dog, Charley.

Gyongyi Hamori was born in Hungary in a small village called Kek. She arrived in Toronto as a refugee claimant on June 12, 2000, and is now a Canadian citizen. Professionally trained as a bookkeeper, statistician, and later as a social worker, Gyongyi is a community volunteer. She also works on an occasional basis as an interpreter for a lawyer. As a settlement worker and outreach worker, she served as advisor and coordinator of a children's traditional dance program. Other experience includes work as an international language teacher (Hungarian-Romani), and as a cleaner. Gyongyi wishes to share her experiences and knowledge with Romani people, especially children and youth. Her message for her people is, "I encourage you all to keep fighting! We can have victory over discrimination. It is never too late to learn; do your job with honesty and to the best of your ability; love and respect each other!" Gyongyi lives in Toronto, a city she loves.

Lynn Hutchinson Lee, daughter of a Canadian mother and an English Romanichal father, is a multimedia artist living and working in Toronto. Co-founder of Red Tree and chirikli collectives, she has exhibited in Canada and Latin America. European exhibits include chirikli collective's *Canada Without Shadows* at the Roma Pavilion, 54th Venice Biennale in Italy, *bak* (*basis voor aktuele kunst*) in Utrecht, Netherlands (2011), and Romania's National Museum of Contemporary Art (2013). Lynn was artistic director of chirikli's community arts project *Musaj te Dzav,* exhibited at Gallery 50 in April, 2015, as part of Toronto's Opre Roma Festival. Her poetry was published in *Drunken Boat – Romani Folio* in 2015. Her current mixed media piece, *Shelter, Provisional – Awaiting Permanent Structure* is included in *Enraged, Inertia Ran Off,* a year-long Red Tree Collective intervention in a Hamilton, Ontario, park (September 2016-2017). Lynn is a member of Toronto Roma Community Centre.

Delilah Lee is a Canadian Romani woman who was born in Canada and has travelled extensively throughout her life. She has lived in China, Ukraine, Georgia, Angola, and England, and has travelled to many parts of the world for pleasure. Having earned a degree in fashion design and art history, Delilah has held jobs mainly in the fashion and teaching vocations. In her youth, she moonlighted as a belly dancer in the evenings. She likes to write for pleasure; her essay in *A Romani Women's Anthology* is her first publication. Drawing and oil painting are among her other favourite activities. She hopes to some day collaborate on a project for a Romani museum in order to raise awareness and understanding of her culture. Delilah lives in Montreal with her English husband and their adopted Georgian Romani son.

Cynthia Levine-Rasky is Associate Professor in the Department of Sociology at Queen's University in Kingston, Ontario where she teaches courses on social problems and on applied sociology, among other topics. She has published extensively on whiteness, i.e., *Working through Whiteness* (2002) and *Whiteness Fractured* (2013), as well as on education and other topics. Cynthia's work as a community-engaged researcher with the Romani community in Toronto appears in *Patterns of Prejudice, Cultural Studies <–> Critical Methodologies, Refuge,* and the magazines, *Canadian Dimension, Canada's History,* and *NOW.* Her book, *Writing the Roma* (2016), is based on four years of ethnographic research with the Toronto Roma Community Centre. As a Jewish woman and ally, Cynthia continues her work with local Roma as a volunteer and advocate. She lives in Toronto.

Julia Lovell is a Romani activist who was born in Scotland and immigrated to Canada in the late 1960s. She grew up travelling with her family throughout North America and the Caribbean, and finally settled in Vancouver, British Columbia. She established the first Romani organization in Canada, the Western Canadian Romani Alliance, which held the first Romani Conference and Symposium in Canada in 1996. In her work as a consultant for immigration lawyers, she assisted many refugees, speaking on their behalf about country conditions and Romani ethnicity. Her activism led her to filmmaking. In 1999, the National Film Board produced a documentary film about her life and family, *Opre Roma: Gypsies in Canada.* In 2003, with Gillian and Rudy Kovanic, Julia documented the plight of several families living in Rome in the film, *Suspino: A Cry For Roma* (Tamarin Productions). Julia co-founded the Canadian Romani Alliance with Gina Csanyi-Robah in 2014. She is currently working on a Romanichel dialect glossary to be published in 2017. It is her hope that Romani people around the world continue to fight for equality and recognition, and become unified in order to build a stronger global nation.

Born in Berettyóújfalu, Hungary, **Viktoria Mohacsi** is an internationally recognized human rights activist. As a special commissioner at the Hungarian Ministry of Education, she spearheaded numerous initiatives to dismantle the system of educational segregation of Romani children. Viktoria served in the European Parliament from 2004 to 2009 where she was one of a very small caucus of Romani MEPs. Trained as a journalist in her teens and working as a television news reporter at age twenty, she is responsible for the systematic reporting of the fatal attacks on Hungarian Roma in 2008-2009—events that became known as the "Roma Murders," the subject of Director Eszter Hajdú's 2013 documentary, *Judgment in Hungary*. Since migrating to Canada, where she claimed refugee status, in 2011, Viktoria has continued to wait for the Immigration and Refugee Board to render a final decision on her application. She lives in the Toronto area with two of her children.

Hedina Tahirović-Sijerčić was born in Sarajevo in Bosnia and Herzegovina. Active at the Toronto Roma Community Centre in the 1990s, she has dual Canadian citizenship. She was Lecturer on Romani language, literature, and culture at the University of Zagreb, Croatia, from 2012-2014. Currently completing her PhD, Hedina is a Member of the Committee of Experts of the European Charter for Regional or Minority Languages for Bosnia and Herzegovina, Council of Europe, Strasbourg. The first Romani female broadcaster in Eastern Europe, Hedina has published many books of folktales, stories, plays, and poems in Romani, Bosnian, and English. A major contributor to world Romani literature, her publications include two dictionaries, *Romani Folktales* in six volumes; a collection of poems, *Dukh-Pain*; an autobiographical novel, *Rom like Thunder*, an edited collection of poems by Romani women, *Like Water*; and many academic papers.

Bluma Teram is a feminist advocate for social justice with graduate education in social work, health studies, and gerontology. She has management experience in programs serving people who are homeless, women who experienced violence, federally sentenced women, and people living with cancer. Working towards improved provision of mental and public health care, addiction services, and affordable housing, Bluma has served as a member of several Boards of Directors of non-profit organizations. Since 2009, Bluma has been involved with Help the Aged Canada, and the Canadian Institute of Cultural Affairs (ICA Canada) in the development of sustainable livelihoods, food security, and climate change adaptation for older women, and communities affected by HIV/AIDS in rural Kenya. Her current project on women's and girls' health engages Maasai communities in Kenya. Bluma's volunteer work with the Roma Community Centre focused on supporting program development and organizational capacity building.

Saskia Tomkins was born in the United Kingdom. She began playing classical violin when she was seven years old, then discovered folk music at age eleven, and jazz at age seventeen. She enjoys exploring and making connections with her very mixed ethnic heritage through music. Since earning an Honours BA in Jazz from Middlesex University in London, Saskia has travelled the world learning different violin genres. Her recording career consists of over thirty albums and numerous radio broadcasts, including work for the BBC. She is an all Britain Irish Fiddle Champion. Since arriving in Canada in 2007 with her family, she has worked with the 4th Line Theatre Company and the Mackenzie Roe Theatre Company, and as principle viola in the Northumberland Symphony Orchestra. Saskia teaches violin, viola, cello, and nyckelharpa, and performs with her own groups, Cairdeas (an Irish/Canadian trio), and 2ish (a roots/jazz duo), and her family band, Clan Hannigan.

Photo credit: Rizah Sijerčić

Hedina Tahirović-Sijerčić is an instructor of Romani language, literature, and culture. She is an author of *Rodni identiteti u književnosti romskih autorica na prostorima bivše Jugoslavije*, [*Gender Identity in Literature by Romani Women Authors from Former Yugoslavia*] (2016), and major contributor to the world of Romani literature. She lives in Sarajevo.

Photo credit: Eunice Katan

Cynthia Levine-Rasky is Associate Professor in the Department of Sociology at Queen's University in Kingston, Ontario. She is the author of, *Writing the Roma*, published in 2016. She lives in Toronto.